The Counterfeit Coin

The Counterfeit Coin

•••••••••••••••••••••••••••••

Videogames and Fantasies of Empowerment

CHRISTOPHER GOETZ

Rutgers University Press

New Brunswick, Camden, and Newark, New Jersey

London and Oxford

Rutgers University Press is a department of Rutgers, The State University of New Jersey, one of the leading public research universities in the nation. By publishing worldwide, it furthers the University's mission of dedication to excellence in teaching, scholarship, research, and clinical care.

Library of Congress Cataloging-in-Publication Data

Names: Goetz, Christopher, author.
Title: The counterfeit coin : videogames and fantasies of empowerment / Christopher Goetz.
Description: New Brunswick : Rutgers University Press, [2023] | Includes bibliographical references and index.
Identifiers: LCCN 2022039033 | ISBN 9781978825505 (Paperback : acid-free paper) | ISBN 9781978825512 (Hardback : acid-free paper) | ISBN 9781978825529 (epub) | ISBN 9781978825543 (pdf)
Subjects: LCSH: Video games. | Fantasy games.
Classification: LCC GV1469.37 .G64 2023 | DDC 794.8—dc23/eng/20221213
LC record available at https://lccn.loc.gov/2022039033

A British Cataloging-in-Publication record for this book is available from the British Library.

References to internet websites (URLs) were accurate at the time of writing. Neither the author nor Rutgers University Press is responsible for URLs that may have expired or changed since the manuscript was prepared.

∞ The paper used in this publication meets the requirements of the American National Standard for Information Sciences—Permanence of Paper for Printed Library Materials, ANSI Z39.48-1992.

rutgersuniversitypress.org

In memory of my uncle, Larry Edward Goetz (1956–2019)
And my grandmother, Eldrus Ann Goetz (1927–2022)

Contents

Contents

The Counterfeit Coin

Introduction

• •

Feeling Powerful and Getting
Your Way

In 2015, the pop culture website Buzzfeed posted a video titled "Feminists Play *Grand Theft Auto* for the First Time."[1] The video includes a moment when former Buzzfeed producer Claudia Restrepo reacts to a scene set in a strip club by saying she hates videogames because they "appeal to the male fantasy"—words that would enjoy new life as a popular online meme ("Video Games Appeal to the Male Fantasy").[2] The meme juxtaposes Restrepo mid-articulation with game-play moments intended to undermine her critique, such as repaying a home loan in *Animal Crossing* (2001), planting crops in *Minecraft* (2011), dying in *Dark Souls* (2011), sleeping in *The Elder Scrolls V: Skyrim* (2011), or petting foxes in *Ghost of Tsushima* (2020).

Restrepo's language—particularly her use of *fantasy*—evokes the gender-based critique of media representation popularized in the 1970s by Laura Mulvey in her argument about Hollywood cinema as an "illusion cut to the measure of desire."[3] And commercial videogames, with their princess rescue plots and the sexual objectification of women's bodies, are indeed susceptible to a Mulveyan critique at the level of representation.[4] No credible voice doubts this. And yet, by pointing to the odd variety of activities performed in games, the meme suggests that empowerment fantasies might be stranger than we tend to think.

Of course, the Male Fantasy meme's rhetoric falls flat; applying Restrepo's words to moments when power and the objectification of women are not on display says nothing of the many moments when games *do* cater to the romantic and ambitious wishes of (straight and white) male players (e.g., the strip club scene

1

The "Video Games Appeal to the Male Fantasy" meme. This iteration references a fox-petting mechanic in *Ghost of Tsushima* (2020).

referenced in the Buzzfeed video).[5] The meme's politics are problematic as well. It mocks and dismisses a woman's criticism of an exclusionary gamer culture. Nor is Restrepo alone in tying games to masculine fantasy structures; hers follows journalistic and academic critiques of popular games as a kind of "empowerment fantasy"—"fantasies of control" that are especially transparent in gaming's many violent, war-themed commercial franchises.[6] The gamer communities that gleefully circulate the Male Fantasy meme seem eager to remind us that games often truly are about "feeling powerful" and "about you getting your way," to borrow phrasing from Leigh Alexander's unfavorable review of *Grand Theft Auto V* (2013).[7]

It is only with all this in mind that one should turn (with some caution) to the meme's provocative suggestion that games, in their complexity and multiplicity, cannot be neatly assembled under the singular heading of "male fantasy." How could "male fantasy" include activities as varied as riding horses, buying furniture, building cabins, shooting asteroids, baking cookies, rearranging gems, and gardening, to name a few core gameplay experiences frequently repeated in popular game genres?[8] If playing games means entertaining a fantasy, then this fantasy seems not only polymorphous and complex in its relationship to gender, but also sometimes banal and innocuous. In short, it seems that it is only with difficulty that we can situate the fantasy attached to games in a binary, Mulveyan framework.

The Counterfeit Coin explores the notion that games and related entertainment media have become almost inseparable from fantasy, which I understand broadly as a dynamic psychological process related to play. In turn, these media are making fantasy itself visible in new ways. The book's mission is not to relabel games *as* fantasy, but rather to focus on the conditions of this visibility. It offers original theoretical paradigms for thinking about what games are and how they relate to other media. Tracking fantasies that intersect with a game's mechanics as well as its representational layers reveals some of the vital connections that exist between computational processes and narrative contents; between games and principally representational media such as cinema, television, and comics; and between games and the players they enclose within fantasy loops.

As the Male Fantasy meme illustrates, the term "fantasy" has become charged with meaning in the world of videogames. Though apparently asocial and egocentric—an internal mental image expressing the fulfillment of some wish—fantasy has become a key term in recent social contestations of the emerging medium. Not far beneath the surface of the conflict repeatedly registered in this meme lie fundamental questions, such as "What is a game?" and "What is fantasy?" These questions orient us (in Sara Ahmed's sense) in certain directions, toward some objects and questions and away from others. Would anybody lay claim to *every* fantasy that has ever cropped up during idle thoughts? What does it mean for a fantasy to become so closely tied to an external form— something shared with and observed by others—that it becomes subject to a broad critique? How one defines games (or fantasy) will largely determine one's position on the question of whether men who play digital games enjoy ownership of certain fantasy scenarios from which women can be excluded, even in their own fantasies and play.

It is interesting along these lines that late twentieth-century feminist film theory embraced fantasy as a way to reintroduce flexibility into our engagement with media texts.[9] Key to such efforts was a particular definition of fantasy borrowed from Freudian psychoanalysts Jean Laplanche and Jean-Bertrand Pontalis as a "scenario with multiple entries," where we might imagine identifying with the subject who is acting, the object being acted upon, or even the verb, to act.[10] Definitions matter; this one emphasizes fantasy's "absence of subjectivization," meaning that our experience of a fantasy scenario is not "weighted by the ego" or anchored to our waking sense of self, our subjectivity.[11] Instead, fantasy is understood as an opportunity to try something different: it offers latitude for play, for identifying across gender lines as well as subject-object divisions within the supposedly impermeable binaries of Mulvey's gaze theory. For games, fantasy might best describe what it means to identify with a figure such as Nintendo's iconic plumber, Mario, not simply in terms of his masculine appearance, but also (or even primarily) in terms of the verbs enabled through him, such as *to leap*. Of course, the theoretical softening of Mulvey's gender binary was never meant to blunt her (then-and-now) relevant critique of the treatment of women in media and media industries. If anything, fantasy highlights the urgency of interrogating our intimate relationship with media texts.

Regardless of our point of entry to a text such as a videogame, play and fantasy should be understood as social and shared experiences. Even when we play alone, we play before an audience we have long since internalized—one that either approves of our play or scorns us for it. So argues Sigmund Freud in an early essay ("The Creative Writer and Daydreaming") about the consciously acknowledged sort of fantasy, about daydreams or castles in the air. Here, Freud defines fantasy as *play* that has been drawn inward and forced to surrender its connection with "palpable and visible things in the real world."[12] Freud understands both play and fantasy as "wish-fulfilment," or imaginative formations aimed at the task of "correcting an unsatisfactory reality."[13] Why does play becomes fantasy? Because the psyche is unable to forgo a pleasure it has known; it must, at the very least, attempt to "exchange one thing for another."[14] The child, who openly and "constantly plays at being grown up," who "imitates in play what it has gathered about grown-up life," this child has "no reason" to conceal the ambitious wish to be big and powerful—"Not so the adult: *he* knows what is expected of him—that he should no longer play or fantasize, but take an active part in the real world."[15] For Freud, play becomes fantasy so that it may persist in spite of its ambitious wish's "excessive self-regard" and the childish refusal to assume one's proper "place in a society that teems with individuals who nurse equal pretensions."[16] Fantasy is a form of self-regard that seeks to stave off any excessive regarding of the self.

The one topic I might be tempted to explore entirely through a Freudian lens is fantasy, which is, after all, psychoanalysis's "fundamental object."[17] Freud's daydream essay ties fantasy to play and anchors both in a social framework through the internalization of a "social situation" where we become our own "disapproving audience," to borrow phrasing from clinical psychoanalysts.[18] Freud's theory is also helpful for thinking about contemporary digital games, which straddle a number of resonant binary pairs: the tangible and the intangible, play and fantasy, shame and empowerment, and subjectivity and the absence of subjectivization.[19] However, Freud's daydream essay is especially attractive because it does *not* exemplify depth psychology's search for unconscious motives. Conscious fantasy does not necessarily require specialized interpretation.[20] The mystery the essay tackles is not the unconscious mind, but the realm of art—specifically, what Freud calls the "ars poetica,"[21] or the secret technique by which the artist's own fantasy somehow takes hold in the audience, where it relaxes some barrier to pleasure and so "enables us, from now on, to enjoy our own fantasies without shame or self-reproach."[22] Freud is suggesting that the creative work around which we spin our empowering fantasies forms a closely knit pair or ensemble with our own minds.

Though Freud's "ars poetica" provides a helpful starting point for thinking about fantasy, it is necessary to go beyond Freud in facing the broad continuity that exists between our minds, bodies, and the digital games we play. In lieu of an interaction-based conceptual framework (the coming together of "two discrete things, a medium and a mind"), this project follows philosophical and theoretical traditions that understand our relationship with media as, in Daniel Reynolds' words, "a transaction within a continuous field of matter."[23] Because the mind is part of the physical world, Reynolds argues, "the mind of a media user must be continuous with and partly constituted by media."[24] And the reverse must also be true. Reynolds, for instance, draws on models of embodied cognition to assert that "the mental and physical tasks of playing *Tetris*" are "fundamentally indistinguishable from one another."[25] That thing we think of as a game is constituted by a powerful attribution: by how we frame it when we *play* it.[26] And playing it means internalizing its systems. We land a difficult "skill shot" by already knowing where an opponent is heading. The game lives in us. It lives in our fantasies, and our fantasies live in it.

For the sake of descriptive convenience in the pages ahead, I will often refer to fantasy and videogames as though they were distinguishable. But the focus of this book rests on the special conjunction of fantasy, narrative, and software systems that characterizes a broad swath of contemporary entertainment industries. Historically, the project focuses on the past forty years, a period of time during which games became *domesticated*, their hyperstimulating arcade logics and rhythms gradually transformed by new relations with domestic leisure activities, such as reading, watching television, or (repeatedly) viewing movies at home.

Enmeshed with other domestic leisure activities and shoehorned into the daily lives of billions of people around the world, popular videogames have gradually become mechanisms that, as Chris Bateman suggests, *hack* the mind's pleasure centers. Bateman offers the interesting analogy between games and what Ernst Gombrich calls "functional" substitutes, or objects that enable certain valued actions that would otherwise be possible only in special circumstances—the way a cat chases a ball. When Gombrich says the "ball 'represents' a mouse to the cat, the thumb a breast to the baby," the concept of representation is predicated less on a substitute's "formal similarities" (i.e., resemblance to an original) than on "function": "The ball has nothing in common with the mouse except that it is chasable. The thumb nothing with the breast except that it is suckable."[27] In Gombrich's words, the action carried out with the aid of these objects substitutes for or "fulfills certain demands of the organism. They are keys which happen to fit into biological locks, or counterfeit coins which make the machine work when dropped into the slot."[28] Gombrich's framework focuses on tangible things as well as a kind of play that has been restored from fantasy, an internal world revivified by objects. Situating Gombrich alongside Freud's "ars poetica" orients this project toward the art of functional substitution. The key that fits into a biological lock is itself part of our world—something worth seeing, studying, practicing, and knowing. The key is not simply a virtual object; it cannot be reduced to a substitutive function, its illusory relationship to some *other* thing in the world.

The counterfeit coin stands out among Gombrich's examples as likely the best for thinking about an ongoing relationship with the functional substitutes at the center of this book. It is evocative of commercial gaming's coin-operated roots but is also oriented toward home spaces through the promise of costless coin dropping in ads for early home versions of arcade videogames. Moreover, this coin that makes the machine work when dropped into the slot expresses, in its deliberate design, specific ideas about the "machine" itself. Even in those digital games that represent the external world with staggering optical fidelity, a large part of what is being modeled through algorithms, actions, and code is the player's own mind, reflected in the structure of a fantasy that recurs throughout play. Videogames are, in this sense, self-involving: they're about the people who play them.[29]

Fantasy Is a Core Loop

Even in its most conventional meanings, fantasy is associated with repetition and circular temporality. Fantasy is not just any mental image, but one upon which we tend to dwell, to return to again and again. Freud speaks of the staging of a wish in fantasy as a mental representation of a somatic (bodily) impulse or drive, which he understands to inexhaustibly and repeatedly supply the motive force for all mental ideation. Jacques Lacan's influential notion of desire as a demand that can never be satisfied is based in large part on a reading of Freud's drive theory. In Slavoj Žižek's phrasing, "The real purpose of the drive is not its goal (full satisfaction) but its aim: the drive's ultimate aim is simply to reproduce itself as drive, to return to its circular path, to continue its path to and from the goal. The real source of enjoyment is the repetitive movement of this closed circuit."[30] Fantasy does not merely stage and so satisfy a wish; fantasy also *constitutes* the wish: "It is only through fantasy that the subject is constituted as desiring: through fantasy, we learn how to desire."[31] Žižek himself gets somewhat caught up in repetition, referring again and again to fantasy as a circular argument, an interminable searching around a "phantasmic loop."[32]

Fantasy's circular temporality has been discussed in relation to entertainment media as well. Laura Mulvey briefly addresses a voyeuristic fantasy's fetishistic tendencies, which she suggests "exist outside linear time," pulling an overvalued image out of the signifying chain of its narrative sequence.[33] Linda Williams extends this idea to the repetitious spectacle of sexual intercourse in pornographic media.[34] And in their looping, fractal structure, videogames would seem to even better exemplify fantasy's circularity.

Indeed, loops or "self-contained units that may or may not be combined with other loops or non-looping material in a larger structure"[35] are a basic element of design that ties videogames to new media logics of modularity and variability.[36] Games loop music,[37] background scenery, character animation and models, gameplay action, and broader patterns of play across repeated gameplay sessions of variable duration. For game designers, "loop" is often shorthand for "feedback loop," or the idea that play is reinforced as it moves from objective to challenge and reward (then back again). The term "core loop" is often employed to refer to the most frequently iterated actions, a game's central verbs (run, jump, shoot, duck, etc.) that are enacted with real-time feedback and play a central role in determining the game's outcome.[38] The notion of "algorithmic loop" stands as one of game studies' key terms—this is the gameplay loop but with particular emphasis on how a game's procedures and processes are structured by programmed machine instructions (algorithms).

Game studies scholarship has tended to discuss algorithmic loops in prosaic or computational terms. For instance, Ian Bogost argues that game algorithms possess a "procedural rhetoric," that they express some view about whatever aspect of the world they model or simulate.[39] Noah Wardrip-Fruin's notion of "operational logic" makes the case that algorithms express an authorial voice.[40] Such approaches hold games at arm's length. Like recent game studies scholarship by Patrick Jagoda, Katherine Isbister, and Aubrey Anable, *The Counterfeit Coin* instead explores gaming's affective potential.[41] However, rather than opposing the algorithmic loop and its formal machine logics to a game's more sensuous features (e.g., representational imagery, interface design, or player subjectivity), I seek to reintegrate the loop as an affective structure itself—one that moves along with fantasy. The cybernetic loop, the one that incorporates the player into the machine, cannot be made sense of through machine logics alone. With its eschewal of linearity, the gameplay loop is less prose and more poetry, less narrative and more fantasy. When games grip us, looping us into their systems, we struggle to attain critical distance from the repetitive and compulsory movement of a closed circuit.

This project views a game's repetitions, its core loops, as the enactment of empowering fantasies. Following David Mechanic's definition of empowerment as the "process in which individuals learn to see a closer correspondence between their goals and a sense of how to achieve them,"[42] I define empowerment fantasy as a dynamic psychological process in which wish-fulfilling goals and the means to achieve them find a special correspondence that is based less on satisfaction than renewal, and that structures prolonged and repetitious interaction with media objects such as games. Rather than treat any pleasurable gameplay mechanism as an empowerment fantasy, this designation is reserved for especially compelling patterns of play repeated not just in one game, but in many games, across different game platforms, and usually in relation to narrative media as part of a broader cultural concern or even preoccupation.

This book discusses three basic empowerment fantasy categories that motivate the design of core loops in commercial videogames.[43] None of these categories originates with digital games—nor can any be said to exist as the exclusive domain of games. However, each has taken hold in games, has adopted new forms and meanings there, and has become visible in new ways thanks to games. Fantasy loops spread outward from the time and place of play as a powerfully assimilatory force—they forge connections that defy logic and ignore the supposed boundaries separating inner from outer realities, actions from images, and one type of medium from another. In this way, they bridge apparently distinct media and so hold special value for the task of thinking about how media fit into the rituals of everyday life. In Žižek's terms, fantasy provides desire its "coordinates" ("it literally 'teaches us how to desire'"): "Fantasy does not mean that when I desire a strawberry cake and cannot get it in reality, I fantasize about eating it; the problem is, rather: *how do I know that I desire a strawberry cake in the first place? This* is what fantasy tells me."[44] Žižek's example is especially helpful because it emphasizes that fantasy is corporeal, an expression that emerges from the body—and the body is a key term in this book.

A Short Guide for the Fantasies Ahead

In chapter 1, I discuss a fantasy about transcending the limits of what is normally possible, a fantasy about bodies that leap beyond constraint, overcome opposition, and defy expectations—a *fantasy of bodily transcendence*. Especially where digital games are concerned, this fantasy is anchored in the player's *own* body as an internalized pattern of action (or body schema). I do not call it a fantasy of transcendent bodies because it is not always anchored in the depiction of a literal body. Rather, it is often found in a general, even decentralized capacity to act, to intervene into difficult situations, or to cut one's own trajectory through space. Even abstract digital games such as *Geometry Wars* (2003) require players to develop fine-grained body schema for moving and acting within game spaces. Embodied fantasy hails us through our own internalized capacity to transcend opposition. This fantasy is always negotiating—seeking the "coordinates" for—a way to creatively connect an internalized, wish-fulfilling memory of leaping beyond constraint with some present obstacle in our harshly inhibiting world.

Action games such as *Contra III: The Alien Wars* (1992), *Super Punch-Out!!* (1994), and *Super Mario Galaxy* (2007)—representative of shooters, fighting games, and platformers—offer distinct impressions of this fantasy, which assumes many different forms across the diverse terrain of commercial videogames as well as related narrative media. What all forms share in common is a pleasure taken in seeing the self as a *cause*, or as a force that intervenes. Such a pleasure could apply to *any* game, insofar as the power to manipulate and influence an interface (digital or otherwise) can be traced to the player's own willful intervention: the tactile sense of dice skipping across a wooden game board, the satisfying click of a virtual cursor navigating menus or arranging gems in a grid. However, challenging action games may provide the most legible and sustained examples of a broader wish-fulfilling structure that continuously repeats and renews itself. The spatiotemporal play that in these games becomes the object of focus, that becomes body schema, repeatedly connects a visual frenzy with feelings of triumph. Along with the skills that are honed, players make this feeling their own. And the allure of being a cause marks the fantasy as ambitious or egotistical, verging on a belief in one's specialness.

Chapter 2 tracks this same fantasy as a vehicle for convergence (or a condition of mutual influence and development) between games and principally narrative media. The designation of *action-body melodrama* names a narrative mode in which melodrama's need to recognize virtue is cast in especially corporeal terms, and where what is virtuous is ultimately tied to a special body that somehow permits one to transcend constraints or overcome opposition. Narrative permutations of the fantasy of bodily transcendence are perhaps most apparent in plots when diegetic audiences finally recognize a specialness that has gone unheeded. In such moments, misrecognition is dramatically corrected through "the spectacle of the body in exhilarating purposeful action."[45] Consider, for example, the moment that stunned onlookers gape at large dust plumes when Rock Lee drops his heavy training weights in the Japanese anime *Naruto* (2002–2007); when local ruffians bully the wrong dandy in the British American action film *Kingsman: The Secret Service* (2014); or when overlooked characters on the margins of a story dramatically assume center stage in the Hong Kong action-comedy *Kung Fu Hustle* (2004). In such examples, the fantasy seems to work into its mise-en-scène[46] the very same critical voice that structures fantasy in the first place, at least in Freud's "Creative Writer" framework. The fear that others will observe the ambitious wish becomes woven into the structure of the fantasy as a scenario where one's specialness is recognized by others. Such a scenario goes beyond merely inverting the social situation of shame and also drags one's specialness out into the open where it cannot be denied.

Chapters 3 and 4 build upon and, to a certain extent, take for granted the proposition that empowerment fantasy is grounded in the body and functions as a kind of glue for media convergence. These chapters therefore address both gamic and narrative permutations of their core fantasies within a single chapter.

Chapter 3 explores how entertainment media such as digital games have taken on the logic of security-seeking, especially in adventure, role-playing, and survival genres. The chapter defines and tracks a *tether fantasy*, which involves the pleasure of leaving a safe point and venturing into the unknown as well as the pleasure of returning to safety. Tethers entail dwelling on the boundaries that separate feeling safe and feeling exposed and are most clearly exemplified in games where players carefully construct and maintain a protective home base, such as *Minecraft* (2011), *Raft* (2018), and *Valheim* (2021). The fantasy also seems to play a role in a range of principally narrative media, from the adventure stories of Jules Verne, Johann David Wyss, and Robert Louis Stevenson to space operas (e.g., *Star Trek*, *Star Wars*, *Battlestar Galactica*, etc.), medieval fantasy fiction (from authors such as Tudor Jenks, J. R. R. Tolkien, and George R. R. Martin), and apocalyptic narratives of surrender (from zombies to catastrophic weather). Though distinct from the fantasy of bodily transcendence, the tether is also related to notions of embodied fantasy. Tether genres regularly put basic body schema into play, such as our implicit awareness of our relation to a shelter or dwelling (being inside, outside, or transitioning between the two).

The tether fantasy evokes "fort-da," the game Freud discovered when he observed his grandson banishing toys to oblivion and joyfully recalling them.[47] Had the infant been aware of what his grandfather thought of the game (that Freud believed he was observing the symbolized eradication and resurrection of the child's own mother), we might expect the child to have felt shame at so openly attempting to master the pain of separation anxiety. The tether fantasy seeks any occasion to return to such an open display.

If tether play casts security-seeking in spatial terms, then its complement—a *fantasy of accretions*—might be understood as pursuing a kind of protection against time. An accretion is a *thing* that has been actively collected from the world. In a fantasy of accretions, one grows but rarely shrinks. One dies and tries once more without ever losing what has been gained. The accretion is something guaranteed; you can take it to the bank. Encountering the world and gathering its treasured objects—investing them in one's self—means gradually laying claim to that world's total store of power, thereby modifying the very terms of play. Such accrual intersects with other fantasies as well. For instance, a shiny accretion is what players often find when their tethers are stretched to the limit; in turn, that accretion can augment the tether's capacity for stretching out. This reciprocal pairing of tether and accretion is how the fourth chapter makes sense of role-playing games (RPGs) such as *Super Mario RPG* (1996), *Fire Emblem: Path of Radiance* (2005), and *Dragon Quest XI: Echoes of an Elusive Age* (2017).

Chapter 4 argues that a fantasy of accretions acts as a major driving force in game design and development, especially free-to-play markets with in-app purchases that base their monetization strategy on the hope that players get caught in the pleasurable loop of accrual. Neurobiological accounts of reward structures (and the timing of reward intervals) serve as a key discourse in this chapter.

However, beyond what accretions games share in common with slot machine gambling, the fantasy's loops also exemplify a wish for the ultimate defense: to gradually replace life's fragility with armor, to return once again to an inorganic state in order to become shielded not just against time, but against anything which could inhibit or provoke.

On their surface, these three fantasies seem innocuous. They are ambitious but ultimately in accord with the ego, and so not necessarily repressed and disguised in the way psychoanalytic theory understands sexual traumas to be. And yet, each can also be thought of in relation to traumatic experiences, such as abject powerlessness, enforced immobility, separation anxiety, and premature encounters with loss. So it is unsurprising that each is capable of contradictions, inversions, and displacements not quite characteristic of waking thought. In the chapters that follow, I address some implications of this fact in how we understand player agency and identification in games and related entertainment media. There are clear moments in play when the joy of being a cause gives way to the stress of being an effect, when the self-assured act of venturing into the unknown becomes the masochistic pleasure of being caught out and needing to flee, and when a journey's player-directed activity becomes a kind of mindless and trance-like pursuit of constancy (a death drive). Fantasy casts players in multiple, simultaneous, and even opposed roles, dispersed across screen space while playing or spectating a game. In fantasy, we possess the ability to shift fluidly between different levels of subjective engagement: at times entertaining a daydream for its own sake and at other times mobilizing our own bodies in tight correspondence with the structures of a game.

Some Affordances and Limitations of a Fantasy Framework

The following section signals some implications for this book's fantasy framework, beginning with its intervention into conversations about media convergence. Media convergence is often discussed in terms that emphasize overlapping industrial practices, a congruity of aesthetics (e.g., shared optics or the eschewal of montage), or the adaptation of narrative content into new formats.[48] Thinking of fantasy as pre-existing or ready-made schemas through which we assimilate new information (including our encounter with games and narrative media) raises the possibility that it is fantasy itself which coalesces in media convergence. Because fantasy follows a logic of *affinity*, it provides especially flexible ways of thinking about disparate media in relation to one another.

As Kaja Silverman explains, the primary process of the unconscious mind obeys the pleasure principle and "seeks immediate gratification through hallucination," "makes no distinction between internal and external registers," and proceeds by way of affinity, where things that are merely alike can become identified with one another.[49] In contrast, the mind's "secondary process" respects the reality principle and so "traces a more circuitous route to gratification, which necessitates the temporary toleration of unpleasure, but promises a more satisfying conclusion."[50] When fixed to games—their rules, systems, and points of frustration—fantasy might appear more "secondary," as in more capable of observing rational distinctions and tolerating frustration or delay. At other times, fantasy drifts away from stabilizing, secondary systems and is instead capable of connecting or even equating patterns of experience across materially, historically, and culturally distinct domains. Even in its "typical and repetitive scenarios," fantasy freely assembles a "kaleidoscopic material drawn from all quarters of human experience."[51] Like a kaleidoscope, fantasy's formations both draw from but also reassemble and modify their gathered bits of source material. In short, distinct media can *converge* into a shared fantasy without any specific formal similarities. In this sense, fantasy is somewhat indifferent to whether we preserve space for medium specificity (the very "secondary" tendency to seek out essential properties unique to each medium) or else think of media convergence as the merger of "previously distinct forms" (the idea that "it is increasingly difficult to separate or define where one medium stops and another starts").[52] There is generally still little difficulty in distinguishing a videogame from a film (or television series), even in special circumstances when thematic interests and formal systems are shared (e.g., a game such as *Heavy Rain* [2010] or a film such as *Hardcore Henry* [2015]). This book contends that what is unique about our historical moment of apparent convergence has to do with the proliferation of distinct media objects (movies, television series, comics, and digital games) that harness and extend a shared or core set of empowering fantasies. In a related sense, a fantasy framework influences how we conceive of media in the first place. When defining the term "medium," Henry Jenkins distinguishes between a delivery technology and its cultural protocols: "Delivery systems are simply and only technologies; media are also cultural systems."[53] While delivery technologies (such as wax cylinders) "come and go all the time," Jenkins suggests that once a medium (such as the recorded human voice) "establishes itself as satisfying some core human demand, it continues to function within the larger system of communication options."[54] Fantasy would seem to orient discussion of media around their associated protocols or cultural systems rather than their delivery technologies. Further, if we follow Jenkins in imagining core human demands canalized along lines of established media (e.g., recorded voice, moving images, printed words, and so on), then fantasy might well be understood as speaking to some core human demand that runs perpendicular to and often leaps across the boundaries separating disparate media channels.

Along similar lines, fantasy seems to offer new tools for navigating questions of videogame medium specificity—especially the narratology/ludology debates over whether games are best understood in terms of storytelling or as systems of rules.[55] As a term perhaps midway between story and play, fantasy readily speaks to both. It thus helps connect a game's core loops and rule systems to questions about representation, such as those that have been raised by Adrienne Shaw,

Jennifer Malkowski, TreaAndrea Russworm, and Bonnie Ruberg. I highlight this feature of a fantasy framework especially for proponents of ludology (or videogame formalism) who have found themselves resisting critical representational analysis of games along lines of gender, race, class, and ability on the basis that gameplay seems to happen apart from concerns of story, in a game's "extended middles" between narrative cutscenes and their "subject-fixing processes."[56] This book ties concerns about identity directly to a game's algorithmic processes through fantasy. At the same time, fantasy does offer new ways to think about medium specificity, since a fantasy's patterns do seem to change in distinct ways when it leaps between fictional worlds and a game's rule-bound systems.

The flip side to fantasy's tendency to assimilate or emphasize affinities over differences is the risk of eschewing important material and technological distinctions. As a framework, fantasy shifts focus away from a game's status as a fixed object or artifact and toward its status as experience, as something enacted in play. Fantasy may seem to have little to contribute to materialist histories of videogames or platform studies that focus on the relation between a medium's cultural protocols and its delivery technology. However, fantasy is never far from such discussions. For instance, I argue in chapter 3 that *Minecraft*'s use of a voxel-based graphical system with low-resolution textures allows it to prioritize the experience of spatial continuity, which in turn facilitates a particular kind of tether play. Fantasy's often macroscopic vantage speaks more readily to continuities across platforms—across generations of platforms or across media altogether—than to technological distinctions between or within these systems. Fantasy may have little to say about the technical work of porting a piece of software across platforms—an often complex and arduous task. At the same time, however, a tether fantasy can be evoked by this process, such as when we take a Nintendo Switch out of its TV dock and play a ported Super Nintendo game such as *Earthbound* (1994) in handheld mode in a nook on a rainy day (playing the game with a different affective relationship to screen).

As the example of playing (or reading) in a liminal space seems to emphasize, we pursue fantasy in a game or fictional world as well as outside it—fantasy is situated by these texts, but fantasy also situates *them* in time and space. It ties leisure activities to the space and habits of daily life by a logic of repetition, which, as Barbara Klinger argues, "amplifies any domestic medium's ability to become part of viewers' daily lives, even part of their autobiographies, resulting in an intense process of personalization."[57] Fantasy is a sort of fabric that stretches across a series of boundaries in lived experience, connecting the real and the imagined, public and private spaces, and text and audience.[58]

This synthetic function of fantasy enables ambitious transhistorical analogies such as Henry Jenkins's notion of *adventure island*, a fantasy formation that incorporates twentieth-century children's literature, the Victorian doctrine of separate spheres, shrinking suburban environments, and contemporary videogames.[59] Along these lines, however, fantasy also runs the risk of seeming ahistorical and inward-facing, even anecdotal. Psychoanalysis itself has been criticized as constructing a "universal" (aka white, straight, European) subject and at best ignoring (at worst pathologizing) the cultural and historical specificity of anyone who does not fit the mold. Indeed, although there are key exceptions in the form of scholars of critical race, gender, and sexuality studies who engage with psychoanalysis (e.g., Judith Butler, Damon Young, Leo Bersani, Kaja Silverman, Mary Ann Doane, David Eng, Jessica Benjamin, Anne Cheng, bell hooks, Lee Edelman, and others), the framework remains problematic for a number of reasons.[60] Much like the evolutionary perspectives of behavioral psychology I discuss in chapter 3, approaches to fantasy based in Freudian psychoanalysis are not optimized to provide fine-grained distinctions on a historical or cultural level.

There are, however, times when engaging with fantasy is unavoidable. So argues Jacqueline Rose in her study of the role fantasy plays as a kind of social glue for nation-states. Rose notes how fantasy is, "even on its own psychic terms . . . never only inward-turning; it always contains a historical reference in so far as it involves, alongside the attempt to arrest the present, a journey through the past."[61] Because fantasy plays a role in the "forging of the collective will"—as that will's very "precondition or psychic glue"—Rose argues it cannot be understood as entirely "antagonistic to social reality."[62] Quite the reverse. As Jason Bainbridge says of superhero comics, it is precisely *because* they are "a kind of adolescent wish fulfillment" ("the perfect revenge/control fantasy . . . of power without the constraint of law") that studying them means also investigating "the perceived deficiencies in society."[63] In a discussion of digital games, the topic of fantasy is even more strongly justified, as games combine fantasy's role as a social glue with its more common associations with pleasure and play. Rather than only leading away from our outer (historical) selves and into an inner (psychic) space, this book employs fantasy to see the outer deep within the inner.

There is one additional affordance of a fantasy framework: it offers a means of addressing the pleasure of commercial games while also providing new ways to critically examine those pleasures. Almost by definition, however, the consequent limitation is that experimental games often seem situated beyond the project's scope. Experimental games frequently challenge commercial gaming's structures of pleasure, featuring what Patrick Jagoda terms "affective difficulty"[64]—for instance, what Jason Rohrer's *The Castle Doctrine* (2014) does with a tether fantasy.[65] Defining empowerment fantasy as a loop to which we repeatedly return privileges not simply pleasure but also big-budget games that require dozens or hundreds of hours to complete, as well as games sustained by the ongoing labor of large development teams, such as *League of Legends* (2009–present) and *World of Warcraft* (2004–present)—games that have no ending at all. By contrast, consider Anna Anthropy's *Queers in Love at the End of the World* (2015)—an experimental, text-based Twine game that lasts only several seconds, during which time players decide what they would say or do if the world were about to end. The toxic backlash against some queer or experimental games in the wider gaming community can tend to catch one off guard, as if coming out of nowhere. However, as Jacqueline Rose puts it, fantasy "can just as well surface as fierce blockading protectiveness, walls up all around our inner and outer, psychic and historical, selves."[66] Efforts to improve the standing of marginalized groups within this community by empowering them to participate or reimagining the power structures of games have, for some, felt like an encroachment on a protected fantasy space.

This book approaches structures of empowerment from within, and so it is best read in tandem with work that challenges empowerment from without.[67] That it must sometimes venture away from the vanguard of cultural contestations over videogame representations is hopefully counterbalanced by the fresh insights it brings to such discussions when it returns, double-agent-like, from forays into a world of loops where contradictions mingle, meanings are stretched beyond recognition, and empowerment is always stranger than it first seems.

1

The Fantasy of Bodily Transcendence

• •

This chapter introduces and explores an empowerment fantasy at the center of recent film-game convergence. This fantasy, which I term the *fantasy of bodily transcendence*,[1] expresses a wish to exceed constraints, overcome obstacles, and answer feelings of weakness with transcendent displays of power. The *Oxford English Dictionary*'s definition of transcendence as "the action or fact of transcending, surmounting, or rising above" nicely expresses the fantasy's interest in a moment when a limit is overcome. The fantasy does not, however, simply entail the total liquidation of all conflict, an omnipotence of thoughts, or a masculine wish to feel powerful and get your way; rather, transcendence is rooted in the struggle of overcoming. Its exemplar is the determined underdog, and its emblematic form is prolonged training. Key to its designation as a body fantasy is action's internalized pattern: for the game genres discussed in this chapter, gradually overcoming a challenge requires mapping spatiotemporal systems to muscle memory or body schema.

The neuroscientific notion of body schema refers roughly to an internalized map based on patterns of past experience that is used to make sense of the body's spatial coordinates and its capacity to interact with objects in the world. The concept has played a role in philosophical efforts to rethink mind-body dualisms. Mark Johnson, for instance, emphasizes the active part played by the body in ordering our experience of the world and providing conceptual metaphors necessary for thinking itself. In short, we think with and through our bodies. Playing a videogame means developing body schema specific to that game. And, as

Paul Ward puts it, every videogame is "totally created," and each instance of play is in a sense also unique—it exists *only* at the point of playing the game."[2] That a game's action is utterly idiosyncratic is one of gaming's central appeals. And yet there is a surprising variety of uses for these maps or plans outside the context of videogame play when body schema recurs as fantasy. The sudden intrusion into our consciousness of clever gestures and useful maneuvers that have altered our relation to space and time somehow expresses a wish.

Like riding a bike, the mastered skill or dexterous maneuver is retained, paired in long-term memory with the challenge it helps us solve. And the vanquished limit remains: a skill is an identification that preserves a limit in its moment of being overcome. In her discussion of Hegel's notion of habituation, Elisa Magrì notes that in honing a skill, the soul is "empowered" by the specific context in which the habit was formed, a context that endures as "a possibility or an outward projection" of the past into a present moment.[3] And this moment becomes "a field of possibilities for action that the body seeks to actualize spontaneously."[4] Skills enable meaningful material change in the world. However, as Brian Sutton-Smith notes, even skills (or any "serious, adaptive, externally controlled act") can, when controls slacken, become "taken over" by play.[5] Play in the first place means, for Sutton-Smith, an "extrusion of internal mental fantasy into the web of external constraints."[6] Skills learned from playing videogames may find their clearest and most frequent application in related gameplay scenarios. But we carry the game's embodied context with us as a possibility for action or outward projection wherever we go. Fantasy represents the hope for a spontaneous actualization of these possibilities that we always carry with us.

Lunge and Leap: Our Playlist of Body Memories

We each possess a personal "playlist" of extreme body memories that entertainment media happily feed. Fleeting glimpses of bodies running along the wall or leaping through the air—in short, images of bodies "functioning at the extremes of what is physically possible"[7]—intrude upon consciousness in daily life while our bodies are somehow occupied: walking down hallways, jogging the treadmill, or sitting in a train. Such internal imagery is clearly influenced by and takes as its source moments in media consumption when we might collectively cheer, such as when bodies appear to defy gravity in *The Matrix* (1999), leap into orbit in *Super Mario Galaxy* (2007), or emerge suddenly from out of frame in *Game of Thrones* (2011–2019). One thing videogames and action cinema clearly share in common is the promise of implanting new kinetic possibilities into the bodies of their audience. What does it mean for such kinetic imagery to repeat in imagination for weeks, months, or even years? Is such repetition—a kind of bodily mantra—simply an afterimage like the "Tetris effect"?[8] What role might embodied echoes of internalized action play in orienting us toward future acts of consumption?

In pursuit of the hacker Trinity, an Agent leaps an unbridgeable gap and strikes a lunge landing early in *The Matrix* (1999).

The "bodily hook," or the snippet of unique kinetics the game or film succeeds in embedding within us, seems largely personal and idiosyncratic. My own imagination compulsively repeats choreography from *The Matrix*: the Agent's rooftop landing (lunge position) early in the film as he jumps the gap between two buildings in pursuit of the hero, Trinity. This gesture does occur at a significant moment in plot: when law enforcement is left behind, immobilized in disbelief before an unbridgeable gap, which is also a symbolic boundary establishing the arena where the story's heroes and villains clash. But the scene is otherwise not strongly emphasized—nor is it entirely clear why it would stick in memory. Anecdotally, the lunge position (itself a regular bodily configuration from exercise classes) has taken on an "obtuse" significance—in Barthes's sense of the word— that exceeds the meaning given it in the film. As a repeating memory, it seems to somehow encapsulate what I would describe as the wish to hold oneself over a limit. Along with the rest of my own compulsively repeating internal imagery, the lunge is part of my own ongoing body project.[9]

At the same time, my storehouse of body motions is also culturally and historically negotiated in relation to preexisting trajectories of meaning. And this chapter's analysis of videogame kinetics takes as its focus widely shared experiences of embodied action repeated across entire genres of videogame play. Key examples of these kinetics include the way Mario, in *Super Mario Galaxy*, soars through space and summersaults just before landing at the start of each mission (this happens dozens of times throughout the game and is featured in promotional materials); the way Hoy Quarlow jabs then pivots 360 degrees, counterclockwise, to strike Little Mac with an opposite backhand (an oft-repeated attack that is initially difficult to avoid) in *Super Punch-Out!!* (1994); the way Alucard back-dashes while attacking forward (a valuable maneuver for positioning) in *Castlevania: Symphony of the Night* (1997); or the surprising motility that stems from "wave-dashing," an advanced exploit used frequently by competitive *Super Smash Bros. Melee* (2001) players. Wave dashing is an alternative means of conveyance that repurposes the game's midair dodging mechanic in order to glide along the ground while stringing together attacks not normally possible while simply running. Though a technique available only to a skilled few, it exemplifies the affectively charged motion under consideration by introducing an entirely new field of possibilities for action.

Each of these examples might be described as *collective body memories* imparted through virtual exchanges. This is Thomas Fuchs's term for describing cultural practices that are widely shared (which he terms "participation genres"), "such as joint play, shared meals, salutations, queuing, bedtime rituals, and the like."[10] As Marcel Mauss has argued, bodies both are shaped by cultural practices and, in turn, carry their own cultural memories or *techniques of the body*. Within the participation genre of competitive videogame play, there are many YouTube videos devoted to analyzing specialized techniques such as wave dashing.[11] Those who only study videos of the technique and never attempt it themselves are nevertheless able to join this participation genre and take possession of certain aspects of its movement.[12]

This is true also of widely shared experiences of embodied movement detached from skill communities altogether, such as the image of Mario soaring through space in *Super Mario Galaxy*: something that happens frequently in cutscenes, does not involve player skill or control, and has been repeated in advertisements for the game as well as in online video compilations. Such imagery evokes gaming's arcade era, when games hailed passersby through an "attract mode" (aka "display mode"), or prerecorded snippets of in-game action played on a loop to entice potential players. A tension takes hold in the body while watching fragments of gameplay that begin but never conclude; the video loop itself may continuously repeat, but one is implicitly aware that play's action is interrupted and held in suspense. In this way, attract mode is akin to the action movie trailer's bodily provocation: both stage a wish to learn an action's meaning, its relation with what comes before and what comes after.

Once a hook has become embedded in a collective body memory, there seems to be a market incentive to foreground its repetition. For instance, in the early 2000s, there appeared a series of references to *The Matrix*'s "bullet-time" effect, when time briefly stops midaction and yet the camera continues to move freely.[13] The provocative technique was briefly lodged into our collective psyches, leading to what Bob Rehak has called a microgenre. As a foregrounding of style during a moment of narrative pause, bullet time's quotation in another text is easy to recognize. But even subtle gestures can become lodged in body memory for reasons that interweave personal and shared associations.

It always struck me as odd that the Agent's lunge landing was what compulsively repeated in my own memory, and not the effect that made the auditorium cheer (bullet time). The lunge can be spectacular and enthralling—an ostentatious pose. But it can also signify struggle, submission, or defeat. In *Underworld*'s (2003) final moment of action, the protagonist leaps and slashes a sword at the villain near the start of her jump. The reverse shot contains the remaining jump arc and a graceful lunge-landing pose, which is held for a moment before the deferred effect of the slash is revealed in the villain's partially severed head. The lunge seems to depict the literal absorption of the force generated by a leaping body's return to earth. It lends figural representation to the suspension of action required for others to properly absorb the situation. In such moments, the lunge becomes a container for power (a power pose). The pose is reinforced in the moment in *Watchmen* (2009) when Adrian Veidt, having dodged an assassin's bullets in spectacular slow motion, disables his assailant with a stanchion from the lobby in a spiraling arc that culminates in a deep lunge. In *The Matrix: Reloaded* (2003), Neo lunges, builds force, and launches into flight—a moment mirrored in Superman's slow (ground-shaking) takeoff in the trailer for the *Man of Steel* (2013). And the lunge position is made into an explicit, self-reflexive element of the superhero genre by *Deadpool* (2016), which deems it the "superhero landing." The lunge represents a buildup of muscular tension, including moments when the earth is left behind or reencountered in order to be challenged as a limit (a powerful landing). As an expression of the tension between mobility and stasis, it can also represent moments of misrecognized strength. It is the position the Beast is forced to adopt for stability when a more skilled opponent coerces him to bow in *Kung Fu Hustle* (2004). When Little Mac (from the 2009 series reboot *Punch-Out!!*) suffers a knockout blow, he sometimes rebounds off the ropes and catches himself in a standing lunge that grants players one more chance to prevail, marking the position as one that mediates between falling and standing. Like Yoga's warrior pose or the quarterback's kneel on the football field, the lunge can be a symbol of control (of one's body, of the ball, of the clock, of the game), a posture that activates a rule and serves a clear function in play, often in a moment of pause or at the threshold separating play from nonplay.

The lunge in these mostly cinematic examples accumulates a set of meanings that stem from but also exceed the bodily posture itself. It differs from the compulsively repeated videogame gesture (e.g., Mario's acrobatic leap over obstacles), which is generally not stylized in a moment of pause or imbued with specific textual meanings, and which can and does occur hundreds or thousands of times per play session in an always-evolving spatial situation. Developing skill at videogame play means assembling these repeated actions into larger patterns or "chunks": the term "chunking" refers to when any variously complex pattern is stored in long-term memory as a *unitary whole*.[14] Chunking in videogames is usually understood in terms of skill development—so, it would seem to pertain to Mario's manner of jumping in response to certain spatiotemporal scenarios that repeat across play. At first, new players must actively process each part of a complex situation: the enemy above, the pit below, the projectile moving right for us, how high or quickly Mario jumps when the button is pressed, and even where one finds this jump button on the controller itself. After time, we learn to see the entire situation as a unitary whole that is recognizable at a glance, and we react implicitly, without thinking. But to this unitary whole, we should also add the *feelings of triumph* attached to the experience of overcoming a difficult challenge. Doing so moves us one step closer to thinking of an embodied memory as fantasy.

In play, repeated actions gather in body memory as gratifying, useful, and empowering competencies, as the summation of a thousand challenging situations as well as the feeling of satisfaction tied to a skill that has gradually grown. Though they emerge and recede over a digital horizon, a videogame's many situations form a "habit structure" in our lives—this is Fuchs's chunk-like term for the "implicit bodily knowledge and skill" that results from "well-practiced motion sequences" and "repeatedly perceived gestalten."[15] What is most helpful about this concept is how habit structures exceed the literal bounds of our body as part of the wider "sensomotoric, libidinous and interactive field in which we, as embodied beings, constantly move and conduct ourselves."[16] Through habit structure, the past persists in a present situation as *"open loops* of potential interactions," loops that "are only closed to full functional cycles by suitable counterparts in the environment that the body currently connects with."[17] Skills developed while playing a videogame are *open loops* that are closed or completed by specially designed challenges ("suitable counterparts") in the game. Games differ from the rest of our lived reality, perhaps, for the especially tight and enabling correspondence that exists between the open loops of habit and the counterparts that close them. But what if we never cease searching for these suitable counterparts in the wider field of our lives? What is intended by the notion of a playlist of body memory is the playful act of imaginatively applying accrued body schema to our environment, seeking ways to close the loop of potential interactions that exist around us. To close the loop is to feel empowered, to experience both connectedness and agency within *any* libidinous and interactive field of experience.

Body Fantasy: The Tetris Effect as Envoy

In a sense, it is redundant to refer to fantasy as "embodied." The Freudian mythos understands fantasy, like sexuality, as something fundamentally *propped* upon a vital, somatic function. In Freud's discussion of fantasy's earliest infantile manifestations, the baby responds to a bodily tension (hunger) by recalling an embodied memory (the pleasure of nourishment) with an embodied wish (for the *lost* object, the mother's breast).[18] If nevertheless there is a tendency in Western thinking to view the ego (and not the body) as the seat of subjectivity—and to view fantasy as an imagined and consciously authored and arranged tableau (the mise-en-scène of desire)—then this discussion of fantasy will benefit from a narrowing of the term that situates fantasy beyond the realm of conscious authorship.

In their clinical practice, psychoanalysts Nicolas Abraham and Maria Torok define fantasy as a *"fleeting imaginary representation intruding upon the ego's activities"*—in short, as a *"total misfit"* to conscious thought.[19] Though psychoanalytic theory has discovered fantasy at every level of mental functioning (including fantasies that entirely elude conscious awareness), Abraham and Torok's method selects only the *"conscious experience of fantasy,"* where the conscious self becomes "the site and spectator of inner events emerging from a realm not authored or controlled by the ego."[20] Fantasy of this sort is untimely, it "catches one unawares" and "removes the ego from its immediate concerns": "the ego, absorbed in its current tasks, has suffered a break in its continuity."[21] The notion of fantasy as misfit aids clinical analysis because of its implied "ambassadorial function": it conveys wishes between different strata of the psyche—wishes that can then be integrated into analysis.[22] In their example, the image of a knife falling through a gingerbread cookie intrudes into conscious while pouring a drink for a guest. The fantasy poses two key questions: Why this image? And why now? Analysis attempts to answer these questions, to tie the image and its wider associations to the moment it has interrupted.[23]

Most likely, the experience of being the "site and spectator of inner events emerging from a realm not authored or controlled by the ego" returns one to the body: a full bladder, an empty stomach, a muscle memory, a reflex. Fantasy may begin here as a wish that responds to an internal stimulus, a bodily tension, that has been refused satisfaction. But the meanings attached to such a fantasy are perhaps too apparent (wish fulfilment, pure and simple). The body says more, perhaps, when the misfit image seems to express a wish that has come to the body from the outside, such as the image of Trinity's spectacular leap across the chasm. The misfit can also express a "somatic complaint" by conveying the troubling flashbacks of traumatic repetition.[24]

The misfit model of fantasy occasions further consideration of what is evoked by commonalities such as the "Tetris effect," which Tannahill, Tissington, and Senior define as "a form of hypnagogic imagery resulting from playing Alexey Pajitnov's *Tetris* [1984] that affects the player first during play" and again later when consciousness is relaxed.[25] In the Tetris effect, players once more experience "falling Tetriminos in their peripheral vision and while dreaming"—and some have even reported "attempting to mentally interlock real world objects" as if they functioned like the game's blocks.[26] Of course, the term need not apply to the game *Tetris* alone, nor even to gaming itself; rather, the phenomenon refers to the "hallucinatory replay of" any "novel physical or mental activit[y]" that one has pursued "for extended periods of time."[27] The example of catching oneself interlocking real-world objects after playing *Tetris* evokes Fuchs's *open loop*, which describes an embodied competency always seeking suitable counterparts in our lived environment. Not consciously authored, the Tetris effect is a corporeal reverberation that has been found to persist even in patients suffering from amnesia who have no recollection of even playing the game.[28] To explain our capacity for it, media psychology has drawn on simulation theory, or the idea that in order to understand and predict the outcome of events, our minds process internal simulations of experience through a "continuing private rehearsal process" that extends beyond direct participation in the events themselves.[29] As described, the Tetris effect is a live simulation following from motor skill learning that is mapped to the central nervous system.[30] However, the parallels with Abraham and Torok's model are sufficient to note that the Tetris effect also seems to behave just as fantasy does—as a communiqué from nonconscious strata in the psyche (i.e., central nervous system) that intrudes into consciousness as a misfit, removing the ego from present concerns. Does this intrusion also stage a wish of some sort?

Like a traumatic repetition, body fantasy likely returns for a reason. In both common and clinical parlance, a trauma is something we must "process," meaning to reduce the intensity of a sensory impression while drawing meaning from the experience.[31] The relation between trauma and fantasy may seem tonally inappropriate, but there is a tradition within psychoanalysis of viewing fantasy as a defensive formation—as a scenario that screens or "obfuscates the true horror of a situation" to use Slavoj Žižek's phrasing.[32] Fantasy conceals the Real, or at least the relation between subjectivity and reality.[33] And Žižek refers to a specifically embodied sensation in his example of safety instructions for air travel that imagine "a gentle landing on water" followed by a toboggan slide and "a nice collective lagoon holiday"—he calls these images fantasy's "'gentrifying' of a catastrophe."[34] It is no stretch from here to think of the sensation of gliding masterfully over chaos and destruction in games and action films.[35] As has been remarked of the tendency to perceive the terror attacks of September 11, 2001, *like a movie*, so too does fantasy seem to mediate our encounter with actual trauma.[36]

Experiencing trauma "as a movie" is an example of *miniaturization*, or emotional "strategies that help bolster a sense of control" when control has been unexpectedly lost.[37] Imagining Keanu or Bruce coming to the rescue is an effort to reintegrate the traumatic memory within a familiar (and safe, controlled) narrative frame. Along these lines, fantasy and play seem to enact the active, integrative, and adaptive response to (or defense against a potential) trauma.[38] It is as if trauma represents a challenge to Fuchs's open loop (the embodied competence that feels its way around for suitable counterparts in the environment); with trauma, we search for some inbuilt capacity to respond to a shocking or challenging situation, and we come up short. Our ability to *close the loop* would represent an integration of body with mind and world in a moment when these connections feel most threatened.

The analogy between trauma, fantasy, and play has limits. Although each involves the repetition or looping of implicit memory, it is necessary for the sake of description to distinguish between a traumatic event that might occur only once, evocative movements glimpsed a handful of times in a movie such as *The Matrix*, and actions performed hundreds or thousands of times while playing a videogame. There are different kinds of embodied memory at play as well: memories we are not yet prepared to integrate with consciousness (trauma), memories we recognize as significant but for reasons we may not initially comprehend (in a film or a catchy song), or memories the significance of which is mandated through sheer force of repetition (as in a game). Embodied memories involved in gameplay are not only drilled into muscle memory but also called upon and tested openly. These memories are available at a moment's notice even after significant time away from a game (*like riding a bike*), and they intrude into consciousness as an apparent misfit very predictably, following any prolonged period of heavy play.

The question of why certain actions might recur as fantasy more readily than others—what ambassadorial function they serve—likely also speaks to factors motivating what we play or watch in the first place. The fantasy of bodily transcendence represents a broad and synthetic attempt to answer the question of why such imagery intrudes following play, if play is not quite like a trauma. At stake is the meaning of *closing the loop*, not just in Fuchs's sense of a habit structure finding some suitable counterpart but also regarding the broader loops that ensnare us in habitual encounters with media.

The Joy of Being a Cause

One of the central ideas in Karl Groos's 1898 study of animal play is what the German philosopher and psychologist describes as the "joy in being a cause."[39] This joy is understood as a direct, embodied experience: the "*feeling* of pleasure arising from the consciousness of being a cause and culminating in the feeling of freedom."[40] Such a feeling lies at the heart of a fantasy of bodily transcendence. The breadth in Groos's concept implicates a range of impulsive behaviors:

> The little polar bear that delightfully tore the paper bag to bits certainly felt the pleasure of "being a cause"—"in working his own sweet will" . . . I wish to call attention to the absurd form this pleasure in being a cause sometimes takes even in rational beings. How many of us want to scribble or whittle or do something with our hands all the time, to break a twig and chew it while we walk, to strike the snow off walls as we pass, to kick a pebble before us, to step on all the acorns on the pavement, to drum on the window pane, to hit the wine glasses together, to roll up little balls of bread, etc.[41]

The elegant notion of being a cause is helpful for talking about pleasure taken in the low-level and non-goal-directed actions that all games provide. It serves as the conceptual foundation for French intellectual and seminal play theorist

Roger Caillois's formulation of *paidia*, or the raw instinct for play that has not yet been refined or disciplined by rules.[42]

The creative, spontaneous, and embodied joy of being a cause speaks to design aesthetics, from food packaging to the computer-user interface. It pertains to the experience of navigating virtual menus, especially with respect to how screens register user inputs. One of Steve Swink's fundamental elements of *game feel* is real-time interaction, which could itself be thought of as the pleasure of seeing the effects of one's actions in a virtual space without delay. Consider also the skeuomorphic clicking sound effects when texting on a smartphone or the built-in force feedback on a MacBook Pro trackpad. In the context of videogames, the joy of being a cause is helpful for addressing diegetic actions where players (beyond simply having agency) are able to work their *own sweet will*, experiencing the thrill of being the source and cause of explosions, streams of bullets, or dramatic leaps across chasms.

The joy of being a cause can be understood as a foundational element of our engagement with most commercial games. It is reflected in Dan Fleming's assertion that playing *Mario* games means identifying not as the character, Mario, but rather as a "powerful intervening force on his behalf."[43] Consider also James Newman's claim that we may not always identify with videogame avatars as fictional characters, but we do always identify with the feeling of "vehicular embodiment" the avatar provides.[44] Along similar lines, Henry Jenkins argues that videogames are an "art of expressive movement": although characters such as Mario and Sonic are reduced "to a limited range of preprogrammed expressions, movements, and gestures," they are nevertheless "enormously evocative" for their power to move *us*.[45] Players of *Mario* and *Sonic* games are stitched into play's fabric while dashing through tunnels, leaping chasms, breaking bricks, launching fireballs, stomping enemies, or knocking shells into walls. For each action, the joy of being a cause is marked by distinct, in-game sounds that acoustically register the player's experience as a powerful intervening force acting upon the space of play.

The fantasy of bodily transcendence often situates the joy of being a cause in the context of overcoming difficulty. This context can be spatial, mechanical, or narrative. Either way, the fantasy is self-reflexive—at least in terms of Freud's own account of the child at play who is ultimately forced to forfeit the pleasure of magically controlling "palpable and visible things in the real world."[46] Freud's theory is that in order to protect ego-aggrandizing wishes from observation, the child learns to limit their expression to internal thing representations (aka fantasy). In each of Groos's and Caillois's examples, tangible objects register the experience of being a cause; in contrast, when fantasy is an envoy from elsewhere, one is not so much the *cause* as the *recipient* of fantasy's imagery. The fantasy of bodily transcendence is a fantasy about being the cause once more.

Videogame play motivated by the fantasy can be understood as an effort—usually difficult and protracted—to return to the practice of staging wishes in a world of objects. This time, objects are assembled for play through the development of skills and a discourse of mastery. Play's connection with tangible things in the world is not simply exchanged for internal objects, as Freud suggests, but rather likely becomes displaced onto the body, that "first locus of intentionality"[47] and the primary object we both do and do not possess, do and do not control, and must work to improve before we can hope to manipulate the material world in such a way that we can experience the joy of being a cause once more. In their unquestionable rules and mechanical systems, videogames offer the fantasy a path back to palpable and real things. Their structure as competitive and progression-based systems (e.g., winning the match or advancing toward a goal) also supports fantasy through a socially affirmative framework about overcoming difficulty.

In fact, one common form given the fantasy is what Hal Niedzviecki terms "I'm Specialism," where a longed-for specialness (extreme individuality) represents a new kind of consumer conformity. I'm Specialism (or specialism) is best captured for Niedzviecki in the immense popularity of reality television programs such as *The Osbournes* (2002–2005) as well as in the phenomenon of people lining up by the thousands to audition for programs such as *Canadian Idol* (2003–2008). Specialism entails imagining oneself as a powerful causal force that has not yet been unleashed. It is as though one's banal daily existence could, at any moment, be punctured by the thunderclap of sudden recognition (followed by the arrival of documentary crews knocking at the door). Specialism is mobilized when we take time to fill out a personality quiz, when we imagine being sorted into a preferred house at Hogwarts, or when we fantasize that we have been the subject of surveillance all along, as in *The Truman Show* (1998). It can take on positive or negative valences—notoriety is a kind of specialism as well.

The fantasy of bodily transcendence's especially kinetic imagery of leaping, dodging, or entirely inverting oneself in relation to a given world's spatial coordinates reveals a wish to stand apart from the crowd in which one feels lost. Games are spaces where special rules apply—where we can break the usual laws of physics and transform material and social realities. Though Niedzviecki does not consider them, videogames do broadly exemplify specialism by centering players in worlds where they are unique and possess, or may directly pursue, the power to transcend all constraints, even when armies stand in the way—or *especially* when they do. Rather than needing, as Freud says, to find one's "place in a society that teems with individuals who nurse equal pretensions," games offer worlds of resistance that gradually give way to the player's singular efforts.[48]

It is hoped that the reader, by this point, has recognized in their own media consumption something resembling this fantasy. The personal connection is important to keep in mind when considering the fact that our media industries do not authorize everybody's thrills equally. Because Niedzviecki does not engage with the concept of fantasy, he also does not address the gap that exists between fantasy and social reality.[49] As Richard Dyer argues, fantasy is central to efforts at understanding the gendered and racial dynamics of the media we consume. Even supposedly escapist media experiences are in fact always related "to the human coordinates of the real world: the environments we live in, the social categories in which we have our being."[50] Writing about action cinema in the mid-1990s, Dyer argues that fictions "situate the thrills" and "refer us to the world"—a formulation that has two important meanings.[51] First, we rework in fantasy the frustrations that arise from our social and spatial reality.[52] Second, there are long-standing disparities in whose thrills are "legitimated," "who gets them" (who is special), "and who pays the price."[53] As Dyer puts it, "To feel that it is OK to be unrestrained, to kick against what surrounds you, to thrust out into the world is what boys learn, not girls. To see women strain against the world may be inspirational, but also at some psychic level unbelievable. Heroes of action who are other than male and white (and straight and able-bodied) are still going to feel exceptional for some time to come."[54]

What Dyer describes is effectively the joy of being a cause: "a deeper, underlying pattern of feeling, to do with freedom of movement, confidence in the body, engagement with the material world."[55] Boys are taught to take pleasure in being a cause ("to thrust out into the world") more openly than girls—a gender disparity that is nothing new in a historical or theoretical sense.[56] The videogames discussed in this chapter are, at a structural level, decidedly part of boy culture. It follows that the body transcendence fantasy, when reinforced in popular media, tends, as Dyer puts it, to be "coded as male (and straight and white, too)," even if it is something "to which all humans need access."[57] If Groos is correct, then animals need it too. There are material differences in the freedoms people experience to move about in the world, to kick out against that which constrains them. The freedom or license to lash out seems almost more important than the legitimacy of the target.

It is possible to detect the joy of being a cause lurking somewhere within what Jody Carlson describes as a "politics of powerlessness," which operates on an electorate eager to perceive itself as *any* causal force whatsoever, even one destined to fail. Carlson's study of the (conservative and white) supporters of George Wallace, who unsuccessfully ran for president four times, argues that Wallace's supporters stuck with his unlikely candidacy as a protest to their shrinking sense of power in Washington following political gains by minority groups in the 1960s as a result of second-wave feminism, the civil rights movement, and the 1960s counterculture. In Carlson's assessment, Wallace's supporters' "sense of powerlessness" was deeply ingrained, since they were aware that a party-wide opposition to social progress was not possible. However, they nevertheless supported a splinter candidate whose tactics expressed a "show of outrage" with little chance of producing policy change—tactics that included overt race baiting, the unrestrained expressions of sentiment, and the vilification of the press.[58]

Like congressional Republicans in the 2010s who voted unsuccessfully to repeal President Obama's signature health care law more than sixty times, Wallace's supporters "[chose] to remain in the same kind of lonely, individual struggles that Wallace dramatize[d] rather than participate in the kinds of actions that would solve real human problems as well as dispel feelings of powerlessness."[59] In short, Wallace's supporters chose to enjoy the fantasy of being a cause—a show of force for its own sake—over the option of joining a cause (a foreclosed possibility at the time). This historical context is helpful for understanding Donald Trump's shocking ascent in U.S. politics in the 2010s. Trump has proven the continued potency of the fantasy of preserving American exceptionalism (aka specialism) and a white national worldview. In fact, Trump performs an extreme form of the politics of powerlessness where substantive policy issues are replaced with a show of force and an obsession with being a cause: interrupting news segments via telephone, controlling the news cycle via tweet, perpetually reliving past electoral victories, inflating crowd sizes, and building a border wall and "making Mexico pay for it."

In truth, nobody can claim exclusive ownership of the joy of being a cause. However, Trump's rise parallels the disturbing harassment facing women, sexual and racial minorities, and their supporters known as "Gamergate" or "#GamerGate" that has unfolded over the past decade as these groups have sought better representation and fairer treatment in online culture. The joy of being a cause seems like a common factor between a politics of powerlessness and a competitive videogame space. In both, the pleasure of feeling like a powerful intervening force has become a refuge for people who have felt powerless to stop unwanted social change. Such powerlessness may seem unfamiliar to young men who are accustomed to transcendence, both in games and in their own bodies: the sort of transcendence Merleau-Ponty attributes to the lived body as intentionality, or as Iris Marion Young puts it, as "pure fluid action, the continuous calling-forth of capacities that are applied to the world."[60] Young argues that women, on the other hand, tend to experience "ambiguous transcendence" because they are often caught up in thinking of their bodies as a *thing* rather than a capacity. Their intentionality is inhibited, the "I can" constrained by a "self-imposed 'I cannot.'"[61] As Gamergate makes clear, these constraints exist in the world before they impinge on the body. And fantasy is the contested domain in this conflict. If, as Merleau-Ponty suggests, the body is the foundation of intentionality, then it achieves this sense of what it will do (and how) through an anticipatory act that resembles fantasy—this is what Žižek means when he says fantasy provides us the coordinates of desire.

The exclusionary online cultures exemplified by Gamergate target fantasy so that it becomes difficult for some to orient themselves in the space of games and game culture. However, fantasy can also be a site of resistance—because misogynist, homophobic, and racist players cannot completely monopolize the actual joy of being a cause any more than they can control who enjoys transcendence in a kinetic action game. Such sensations would be empowering to anyone made to feel inhibited socially, economically, or physically. When given tangible form and social expression through digital games, the fantasy of bodily transcendence represents an especially resonant nexus of social, political, and historical forces as they intersect with bodily memories of power, specialness, and victory. The second half of this chapter approaches such an embodied nexus through the lens of arcade-style action videogames, which it breaks into three categories.

Action Game Genres: Platformers, Fighters, and Shooters

Through much of the 1980s and 1990s, the *Mario* platformer was the most visible genre of videogame played at home. Also vying for visibility in popular references to games at this time were arcade-style "fighters" such as *Street Fighter* (1987) and *Mortal Kombat* (1992) and "shooters" such as *Gradius* (1985) and *Contra* (1987) and their progeny. While far from exhaustive, this broad industry slice of platformers, fighters, and shooters is fairly representative of arcade-style "action" videogames known for "sensory bombardment with intense, high volume and velocity play."[62] Playing these games well requires skill (hand-eye coordination), a bodily absorption in the act of play at the level of muscle memory, an intuitive understanding of the rules governing play, and a continuous awareness of the state of play as conveyed (mostly) through the game's images. Playing may also require, to some degree, having grown up and felt welcomed within the (typically very masculine) gaming cultures that played these games while trading secrets, strategies, and stories. What follows is an account of the kinetic themes (patterns of affectively charged bodily action) these game genres seem built around and—where possible—discussion of how structures of play might cater to body fantasy. Though the following headings are organized as three arcade-inspired genres, each describes broad tendencies in recent commercial gaming as well.

Transcendence in the Platformer: Eliminating the World as Resistance

The genre of the platformer is aptly named for the innumerable platforms players must land upon and depart in play. A platformer's world is one thrown into disarray, a ground that has been torn asunder and so must be left behind; only athletic leaping can bridge the spatial discontinuities imposed between start and finish. In this genre, epitomized by early *Mario* games, players typically move along a side-scrolling horizontal axis and progression is contingent upon first overcoming opposition cast along the vertical axis. But "progression" is perhaps too prosaic a description for what Nathan Altice suggests of *Super Mario Bros.*'s computational "engine": that it is "built for athletic platforming."[63] In contrast with the once-and-for-all logic that Roland Barthes attributes to Japanese pachinko machines, platformer videogames offer an ongoing latitude for engaging the world.[64] In *Mario* games, players can usually change their mind and influence the arc of a jump midair by pressing forward or pulling back, by holding the button down longer to go higher, or pressing it briefly for a shorter hop—a logic preserved when bouncing off an enemy or certain obstacles. Platformers situate players in an always-evolving spatial scenario.

Mario's side-scrolling "geometry of playability" is rectilinear,[65] prompting players to work through the spatial problem before making their first move. One could say the genre's embodied action is slow or contemplative by comparison with Mario's 1990s rival, Sonic, whose games seem to encourage improvising solutions to spatial problems on the fly. The sinuous stage design of *Sonic the Hedgehog* (1991) creates a rush of impressions. Promotional materials for *Sonic* games emphasize velocity to such an extent that Dyer's essay on *Speed* really ought to have been about these games as well.

The platformer genre waned in prevalence in the late 1990s and early 2000s (games touted as platformers, through and through, nearly disappeared). However, other popular genres incorporated platforming elements into their play, from the first-person exploration game *Metroid Prime* (2002) and the first-person parkour game *Mirror's Edge* (2008) to the cinematic *God of War* series (2005–2018) and the superhero game *Infamous* (2009), which is in several ways exemplary of bodily transcendence.[66]

Like most superheroes, *Infamous*'s Cole MacGrath possesses a special power. His body can store and channel electricity. This grants the ability to zap foes, slide conductively along powerlines, cannonball off skyscrapers, and much more as the game progresses. The fate of the game's fictional metropolis, Empire City, will depend on Cole's growing capacity to move freely through fraught urban spaces. What is certain is that players will work their *own sweet will* on Empire City's transportation infrastructure, that "great frustration of modern urban living."[67] One ability even repurposes idle vehicles as bombs with a large area of effect. The game uses a morality system, where players make narrative choices that influence whether they accrue good or bad karma—this, in turn, affects what sorts of powers they gain. What they choose matters less than the joy of being a cause each option shares in common. Whether leaping over cars or blasting them skyward with a radial pulse, using static thrusters to hover short distances or traversing obstacles with parkour, binding enemies to the ground with electrical restraints or leeching their life force, players will discover many clever means of "eliminating the world as resistance," to borrow Max Frisch's phrasing.[68]

Cole MacGrath might even seem to exemplify the wish to transcend embodiment altogether, to become pure energy.[69] It is important to keep in mind, therefore, that platformers are no more invested in *worldlessness* (the tendency toward "diluting" our encounter with the world, such as "by speed, so that we don't have to experience it") than in completely phasing out the body.[70] The player's own body is doubly involved in the action videogame's pleasures: in the game's staging of a fantasy about a body that transcends space, and in the player's simultaneous bodily training. *Infamous* emphasizes this double involvement of the body through a mimesis of familiar urban spaces and their concomitant frictions and anxieties. The game uses fantasy to refer us to the world. Its action maintains contact with banal, everyday reality, even if this contact stages the confrontation of the "normal with the superpowered," a staple of superhero narratives.[71] Cole certainly enjoys a magical continuity with and mastery over structures that inhibit, confine, and control—he glides along elevated train tracks; Cole does not need to wait for the train, he *is* the train. And yet Cole's body dilutes the world as resistance only by fusing with and repurposing an existing urban infrastructure (and that only after some practice). The cyberspace logic of instantaneous telepresence may represent the wish to escape the strictures of body and world. *Infamous's* platforming, on the other hand, inaugurates the joy of being a cause that originates *in* the body and is directed outward, confidently, toward the world.

In contrast with *Infamous*, *Mario*-style platformers seem to prefer more abstract settings. Abstraction helps these games emphasize the importance of novelty to body-transcendence play. And this is perhaps nowhere clearer than in the *Super Mario Galaxy* series (2007, 2010). At the outset of *Super Mario Galaxy* (2007), the Princess's castle is torn from the ground and Mario is blasted into space. The game's narrative premise barely justifies its presentation of a universe of disjointed spaces, textures, objects, and challenges that are reassembled into bizarre juxtapositions: blocks, cylinders, spheres, and donuts that are clustered but adrift, floating at just the right interval for making the jump slightly uncertain (and interesting). What more clearly motivates spatial arrangements is the novel form of embodied motility each brings into play. Motility is a function not merely of space but of texture as well, in that each floating object can be made of different materials that impact movement, from grippy tread-plated metal to squeaky glass and crystalline ice that Mario can pirouette across. *Super Mario Galaxy* (hereafter *Galaxy*) exemplifies how objects in platformer videogames (enemies, obstacles, spaces) do not merely form the mise-en-scène and are not simply assembled in a scene and defined by their position there (what Merleau-Ponty would term a "spatiality of position").[72] Rather, they constitute a "spatiality of situation," activating the body's own situational awareness of potential actions and goals.[73]

Galaxy's unique physics system allows Mario to circumnavigate small objects as if they were miniature planets, each with its own gravitational pull. Often, the camera framing the planetoids is static, which means Mario's gravity play has a variable relation with the screen's vertical axis. A jump away from gravity's center can send Mario downward. And, if timed properly, Mario can slingshot into the overlapping pull of nearby objects, resulting in orbital figure eights and the temporary illusion of flight. The game's special physics enable the discovery of novel bodily positions, such as a jump that becomes inverted as an upward fall (toward the "ground" of an orbiting object above)—just one example of the many ways *Galaxy* disorders the side-scrolling platformer's typical spatial arrangements.

Though perhaps the exception that proves the rule, *Galaxy* seems to challenge the notion that vertically oriented movement "gives dynamic, hyperkinetic

Standing on the ground above in *Super Mario Galaxy* (2007).

expression to power and the individual's relation to it," to borrow phrasing from Kristen Whissel's argument about verticality in CGI cinema that has been influenced by the "visual logics of video games and virtual reality."[74] As Whissel suggests, "because verticality automatically implies the intersection of two opposed forces—gravity and the force required to overcome it—it is an ideal technique for visualizing power" in cinema.[75] And, indeed, contestations over power do map to the vertical axis in a surprising number of cinematic examples, not to mention most platformer videogames.[76] *Galaxy* seems an outlier in the same manner as *Gravity* (2013), an effects-heavy film set in Earth's orbit: both reorient "our perceptual coordinates" so that "screen directions of up and down no longer hold any weight."[77] As Scott Richmond puts it, we become so accustomed to *Gravity*'s untethered, free-floating camera that the horizon of the looming planet Earth in the background stops doing the usual job of horizons: "it no longer indexes *the horizontal*."[78] As a platformer videogame, *Galaxy*'s power dynamics are not merely mapped *onto* its physics systems; its prevailing order *is* its laws of physics. In *Galaxy*'s visualization of power, Mario may be transcendent—the lowly Goombas subordinate. But Mario does not merely leap over slow-moving, grounded enemies; he exceeds terrestrial spatial ordering altogether.

In the absence of other orienting structures, *Galaxy* exemplifies the way spaces and objects in platformer games truly cohere only in the path that the hero cuts through them. Each time Mario leaps, blasts, or glides from one seemingly random bit of floating space debris to the next, his smooth trajectory stitches together and lends highly fragmentary spaces a kind of legibility through the action they enable. Though platformers may adopt an autonomous fictional setting—such as *Infamous*'s Empire City—their spaces ultimately reflect the transcendent bodily capacity of the avatar itself. The two form an irreducible figure-ground pairing—each is built with the other in mind. And neither has much meaning without the other. Playing a platformer well entails incorporating both into your own body as a core set of competencies and possible interactions.

It is helpful to recall that Merleau-Ponty's phenomenological method locates intentionality in the body, in its motility (rather than in an abstract, disembodied concept such as "will"). Intentionality always pairs body with world. When body and world pair well, the "body's movement and orientation organizes the surrounding space as a continuous extension of its own being."[79] Such a synthesis of body and surroundings also results in a synthesis or unification of the self.[80] In relation to a harsh, alienating, and unassimilable world, the platformer game exudes a powerful "I can." This is what the transcendent leap enacts over constraints both external and internal.

Transcendence in the Fighter: Special Moves and Special Players

Compared with other action game genres, the *fighter* is distinct for its structure of prolonged, diametric opposition between bodies that can do nothing but face one another until only one remains standing. The basic aim of such games is usually to deplete an opponent's health bar. A cohesive genre, the fighter has changed relatively little between the age of the video arcade and today. Many of the most prominent ports of arcade titles into homes in the 1980s and 1990s were fighting games, such as *Punch-Out!!* (1987), *Mortal Kombat* (1992), and *Street Fighter II* (1994). The fighter's action is mostly linear and horizontal; players may hop into the air or duck momentarily to avoid an attack, but the vertical axis is not typically as meaningful a part of play as with platformers. The fighter's combatants chip away at one another's health bars and vie for control of the arena's center in a flurry of maneuvers that represent in both image and effect a power emanating from the body. In contrast with platformers and shooters, which tend to be single-player and progression-based, fighting games are usually player-versus-player and are emergence-based in that their agonistic situations emerge dynamically and unpredictably from the exigencies of play.[81]

In spite of thirty years of technological change affecting computer processing power and memory capacity, the design and mechanics of early arcade fighters are still largely intact today in games such as *Street Fighter V* (2016) and *Mortal Kombat 11* (2019). The *Super Smash Bros.* series (1999, 2001, 2008, 2014, 2018) represents perhaps the most significant deviation from the standard formula in that input commands are simplified, the vertical axis is more open to play, and, rather than depleting health meters, players instead launch opponents past the arena's boundaries and out of play by first dealing damage and then landing a strong, finishing attack. In most fighters, though controller buttons are mapped to specific actions consistently across many games (e.g., "A" is a strong kick, "Y" is a quick punch, etc.), each combatant's powerful special attacks involve these same buttons in arbitrary sequences (e.g., hold back for a moment, then press forward and punch) followed by a sometimes lengthy prerendered action (e.g., E. Honda's "Sumo Headbutt" where the *Street Fighter II* combatant flies head-first across the screen). During the prerendered animation, button inputs are temporarily ignored and the player is rendered a spectator to an energy that seems to emanate from the fighter's body or that propels that body across the screen.

Fighters are the limit case in Dan Fleming's argument that games decouple representational contents (and their implied subject positions) from an "underlying geometry of playability."[82] Representations cling tightly to the fighters' bodies, which loom large in the frame as the very focal point of play. Each fighter's corporeal form is distinct from the others; characteristics of race, gender, national identity, and body type are all exaggerated. In contrast, the small and nondescript avatar of platformer games tends to recede from attention so focus can fall on the obstacle course ahead. The importance of a fighter's appearance may wax and wane as players learn each underlying move set. A compromise must often be struck between choosing a fighter whose appearance is preferred and a fighter whose moves seem the most intuitive or effective. The maneuver that is useful and recurs repeatedly across many hours of play becomes not only muscle memory but also a proxy for character personality, which is always partly expressed through such maneuvers. Practicing the move cements this relation and renders it an anchor for player involvement. The play style it affords is chosen as a player's preferred approach to the game, a point of entry, a means of orientation, an open loop, an "I can."

Insofar as a compromise is struck and a player settles on a particular character—and by extension a style of play (e.g., aggressive, reactive, strategic)—the fighting game captures the experience of Niedzviecki's "I'm Specialism" better than the platformer. In *Super Smash Bros. Melee* (2001), for instance, I play Captain Falcon. Some readers will already be able to surmise much about me (or at least my approach to the game) from this statement alone. One unassuming childhood friend always gravitated toward Luigi, the consummate underdog. He rarely won, but cheers erupted whenever he landed Luigi's Super Jump Punch and sent an overconfident opponent sailing out of the arena. Surely I am not alone in having encountered the very embodiment of chaos in the opponent who avoids learning the game's mechanics and instead simply inhales opponents with Kirby and walks them off a ledge. As Captain Falcon, I identify strongly with the meteor smash (Stampede Down) into Knee Strike combo—these are directional attacks performed while airborne: the first has generous hit detection and drives opponents straight down, into the ground with enough force that they will likely rebound into the air for a moment before regaining control; the second requires precise positioning but, if struck, launches the airborne opponent a great lateral distance toward the edge of the arena. Falcon is one of the fastest fighters in the game and drops through the air like a rock—the untrained eye cannot track his movement. The combo, therefore, requires very precise timing and positioning.

And I have practiced it thousands of times. Whenever I play *Smash Melee* on a regular basis, I am flooded by hypnagogic imagery of different scenarios in which I might perform it—from above, while standing still, while running at top speed, over and over until a shield breaks, and so on. In the simulated action, I know I press the "L" button the moment my fighter lands on the ground: doing so precisely shortens recovery time, an "L-cancel," which is needed for the second part of the combo. However, it is not the responsible digit, my left index finger, that twitches in the body fantasy as Falcon's Stampede Down melts into the ground with an L-cancel; rather, I feel this button command as an impulse stemming from my chest and rebounding across my entire body as a broad, implicit awareness of the timing of things.

Fantasy may find its greatest incentive for dwelling upon embodied capacities when these intersect so explicitly with the social realm of a competitive scene. There, a skilled player's body fantasy finds an affirmational path back to palpable and visible things—real-world spaces (arenas, stages), real time (shared time, scheduled time), and, of course, real prize money. Like most who play *Melee*, I am nowhere near skilled enough to compete in tournaments. Highly skilled players can come to be identified internationally with certain fighters as well as with certain move combinations or strategies. For example, famed American professional *Melee* player Ken Hoang is known for playing Marth (a sword-wielding fighter in the game) as well as for a distinct style of play; he is the namesake for the "Ken Combo."[83] Identification with a useful move or strategy is powerfully reinforced by fame in the community (local or international) that has formed around a popular videogame. Such a community is capable of both recognizing and valuing a special demonstration of skill. In the competitive scene, the superlative player's own embodied fantasies are recognized, accepted, disseminated, and celebrated.

Whether we play for an international audience on a stage, for a younger sibling in the living room, or by ourselves, fantasy is *always* social, at least in terms of Freud's notion of internalized observation. We always play for at least an implied audience. The social aspect of games, then, does not rely on network technology, the presence of formalized competitive play, or the existence of multiplayer options within a game. It is not remarkable that one of the most interesting examples of body transcendence in a fighter comes from a mostly single-player game: Nintendo's *Punch-Out!!* series (1984, 1987, 1994, 2009).

Punch-Out!! epitomizes the fighter's tight clustering of personality, affectively charged motion, and muscle memory. The series adopts an over-the-shoulder point of view—opponents still face one another in a linear manner, but along the screen's z-axis—so that the player's avatar (Little Mac) fades from view in the foreground, reflecting the game's focus on the motions, manners, and tempos of each unique, computer-controlled opponent. *Punch-Out!!* games are about learning the cues, timing, and behavior of each opponent's patterned attacks so that dodging them ceases to require conscious thought. Some attacks are even designed to take advantage of habitual play patterns. Hoy Quarlow from *Super*

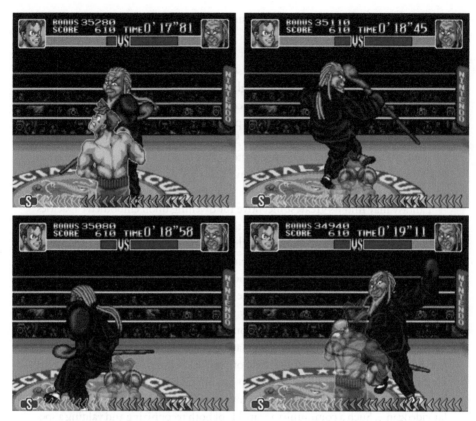

Top left to bottom right: Hoy Quarlow's hypnotic, 360-degree attack in *Super Punch-Out!!* (1994).

Punch-Out!! (1994), for example, begins a particular attack by swinging his glove in a 360-degree arc away from the player (reaching into the background of the ring) before returning to the player's opposite side. One's initial reaction is to dodge the moment the attack begins, which leaves Mac exposed when the move finally lands. Having to accommodate, to preserve space in one's muscle memory for this sort of exception to the game's general rules about dodging, leaves a mark on embodied memory.[84] The move becomes an expressive centerpiece of Quarlow's repertoire as well as (at least in my case) an affectively charged rhythm that recurs in the player's imagination long after the game is complete.

To progress through a *Punch-Out!!* game, each fighter's patterns must be learned. And each opponent presents his own embodied tells: a raised eyebrow, a catchphrase, a small twitch of the glove, and so on. When these tells are understood only cognitively (i.e., when first learned), there is insufficient time to respond: the player must interpret the tell, remember the attack it signals, and decide on and execute a response—all within a fraction of a second. When an opponent's tell becomes muscle memory, however, it joins a larger preformed pattern or chunk that includes the full attack underway as well as the effective response—the whole circuit is immediately evoked by the tell alone (stimulus-response). In this sense, Fuchs's open loop of potential interactions contains not just the player's own limited movement options (i.e., the ability to dodge in three directions, block, or punch high or low with either glove), but also the opponent's tell, which must also be made our own and resolved (closed) with a proper response in each new situation.

Bodies in *Punch-Out!!* are defined by their unique manner of moving. Players thrive only through the precise acquisition of these kinetics. The series makes especially clear that players identify not merely with their avatar in action game genres, nor even with the way their avatar moves (vehicular embodiment), but rather with the entire fabric of the game's potential motions. Playing the game involves an active working and reworking of body memory and posits the body as a dynamic, postural interface capable of accommodating itself to a variety of challenging situations in the world.

Transcendence in the Shooter: Bodies in Flux

Shooter games are so named for the gunfire players both release and must dodge. The genre's earliest titles, such as *Space Invaders* (1978) and *Galaxian* (1981), involve manipulating tiny vessels and firing at enemies in one direction along the arcade screen's vertical axis. Many subsequent space- or aircraft-themed shooters have retained this bird's-eye view. But in games such as *Gradius III* (1989), the screen scrolls along the horizontal axis and gunfire is concentrated forward (toward the right). That enemies still emerge from all margins of the screen (even from behind) emphasizes the need for careful positioning. Of the three genres discussed in this chapter, the shooter most clearly demonstrates the flux of a body in play. Though the protagonists' bodies do not literally transform in shooters such as *Contra* (1988) or *Gradius III*, the points of vulnerability and power they represent do fluctuate, or contract and expand across the screen. In fact, shooters exemplify Sianne Ngai's notion of "animatedness," an affect that measures the elasticity of animated bodies.[85] This may seem counterintuitive, since the shooter's avatar is typically small in scale, limited in its animation, and streamlined in its physics when compared with platformers. However, its simplified movement options help facilitate the shooter's dynamic participation in action spread across the entire screen. Against enemy fire, the shooter body seeks to minimize itself, to shrink away from a barrage or weave through small openings in a radiating wave of shrapnel. At other times, it projects force outward in centrifugal gunfire that stretches to the boundaries of the frame.

The shooter's general lack of simulated gravity means verticality plays a less significant role in its spatial dynamics than is the case for platformers, which stage the conflict between a leap and the force of gravity that counteracts it, and where every vertical inch is fought for and achieved with careful timing and placement. For the same reason, shooters open the screen's vertical axis more than

The player character is forced to the frame's periphery by Big Fuzz, the third boss of *Contra III: The Alien Wars* (1992).

platformers do, often permitting players to roam the screen's full dimensions at will. Even grounded (anthropomorphized) shooter bodies (e.g., in *run-and-gun* shooters like *Contra*) make frequent use of the vertical axis to evade enemy fire.

The run-and-gun shooter's spatial logics are often radial. In *Contra III: The Alien Wars* (1992), for instance, bullets spiral away from the protagonist in 360 degrees as a way of policing the screen's dangerous margins, managing a hostile frontier that continuously spawns new threats from all sides. Bosses, when they arrive, displace players from and then occupy the screen's center. Players must dodge around the screen's peripheries, shooting centripetally toward the bullseye: the boss's glowing point of vulnerability, often a sensitive internal organ protruding from a monstrous, fleshy body. The boss's expulsion of players from the screen's center introduces a tension to the game's spatial logic: players orbit the periphery and plan their return (with vengeance). The boss fight's tendency to locate vulnerable bodily organs at the screen's nucleus reflects how the game is casting the player's own embodied participation as a dance of center and periphery, threat and vulnerability. The avatar's body is akin to the boss's weak point: a fragile core ensconced at the center of the screen, which pulsates and flashes as it is shot, slashed, and burned.

At its most demanding moments, the shooter becomes what is referred to as "bullet hell," exemplified in games like *Ikaruga* (2001) where the screen is overwhelmed with countless lasers, blast waves, and bullets—projectiles known collectively as "dakka" (onomatopoeia for the sound of machine-gun fire). Popularly associated with notions of thoughtlessness, with players entering autopilot and ceasing to navigate with intentionality, bullet hell games require pure flow.[86] As with the experience of making one's way through a densely crowded space, movement through dakka in bullet hell requires a fluid compromise between intentions and the unpredictable, always-changing exigencies of the spatial situation. Chris Goto-Jones's evocation of the Zen arts in relation to action videogames is especially apt here.[87]

As a shooter subgenre, bullet hell games call for a reflection on the player's supposedly active participation in action games. *Geometry Wars* (2005), for instance, employs particle and lighting effects to increase the sense of chaos onscreen beyond the point of visual intelligibility, revealing a vertiginous pleasure that disrupts legibility and control. One of Roger Caillois's four categories of play, vertigo—or a pleasure taken in experiencing a loss of bodily equilibrium—expresses something nearly the opposite of the experience of *being a cause*. If the radiating waves of dakka were ripples in pond water, the shooter avatar would most often be caught in someone else's undulation, forced into going with the flow and surrendering to the experience of vertigo, a kind of empowering passivity in response to complex visual stimuli. Reading shooter games this way cuts against the grain of a genre ostensibly about violent self-assertion. And at least one self-reflexive bullet hell game—*Undertale* (2015)—provides an environment where players can progress through the entire game without ever enacting violence.[88] However, doing so requires especially nimble navigation of the game's many bullet hell encounters, and the effect on body memory is the same as in any such game. As William Cheng says of games more generally, "Players of games oscillate between being in and out of control, between acting and getting acted *upon* by a game's barrage of audiovisual stimuli."[89]

Bullet hell shooters might best illustrate the bipolar qualities of a fantasy of bodily transcendence, which the games discussed in this chapter suggest is about powerlessness as much as power, about being an effect as well as being a cause. In platformers, players seek to resolve spatial tensions separating a present position from a destination. As Scott Bukatman says of superhero bodies, the platformer's acrobatic form may seem like "a body transcending bodily limits, defying gravity, mocking the real," a body that is "lighter than air, liberated from earthly constraints"—when, in reality, it is *"a body in space, . . .* a body that belongs to the space that it masters."[90] Leaping beyond constraint requires first installing that spatial tension in the self: learning to field the obstacle by accommodating one's own body to it. Likewise with fighters, where an entire domain of possible attacks and responses becomes invested with the potential for immediate activation. The useful maneuver is the one that wins the day, the one that is practiced and applied countless times.

Experiencing the compulsive repetition of the useful maneuver as a body fantasy renders players lost to an entire field of kinetic interactions, as if *"assimilated into the environment,"* as Roger Caillois says of an insect's defensive mimesis.[91] This is as clear as Little Mac himself in *Super Punch-Out!!*, as he transparently dissolves into surroundings, ostensibly so attention can fall on the unique opponent and their tells. Caillois provocatively claims that mimicry is not a survival mechanism but rather a crisis of identity, a dissolution of the coordinates of the self, and a submission to the "veritable *lure of space*."[92] The insect is mysteriously drawn to the place in the world where it blends in and is there lost. Such is a fantasy of bodily transcendence, even (or especially) in games with no avatars, including puzzle games such as *Tetris*, for instance. It is as if the avatar were already consumed by the environment, spread across an entire field of play mechanics. Game interactions repeated as body fantasy mark for players the locus of our embodied investment in the world, the place where we are mysteriously drawn. Such an investment can take hold at any point in the player-machine ensemble or interface, not simply in our relationship with the avatar.

Embodied fantasy does more with the body than simply manage the uptake of patterns from the world; nor is fantasy merely the pure, outward extrusion of will into external constraints. Rather, fantasy is the summation of both processes, when the "open loop" of potential action is closed, a completed circuit. Body fantasy may be understood as a loop always in search of that which permits closure. In games, mechanisms that might be called "closing structures" recur repeatedly and without much fanfare. In cinema, closing structures are few and far between, but their closure can be especially powerful. And these structures are with us throughout our day as we move our bodies across a variety of spaces that might make us feel small or constrained and unable to alter our circumstances. Perhaps by converting a present obstacle into the same spatiotemporal terms that define the transcendent body in its capacity to act, the fantasy could express an empowering passivity in the face of—and thus may help mediate—overwhelming complexity, high-stakes scenarios, or social anxiety. Of course, if there is no "open loop" that allows us to respond to a catastrophic event, the result might well be the cessation of all fantasy, the shattering of the façade covering the Real (in short, trauma).

2

The Fantasy of Bodily Transcendence in Narrative Media

● ●

If one were to juxtapose Remedy Entertainment's recent game *Control* (2019) with the action film *Push* (2009), a shared image would emerge of a person directing telekinetic energy through an outstretched hand. Such an image expresses the wish to control the world in the same way we have learned to control our own limbs. One might wonder whether there could possibly be a more direct expression of a *fantasy of bodily transcendence*, which chapter 1 defines as the wish to overcome difficulty and leap beyond constraint in pursuit of the "joy of being a cause."[1] In fact, such an image might be too direct, too overt an ego-aggrandizing wish. Before it, we might throw up our own hand and imagine stopping the fantasy in its tracks.

This chapter considers the fantasy of bodily transcendence as a kind of convergence—a significant commonality—between games and principally narrative media. The fantasy's nexus (the texts it connects together) is far-flung and stretches across both media industries and national borders, incorporating videogames, cinema, television, and comic books produced in Japan, America, Hong Kong, and elsewhere—all of which circulate globally with help from online distribution and e-commerce platforms such as the Nintendo eShop, Amazon, Viz, YouTube, Netflix, and Crunchyroll. What the media in question share in common is the way they situate the joy of being a cause within a narrative framework about overcoming difficulty, defying expectations, and ultimately winning recognition of one's specialness—all thanks to spectacular feats of embodied action. The cinematic component of the wider fantasy nexus accounts for the majority of the most profitable cinematic events of the last forty years.[2] Its most high-profile manifestations are blockbuster superhero films—especially those following what Shaun Treat terms the "superhero zeitgeist" of the early 2000s.[3] But games are an essential component of this nexus as well—their relationship to the fantasy of bodily transcendence is unique because they require its active installation in the player's muscle memory.

There is a long-standing question in film and media studies about how videogames have influenced narrative media such as cinema. As Jay David Bolter and Richard Grusin suggest of any medium that becomes a transformative cultural and economic phenomenon, games have certainly borrowed from or *remediated* other media,[4] incorporating (for instance) cinematic devices in their cutscenes.[5] So too, as the theory goes, have videogames influenced *other* media ever since they moved into our homes and became part of everyday life there between the 1970s and 1990s. For instance, Henry Jenkins suggests that videogames inspired a formal playfulness in films from the late 1990s that experimented with fragmented or nonlinear plots and so required especially active engagement from spectators.[6] Thus, Jenkins's answer to the question—What is game-like or *gamic* cinema?—orients us toward films such as *Run Lola Run* (1998), *Memento* (2000), and *The Sixth Sense* (1999).

This chapter explores the possibility of reframing the question "What is gamic cinema?" as a question about the role cinema plays in that wider fantasy nexus. In one sense, fantasy does not help answer this question at all. Simply because the fantasy is shared between games and cinema does not mean its presence in a film brands that film as *gamic*. Nor would its presence in a game render that game *cinematic*. However, fantasy does offer a unique perspective on this question because games and cinema structure this shared fantasy differently. Jenkins is likely correct about the relevance of a game's nonlinearity—its looping structure. However, rather than seeking repetition directly in the structure of a movie's plot, it is perhaps more productive to adopt a holistic view of recursion in videogame play—especially in light of the role repetition plays in the development of a player's skills, what Fuchs refers to as those "*open loops* of potential interactions."[7] When we play a game, we do not necessarily keep track of each attempt as if it represented a different path through a story. Rather, the *skill* is what we carry with us from one attempt to the next (and the next...)—across dozens, hundreds, or even thousands of play sessions. Even for the most avid repeat viewers, narrative cinema will never function this way. What narrative media can and do capture of gaming's open loops is a foregrounding of *process*, and a clear and legible articulation of the rules governing the interaction of bodies. Process-oriented stories that employ a fantasy of bodily transcendence approach games more closely than even Jenkins's own examples of nonlinear cinema.

This chapter seeks to accomplish two goals: First, it builds on the discussion of games begun in chapter 1 in order to flesh out what it sees as fundamental precepts for a visual narrative mode that has been influenced by the logics of videogames. It then explores key examples of narrative media that host a fantasy of bodily transcendence, with special attention given to the melodramatic mode behind each example. Though not every film in this chapter is branded *gamic*, each does share an affinity for games through a fantasy tradition that has become compounded and reinforced in our current era of media convergence.

Toward Gamic Cinema

Like the melodramatic mode of which it is a part, gamic cinema transcends generic boundaries; its examples are drawn from martial arts cinema, action blockbusters, Japanese anime, and superhero films—insofar as these global action genres can always be distinguished from one another in the first place. Perhaps counterintuitively, gamic cinema need not explicitly reference gaming as a medium; in fact, neither game-to-film adaptations nor films explicitly evoking the aesthetics of gaming tend to best exemplify the mode of storytelling this chapter argues has been most meaningfully influenced by games or the fantasies games stage. In contrast with *Doom*'s (2005) halfhearted subjective optics, *Gamer*'s (2009) disorienting shaky camera, and the playful (though superficial) use of retro gaming aesthetics in *Scott Pilgrim vs. the World* (2010), gamic cinema demonstrates a genuine eagerness for process and takes its action seriously in ways most videogame-themed films do not. Gamic cinema *may* prioritize continuity in its optics, as Alexander Galloway suggests of "gamic vision," *if* such a style helps render its action legible.[8] And it *may* contain moments of levity in its references to gamer culture, such as with the boastful "EZ" the first-person protagonist scrawls with his own blood at the end of *Hardcore Henry* (2015). But what distinguishes cinema as gamic in the first place is also what facilitates the intermedial transfer of a body fantasy sustained primarily through videogame play: a film's clean elaboration of complex agonistic situations and its prioritization of the fluid trajectory of bodies moving through a highly legible space.

In related terms, the extent to which a narrative is gamic might be assessed by considering how carefully it introduces and attends to the rules—both affordances and limits—governing the interaction of bodies. Clearly communicated rules help render action legible and so facilitate embodied participation in events regardless of whether there are human bodies on-screen (or whether those bodies adhere to Newtonian physics). As with nearly any virtual camera in a videogame, the mechanics of image in gamic cinema must be subordinated to the task of generating "Constant and unpredictable definitions of the situation" as the situation changes with "each attack and counterattack," to reference Roger Caillois's discussion of what is required in order to participate in games due to their necessarily uncertain outcomes.[9] Definitions of the situation are a key part of any game's most basic feedback loop between player and system (or player and opponent). Even spectators must produce their own definitions of the situation in order to participate in sporting events. When viewing (or listening to) a game remotely, spectators inevitably do so through the focalizing efforts of sports commentators who provide elaborate definitions of situation through the introjection of statistics or by overtly manipulating the replayed image itself. And games tend to contain rules and systems that implicitly facilitate focalization—the way, for instance, game situations tend to hinge upon some principal object (e.g., a ball, a puck, a die, etc.).[10]

Gamic cinema is distinct from sportscasting in that its "situation" is also melodramatic, at least in Lea Jacobs's sense. Ben Singer helpfully synthesizes Jacobs's slippery concept of "situation" in melodrama as "a striking and exciting incident that momentarily arrests narrative action while the characters encounter a powerful new circumstance and the audience relishes the heightened dramatic tension."[11] For critics of melodrama, situation is an implausible contrivance that undermines character development, violates conventions of realism, and destroys pacing. The stunning peripety (aka a sudden reversal of fortune) in plot twists creates a "dramatic impasse" as well as "a momentary paralysis"—a pause in plot's unfolding that permits the full emotional significance of events to register for characters and audience alike.[12] In other words, situation prioritizes the legibility of a complex and surprising predicament. In gamic cinema, situation can puncture and transcend diegesis through a range of temporal manipulations—slow motion, freezing or reversing time, or dilating plot to provide time to process the emotions generated by new circumstances. Japanese anime is often the boldest in its willingness not only to pause plot at crucial moments but even to introduce pedagogical diagrams that specify situation in both its ludic and melodramatic meanings.

Admittedly, there is nothing in these preliminary qualities of gamic cinema that relies on the medium of the videogame for intelligibility. Few films foreground a more genuine interest in process than Robert Bresson's *Pickpocket* (1959), which is riveted by the thief's hand as it nimbly lifts from its mark. And when it comes to the feelings of empowerment underlying gamic cinema's legibility of situation, even a horror film such as *Carrie* (1976) exemplifies the joy of being a cause. In *Carrie*'s narrative climax, the titular protagonist intervenes on her own behalf: she answers the cruelty of classmates with the projection of a cathartic telekinetic force in *all* directions. Though spectators are given recompense for all Carrie has endured, we are also perhaps caught off guard by the moral indiscriminateness of the carnage.

In part, it is the manner in which the moral justification for action is organized that differentiates a videogame-inflected cinema from prior examples that seem to anticipate its forms (i.e., a minimalist cinema of process or a cathartic horror film). A post-1990s gamic cinema not only foregrounds process and situation but tends also to situate the joy of being a cause within a melodramatic framework where the transcendent bodies of heroes and villains struggle in a Manichaean conflict (a stark contrast of good versus evil). This is not just because the plots of videogames are Manichaean in their conflict (though they usually are); rather, it is because the *full articulation* of good's triumph over evil in melo-drama lends the action's moral and ethical stakes a clarity and forcefulness that is necessary for participation and the play of body fantasy.[13] It is as if the accrued tension of the villain's mockery of virtue somehow overwhelms our own inter-nal resistances and so permits the free and full expression of our own ambitious wish to transcend opposition and leap over restraint. The melodramatic plot structure is fundamentally orienting in a way that aligns action cinema with the aesthetics of games—players of games (who skip cutscenes) may not fully appreciate *why* they oppose the game's villain, but they know in their bones that they do.

Although the narratives discussed in this chapter may initially focus on a bodily affordance enjoyed for its own sake as the sheer joy of being a cause (e.g., shooting webbing from one's wrists or gliding through the air with newfound abilities), the body's capacity to overcome opposition is ultimately wedded to a morally clarifying call to action. These films reveal a close relationship between *kinetic legibility* and *moral legibility*, as though the unrestrained articulation of a moral truth permitted the full embrace of the transcendent leap—or, inversely, in David Bordwell's sense, as if cleanly organized and compelling action prepared us to emote.

A key example of gamic cinema, *Equilibrium* (2002), parallels *Carrie* in its aestheticized violence. But there is also a meaningful contrast to be found in how *Equilibrium* organizes its categories of victim, hero, and villain. The film exem-plifies a key point about gamic cinema and, in turn, about games themselves: its focus on process is serious; there is something meaningful at stake in the fight, and the fight itself is taken seriously, blow by blow. Consider, for example, the film's puppy shoot-out scene. In *Equilibrium*'s Orwellian future, all expressions of emotion and sentiment are forbidden by threat of death—a sentence enforced by elite police known as Grammaton Clerics. Following events that lead to his missing a dose of the government-mandated, emotion-suppressing medication, Cleric John Preston (Christian Bale) oversees a raid on the hideout of a group of "sense offenders" who refuse the medication and partake in forbidden pleasures (e.g., listening to music, keeping pets, or consuming alcohol). Preston witnesses the confiscation and destruction of a litter of puppies and his freshly felt emotions compel him to intervene by claiming one of the puppies for an "investigation." At great personal risk, Preston drives the puppy outside city limits to free it, but the dog refuses to leave him. That Preston is unable to abandon the puppy, returning it to the trunk of his car along with his coat for warmth, establishes Preston's virtue (his identity as protector of the innocent) at the precise moment when he is confronted by a patrolling police squad demanding "identification"—the badge that is in the jacket in the trunk with the contraband animal (situ-ation indeed!). Completely surrounded by a heavily armed, faceless riot squad, Preston must attack in order to survive when the puppy is discovered. At this moment, and like Carrie on her stage, Preston projects a powerful force in all directions: he dispatches the two men flanking him with their own weapons and then shoots out the remainder with burst-fire pistols concealed in his sleeves. When a closely huddled reinforcement squad join the fight, Preston leaps through the air, landing directly in the middle of their group, and fires on them radially. The pistol fire's smooth and rhythmic blasts are shown diagrammatically, in a stunning but also highly legible bird's-eye shot; their symmetrical precision marks Preston's elite Cleric training.

The puppy shoot-out's aestheticization of violence represents an empowerment fantasy that meets an anxious feeling of dread and constraint with a transcendent and defiant act. Audiences are encouraged to participate not merely in the stylized action, but also in the film's embrace of Preston as a hero who faces a ruthless police force of greater numbers, who possesses overwhelming power but uses it reluctantly, and who intervenes on the behalf of the innocent and the helpless. Even without the puppy (who reappears from out of frame to bookend this scene), American audiences would likely be closely aligned with Preston's interests, given his emotional transformation in the face of an oppressive state that outlaws personal freedom and pleasure. However, the puppy makes perhaps overly legible the scene's moral stakes—an affective correlate to the kinetic legibility of the action's climax (the top-down shot of the radial pistol fire).

Because of its unique focus on a fantasy of bodily transcendence, this chapter forges an idiosyncratic path through film-game convergence—or, more precisely, through a nexus of closely related popular texts that includes comics, television, cinema, and games. Its governing concern is how narratives might be understood to function like dynamic systems for supporting and extending an embodied fantasy that is often anchored in videogames.

However, there are productive limits to the notion that games and principally narrative media both introduce embodied tensions that recur as fantasy. Accrued body memories differ in each case by their degree of abstraction, and by the nature of their excess to a narrative framework that attempts to motivate or contain embodied meaning. With action videogames, embodied memory may be bound to the corporeal form of the athletic avatar. However, it may just as readily take the form of diffuse geometric phenomena encountered in play. Even in the most anthropocentric examples (i.e., games that explicitly evoke the human coordinates of real-world spaces), a game's mechanics exceed their moral framework in both form and function. Their excess is borne out through sheer repetition of interactions that generate affective rhythms and embodied meanings of their own. Insofar as there is a framing narrative in an action game, it generally works to situate the hero's ability to run, jump, shoot, and dodge as the embodied means to some morally justified end (e.g., the princess rescue plot). However, the means quickly exceed this apparent end, which shrinks away through distance and deferral. When the internalized capacity to act is finally called upon to resolve the game's narrative conflict, the original means-end relationship is inverted: the game's storyline becomes a subset of the joy of being a cause, which emboldens an encounter with the entire field of play, and beyond. In this sense, excess in the game refers to the habit or skill installed in embodied memory that *exceeds* the text's boundaries as a fantasy (an open loop) seeking its counterpart in the world.

Compared with games, gamic cinema's action is more tied to the scale of human subjectivity, or to the coordinates of what Deidre Pribram views as melodrama's "socioemotional individual" ("culturally embedded beings operating within or contesting social institutions and practices").[14] In other words, in gamic cinema, a story's moral framework is foregrounded and virtue's triumph over villainy's repressive force is carefully stitched to dramatic timing. Excess in this case is a tension that is denied release, that gradually balloons over the body as a profound sense of injustice, perhaps even hatred, outrage, or panic; and it is through the body that this tension is finally released not simply as pathos (or tears)—but more often as elation, liberation, joy, or perhaps an agitation that cannot initially be qualified in coherent emotional terms.

This distinction in body and excess is captured in game designer Clint Hocking's notion of analog verbs that games and stories share in common.[15] For context, designers often understand games to have a dual-narrative structure: the story told by their plots and the "story" told through their gameplay. Hocking suggests that gameplay and plot can be described in the same quantitative terms if their verbs are understood to vary in both frequency and amplitude. Gameplay verbs are high frequency, low amplitude; story verbs are low frequency, high amplitude. Consider the action of jumping when playing a *Mario* platformer: some jumps will be tenser than others, but the significance of Mario's acrobatic leap is ultimately divided across hundreds or thousands of repetitions, one following after another. What Dan Fleming terms a videogame's *extended middle* of play (between the "abrupt beginnings" and "always remote finales") entails steady progression and gradual mastery through repetition (i.e., high frequency, low amplitude).[16]

The reverse pattern would find in melodrama's emotional peaks and valleys—not to mention melodrama's logic of the *excluded middle* (moral polarization)—an example superseding the rule itself. In *Equilibrium*'s puppy shoot-out scene, John Preston's single dramatic leap into action tows a significant moral and socioemotional cargo. Such embodied action is reserved for a key moment in plot; there is a once-and-for-all temporal logic to the dissolution of accrued tensions. In this scene, Preston is initially misrecognized—both for the moral truth he withholds (i.e., the spared puppy in the trunk, the pill he has refused to take) as well as the superpowered bodily capacity the police fail to identify in time. The moment of Preston's full recognition is a dramatic revelation for villains and audience alike. But it is also what Franco Moretti terms "agnition," or the reconciliation of two opposed points of view.[17] Moretti suggests agnition moves us to pathos when it comes *too late*—thus melodrama's preference for situating reconciliation at a moment in plot when a character is dying. Gamic cinema, like action melodrama more generally, tends to prefer different timing: agnition occurs both during and *as* the transcendent bodily act, which is often also the revelation of an overlooked or doubted ability that stuns (but also unifies) onlookers. It moves us both affectively and kinesthetically. We are all stitched into the transcendent display, the shared fantasy, through a monopathic (singular, uncomplicated) response. And if we opt to repeat the film's viewing, or if the transcendent leap later recurs as body fantasy, it is as if we were seeking through repetition the hero's open loop, the frequentative skill that might protect us against circumstances of overwhelming amplitude.

The next section briefly introduces the melodramatic mode and specifies within its many generic forms the action-centered stories that best exemplify a gamic cinema. The permutations of body fantasy that flow through this narrative mode become the focus of the remainder of the chapter's consideration of key examples.

Action-Body Melodrama (from Kinetic to Moral Legibility)

Peter Brooks argues that melodrama emerged in the aftermath of the French Revolution as a response to the loss of moral authority once provided by church and monarchy. Thus its goal of producing moral legibility for a post-sacred world— meaning, as Linda Williams emphasizes, not simply "the defeat of evil by good," but rather the "all-important *recognition* of a good or evil that was previously obscure."[18] Every other quality of melodrama that Williams identifies (following Brooks) serves this morally clarifying moment of recognition: moral polarization (the "logic of the excluded middle"); characters embodying primary psychic categories (good and evil); the externalization of moral conflict; the virtue that is connoted by the suffering of innocent victims; and action that is infused with pathos.[19] Significantly, Christine Gledhill, Linda Williams, and others have argued that melodrama is misunderstood when considered a subgenre of popular narrative associated with excessive sentimentality, such as women's "weepies."[20] Rather, melodrama is perhaps *the* dominant cultural mode of storytelling and stretches across many so-called classical cinema genres.[21] Williams is fond of evoking Henry James's image of melodrama as a "wonderful 'leaping' fish" for its protean ability to transcend not only popular genres but even different media as it adapts to and engages with new social realities as an ever-modernizing form.[22]

Despite this, even scholars of cinema can tend to understand melodrama in narrowly domestic and feminine terms—a conception that has the effect of limiting female agency by severing women from action. There are, in other words, political stakes to recognizing melodrama's breadth—what Williams describes as its historical tendency to combine "so-called female-centered pathos" with "so-called masculine adventure and action."[23] In fact, Williams identifies the dialectic of pathos and action as one of the melodramatic mode's key elements, the very "melodramatic glue" that binds together so many different stories and genres, including "contemporary action or superhero films, together with their television variants."[24]

Superhero comics and superhero cinema both exemplify what Williams describes as the "truly modern" aspect of the melodramatic mode:[25] its "reliance on personality—and on the revelation of personality through body and gesture— as the key to both emotional and moral truth."[26] This observation is perhaps reflective of broader cultural trends toward viewing the body as constituting the self.[27] And it is through gesture and the body that melodramatic action and superhero films exemplify Hal Niedzviecki's notion of "I'm specialism," especially in the pervasive trope of budding heroes believing in the specialness of their bodies despite critical and skeptical voices.[28] In response to skepticism, the special body generates agnition by asserting itself as a cause, an intervening force. The threat villainy poses to innocent persons, to a space of innocence, and to the "innocent" belief in one's own specialness spurs the revelation of a previously hidden ability. In other words, the moment the body that had been doubted is finally *recognized* as special is homologous to melodrama's all-important recognition of a virtue that had once been obscured. Often, it seems that what is virtuous in superhero narratives is simply to *be special*.

Since melodrama is already understood as a dialectic of pathos and action, it is perhaps redundant to employ the compound term "action-melodrama"; so too is it redundant to say the body plays a central role in a mode long understood as a *body genre*.[29] Nevertheless, it is helpful to term melodramatic action and superhero films (not to mention gamic cinema) an "action-body melodrama" in order to emphasize the central role of special bodies that enable both action and the recognition of virtue. What bodies can and cannot do, how they move (and how quickly), is the primary preoccupation of a cinema that, as Lisa Purse puts it, "measures progress, failure, and success through the hero's body."[30] As Purse suggests, such bodies indeed push plots forward (in narratives of becoming) and serve as anchors for our own embodied identification ("as the site at which fantasies of empowerment are made physical").[31] As we accumulate the villain's every indignation—the misprision of virtue, the treachery, the apparent victory of evil—the hero's superpowered body becomes the site of a sustained disequilibrium that grows until the reconciliation of opposed perspectives, when doubts about what that body can do are pierced by a transcendent leap beyond all confines. In such moments, what had been contained within bursts forth as externalized emotion—not primarily as catharsis for repressed feelings, but as an excess generated through agnition.

Melodramatic characters need not suffer repression because they are generally understood as distinct from psychological individuals (with internalized conflict). Games, gamic cinema, and action-body melodrama seem to share this in common. Consider Brooks's argument that there is no psychology in melodrama; instead, melodramatic characters embody "pure psychic signs" (e.g., villain, victim, hero), lacking both "interior depth" and internal divided-ness.[32] In other words, melodramatic characters not only carry their moral truths on their sleeves but also express those truths in an impossibly pure form: a villain who is the very embodiment (the *sign*) of evil, a victim the embodi-ment of virtue (e.g., a puppy in the trunk). This accounts for a key pleasure unattainable in reality: the expression of a moral truth in its "full enuncia-tion."[33] So too is gamic cinema less concerned with dramatic realism (and real-ism's representative figure, the psychological individual) than a *psychology of situation* (a concern for situational awareness, for definitions of the situation). Put differently, gamic cinema poses the question, "What is the head inside of?" rather than "What is inside the head?"[34]

Action-body melodrama focuses on what the head is inside of—the structure of the situation itself—in order to reveal what is inside the heart. In short, it is a cinema predicated on the close relationship between motion and emotion, to bor-row David Bordwell's phrasing. In his study of Hong Kong action cinema, Bor-dwell employs the term "expressive amplification" to describe the heightened emotional impact of action when it is rendered legible "at a glance."[35] By care-fully organizing its action sequences and emphasizing each "clean-limbed attack and counter," a film more effectively solicits an audience's embodied participation ("kinetic transport").[36] In turn, our physical investments "prepare us to emote."[37]

Bordwell's idea of expressive amplification (how organized action *moves* us) is clearly relevant to games as well.[38] In fact, Bordwell's language is nearly iden-tical to Roger Caillois's assertion that participation in games requires "constant and unpredictable definitions of the situation . . . such as are produced by each attack or counterattack."[39] Of course, Caillois's words are a serious understate-ment. The need to render an always-evolving situation legible at each moment in play is core to the logic of games. This is perhaps most apparent in videogames precisely because legibility is so precarious there—a videogame's situation of play is often live (synchronous), fluid, and visually and spatially complex. As anyone who remembers their first encounter with a four-player *Super Smash Bros.* (1999) match may attest, it is all too easy to lose one's bearings. Doing so for even a moment can also mean losing the game. As a cultural form, all games tend to make high legibility demands. Being able to follow the specificity of play as well as its broader stakes is a precondition for certain kinds of group identification—as anyone caught off guard by a room's sudden uproar over a spectator sporting event has felt viscerally. As exemplified by such a group bond, one of a game's key pleasures is the presentation of a world that, though complex and often intim-idating (in both its spatiotemporal and social manifestations), does ultimately yield up its secrets and is capable of being known.

Insofar as the wish is to follow the action (and, indeed, this might not be the case),[40] then spectator sports have long understood and reflected the need to clearly focalize their games' events (meaning, to offer a perspective that renders complex action legible). They build focalizing devices directly into game rules, captured in the old adage "keep your eye on the ball," that singular element of the sport that is a necessary participant in nearly all major game events. Spectator sports also tend to stage play within large, open spaces organized by clearly visible boundary lines, and to situate spectators at ideal vantage points for observing the action (within unavoidable strictures of space and time, not to mention socioeconomic factors). Legibility is core to a game's aesthetics—both absolutely required for competition, but also central to its beauty. So suggests the fictional chess prodigy, Beth Harmon, in Netflix's *The Queen's Gambit* (2020). When pressed in an uncomfortable magazine interview to describe her relation to chess in traditional, gendered, and Oedipal terms (the king and queen as substitute parents, "one to attack, one to protect"), Beth (an orphan) responds that what drew her to the game was its absolute legibility: "It was the board I noticed first. It's an entire world of just sixty-four squares. I feel safe in it. I can control it, I can dominate it. And it's predictable. So, if I get hurt, I only have myself to blame."

Videogames focalize their action by building entire worlds around it. The need for legibility of situation (at any moment) is a factor in design decisions affecting the very systems that generate a videogame's images and spaces in the first place. Verisimilitude frequently takes a back seat to legibility's devices: health meters floating above player characters, worlds split diagrammatically down the middle and viewed from the side, cameras that hover in fixed positions high above the field of play, reticles darting around the screen, damage indicators for each successful attack, green and red highlights on character models that help distinguish friend from foe, pickups that flash white, and so on. Bolter and Grusin may see in some of these elements the logic of hypermediacy (meaning they are in tension with the competing logic of immediacy, or optical immersion in a three-dimensional, perspectival space). But the devices are first and foremost the means at one's disposal for an especially powerful immersion in the situation of play, generally only a portion of which is capable of being captured in a virtual camera's optical perspective. Legibility is forged cooperatively between player and game—a key part of the feedback loop. It is the focus of much discourse on games (such as YouTube videos on the minutia of patch updates, emerging strategies, and so on). It is an active element of gameplay that players constantly manage. And the more one plays—and reads, listens, and watches—the more readily one will recognize a familiar situation in play, as well as the circumstances leading up to and away from it. Trajectories of possible action emerge organically from this process.

Highly legible worlds should serve as a mantra linking games to both melodrama and gamic cinema. Expressive amplification speaks to melodrama's externalization of emotion in the socioemotional individual: a melodramatic world is one that is carefully organized for the externalization of moral conflict, a world that is morally legible *at a glance* because it is so strictly patterned. Once more, verisimilitude may at times take a back seat. What Bordwell describes as

"Hong Kong physics"—a midair "kick to the chest" that "somehow drives a man's head down so that a downward punch can launch a midair somersault"—could be described as a *melodrama of action*, where the rules of space and time are bent toward the goal of expressive amplification.[41] Action-body melodrama (like gamic cinema) is bound up with Hong Kong aesthetics, which now refer to a globally pervasive approach to orchestrating not just action (motion) but emotion as well.

Whether considering Hong Kong Action cinema, action-body melodrama, or gamic cinema (admittedly broad categories with considerable overlap), expressive amplification does not denote the use of one stylistic element or formal feature over another. What matters is neither a predilection for long shots nor close-ups, neither an eschewal of montage nor rapid-shot editing, and neither an acceleration of action nor its expansion in slow motion. Rather, the key is the careful and deliberate deployment of all such elements in order to render the action of the fight maximally legible. Likewise, in our thinking about film-game convergence (and composite formations such as gamic cinema), the key commonality is likely not any specific formal or stylistic system—not subjective optics, an eschewal of montage, or modular narrative structures. Instead, what matters is how complex situations are organized. Legibility ties the body to the situation. It is the means by which a narrative can serve as a kind of trellis for the dynamic movement of fantasy. Action that rouses embodied participation can also activate the embodied memory of the transcendent leap. How the body is stitched into narrative is key to the question of how these stories not only solicit our engagement through fantasy, but also how they lend that fantasy freshly evocative movements for our seemingly always-expanding storehouse of body fantasy.

Writing the Action Body into Narrative: *Kung Fu Hustle* and *Naruto*

The 2004 Hong Kong action-comedy *Kung Fu Hustle* contains a blatant reference to Bruce Lee's *The Way of the Dragon* (1972), when Lee's Tang Lung—young and muscled in a tight-fitting white tank top—warns off a crime boss by gesture and demeanor alone. Tang merely locks eyes with the villain and cracks his knuckles, waving a finger and grunting through flexed muscles, but the villain's face conveys emphatic comprehension. *Kung Fu Hustle* repeats Tang's gestures in a similar narrative scenario with one key difference: the envoy of this embodied message is not a young man, but rather a middle-aged woman dressed for bed in a red and white nightgown, curlers in hair, lit cigarette hanging from her lips. The corporeal analogy is striking because this woman—known simply as Landlady—is far more intimidating than Bruce Lee's character from *The Way of the Dragon*. Her confrontation with the crime boss occurs shortly after a surprising transformation, prior to which she had been overlooked and misrecognized. Because of her age, her gender, her casual domestic attire, her pettiness and cheapness—not to mention her exclusive narrative function as comic

Landlady channels Bruce Lee and mugs for the villain in *Kung Fu Hustle* (2004).

relief—nobody seems prepared for the spectacular moment when she defeats the boss's hired assassins, sending them scrambling and whimpering.

Kung Fu Hustle exemplifies Peter Brooks's argument about the body in literature that produces a story (the "signifying body")—especially its relation to identity and affective intensity: how the body is "marked in a significant moment of the person's past history that enables recognition," and how this "moment of recognition is a dramatic climax, a coming into the open of hidden identities and latent possibilities."[42] At the same time, and for largely the same reasons, *Kung Fu Hustle* is an illustrative example of action-body melodrama more generally. As attested by the unmotivated references to American pop culture (which include a burlesque sequence that feels like a Chuck Jones cartoon) the film does not always take itself seriously. However, much like the Japanese anime to which *Kung Fu Hustle* (hereafter *Hustle*) also pays homage, the film *is* serious about its action sequences, which in fact employ the same Chinese martial arts choreographer as *The Matrix* (1999), Yuen Woo-ping. The film's plot twists during these action sequences release a playful energy that seems to transmute into pathos for characters who were previously misrecognized and underestimated.

An early example of recognition's "dramatic climax" occurs when *Hustle*'s Deadly Axe Gang attacks Pigsty Alley, an impoverished, tight-knit tenement community. In response, three skilled martial arts masters shed their identities as local shopkeepers and laborers to fight back. In retaliation for an earlier act of defiance, and to clearly establish the film's Manichaean stakes, the Axe Gang douses a mother and child with kerosene and brandishes a lighter for the name of the culprit. The one who has defied them (Coolie, or manual laborer, glimpsed earlier carrying large sacks on his back) emerges in time to catch the tossed lighter. The revelation that a Pigsty Alley resident is secretly a martial arts master is repeated twice in quick succession, losing a bit of its capacity to surprise each time: Coolie is joined by two others—Tailor and then Donut, the baker—who also cast aside workaday identities and step forward to protect their home. These three experts-in-hiding emerge from an idyllic community of workers and craftsmen (a space of innocence) as its protectors. Villainous threats and intimidation spur each into nomination as a virtuous hero. The true identity of each fighter sticks closely to what their special bodies can do: they are the renowned Twelve Kicks, Iron Fist, and Hexagon Staff.

In this respect, no different is the revelation that the comedic slumlords of Pigsty Alley (Landlord and Landlady) are themselves legendary martial arts masters. However, a far more ambitious hustle is at play with the slumlords. The film hides these characters in plain sight, as clowns who seem immune to the gravity of the situation of escalating gang violence. Both are middle-aged and casually dressed (often in pajamas), and both tend to be animated with cartoonish CGI during moments of physical comedy. When these same bodies step into the film's serious, agonistic arena as a powerful intervening force, we must quickly revise our own grip on them; their entrance into the situation is, itself, an entirely new situation, and one that requires dragging already-established body knowledge back into the domain of working memory. The recent past must be revised at the same time as the spectacular action continues to unfold. There is no time to mobilize doubt or differentiate bodily knowledge and transcendent corporeality from identity and feelings of triumph; everything is mixed together.

The sequence begins when Twelve Kicks, Iron Fist, and Hexagon Staff are fatally ambushed by two skilled assassins (the Harpists) while departing the Alley. Twelve Kicks is killed at the outset, and the remaining two heroes are brought within an inch of their lives by the assassins' unseen, acoustic attacks (sonic objects projected by their stringed instrument). However, the Harpists' finishing blow is deflected and their strings snapped by an obscure, off-screen source. Disarmed, the assassins scale the building to investigate the source of the unseen counterattack ("There's another master?"). However, the pair is inexplicably brought back to the ground by yet another unseen force. In a clever play on continuity editing, the assassins' feet are framed in close-up as they leap upward, out of frame—and instead of the match cut we are trained to anticipate by action that begins in the periphery of the frame and moves off screen, the shot holds on empty space as the Harpists' feet slowly return and float back to the ground, followed by a third pair of feet in the middle. The anticipated shot that never comes might have revealed the presence of a hidden master. Instead, a puzzle of feet intervenes, followed by another briefly enigmatic shot of Landlord (still oily-haired and dressed for bed) between the Harpists, arms hoisted over their shoulders as if too drunk or sleepy to stand on his own.

Perhaps Hal Niedzviecki is correct in that popular culture implants within us "entire decades of made-up memory" that prepares us on some level for moments that suddenly "assert the specialness of the ordinary individual," the "it-could-happen-to-you hero."[43] Nevertheless, Landlord's sudden appearance throws the film's agonistic situation into confusion, posing new questions that are only answered when the Harpists' fists start flying and Landlord's rubbery composition and stringy hip rotations effortlessly repel and redirect their attacks. The assassins pull back for a ranged counterattack, only to be upended (and disrobed) by Landlady's "Lion's Roar," an overwhelming blast of air and sound from her superinflated lungs (now recognized as the source of the earlier interruption). The film's suturing action—its unbroken signifying chain—proceeds by introducing each martial arts master as an initially unseen force intervening into the fight from the battle's fringes, from the space of frightened onlookers; the film repeatedly answers a narrative question with a surprising embodied display of transcendent power so that closure (each question's answer) is simultaneously an opening of new, manifest potential. The fantasy work spurred at such a moment has a dual motion, one part "additive comprehension,"[44] or a reassessing glance backward, and one part "iconic imagination,"[45] or exciting speculation about the direction of movements already underway. So shocking is the transformation that Landlord's and Landlady's bodies—past, present, and future—become the shared focus of a creative reconciliation. Their own bodies become polarized in terms that resonate with a fantasy of bodily transcendence: they stage their own encounter between the special and the ordinary, between virtue and cowardice, and between power and inaction.

Bodies in *Hustle* are freighted with narrative significance, serving not only as anchors for identity and screens that both occlude and reveal major plot twists but also as temporal fulcrums where the past leverages itself on present and future. Like action-body melodrama more broadly, bodies in *Hustle* house the power that is key to resolving narrative conflict. They are tied to identity in a melodramatic fashion in that each character in the central conflict embodies primary psychic categories, even if these roles are initially obscure. Early in the film, Landlord flirts with but also exploits his tenants, often violating their privacy. He is also spinelessness when faced with danger or confronted by his wife for his indiscretions. These tendencies hang on his body as a nonchalance that mirrors the way he guiltlessly exploits the social order he oversees in Pigsty Alley. Even though the selfish slumlord is merely a cover identity that permits Landlord and Landlady anonymity in their retirement from fighting, the truth of the matter is apparent on the surface (on the body itself). Landlord's personality embodies his unique fighting style, based on proximity, passivity, and flexibility; the same is true with Landlady and all her bluster. Though the film's CGI-enhanced effects leave much to be desired, Landlord's and Landlady's bodies exemplify Kristen Whissel's digital "effects emblem," or "a cinematic visual effect that operates as a site of intense signification and gives stunning (and sometimes) allegorical expression to a film's key themes, anxieties, and conceptual obsessions."[46]

Hustle's thematic obsession is a fantasy of believing in and ultimately confirming a specialness of the body: its latent, "natural genius" for martial arts.

Variations of this fantasy occur nearly a dozen times over the film's duration.[47] In truth, a dozen may be one too many for any self-contained, feature-length film: by its conclusion, the body-as-narrative-fulcrum creaks with overuse. That the film comes full circle (i.e., the superlative hero is the man who unwittingly initiated its central conflict in the first place) seems no longer to matter—the plot is not sensible in this way. The loop that *does* matter, the one we retain as the credits roll, is the film's "underlying pattern of feeling"—a highly embodied pattern, to revisit Richard Dyer's language, that has "to do with freedom of movement, confidence in the body, [and] engagement with the material world."[48] We believe in the body by default; doubt is learned, and painfully.[49] As Freud suggests, the child at play stages an ambitious wish; doubt comes from without—a villainous force intruding into a space of innocence. The trope of (mis)recognition through doubt situates the freedom of movement and confidence in the body within a socioemotional context. And in this way, the film's bodies all tell the same story.

Hustle celebrates the innocent belief in the body's specialness, which must be defended against skeptical voices, within and without. The film reflects this (its own) fantasy structure in a flashback, when playground bullies beat and mock its hero, Sing, as a child. Sing witnesses the bullies stealing candy from a young girl and confronts them. What cuts the deepest in this moment is not Sing's utter defeat (how the boys knock him to the ground and urinate on him), but rather the subsequent uncovering of the kung fu pamphlet he has bought with his life savings (from the tramp who deems him special and worthy of training). The boys cruelly point out the stamp on the pamphlet's cover designating it as a cheap, mass-produced product; not only is it worth only a fraction of what was spent, but it ties specialism to conformity through a kind of naïve (mass) consumerism. This narcissistic wound destroys Sing's innocent belief that he is special and apparently sets him on a life path of petty crime. The rest of the film repeatedly imagines the reversal of this situation, where overlooked or misrecognized heroes are spurred into self-nomination and action by the suffering of the innocent.

Of course, *Hustle* does eventually run out of overlooked heroes. In contrast with feature-length melodramatic films, long-form serial narratives (e.g., in print or television) promise to extend and multiply fantasy's forms and structures almost indefinitely through a superabundance of "world and time," as Linda Williams puts it.[50] Rather than returning to the same equilibrial state after each episode or installment, serialized narratives carry their story forward with greater or lesser continuity. For this reason, characters in serial melodrama need not be morally legible at a glance—they do not necessarily embody the very signs of virtue and villainy. Instead, as Pribram and Williams argue, they accumulate ethical and emotional meaning over time through their interactions with others. In this respect, Japanese manga (comics) and anime such as *One Piece* (1997–present), *Naruto* (2002–2007), *Hunter × Hunter* (2011–2014), and *My Hero Academia* (2016–present) not only exemplify action-body melodrama and an especially gamic mode of storytelling but also solicit body fantasy through the promise of an always-developing narrative of becoming that is structured by dramas of (mis)recognition. In these series, heroes defy expectations and reveal their true identities—revelations that are always "a dramatic finding-out from and on the body itself."[51] Fans of the series carry a precise understanding of each character's body and abilities across hundreds of serialized episodes.

To drop a viewer (or reader) into the middle of a single narrative that has been serially developed in weekly installments for more than a decade would be disorienting. The example I often choose for introducing students to these concepts comes early in the *Naruto* series, while basic information about *Naruto*'s world and characters is still being introduced. Based closely on the Shōnen Jump manga, *Naruto* and its continuation as *Naruto: Shippûden* (2007–2017) compose a single, massive, serialized narrative set in a fantastical feudal society where interpersonal, political, and military conflicts are constituted by and resolved through martial arts combat. The secret military technology that often forms the backdrop or motive for war is itself invested in and expressed through special, individualized bodies that, when highly gifted and trained, can channel power that resembles weapons of mass destruction. The emotional energy or agnition generated at the resolution of each story arc's prolonged fight typically hinges on an overtly stated moral truth—such as Naruto's pledge to never leave a friend behind or the Leaf Village's "will of fire" that situates love as central to peace and views social bonds in the village as extensions of familial ties (ties that the villains hope to sever). Inseparably bound to such moral pronouncements is a specialized bodily capacity that is dramatically unveiled during the fight—an ability not yet known to exist, or which a central character has struggled to perform competently during training.

Naruto carefully intertwines moral and bodily truths that have been obscured or called into doubt. This twining often takes place during moments of narrative dilation when single action sequences are extended across multiple episodes (each lasting more than twenty minutes). The dilation of action is achieved through conventional temporal manipulations such as flashbacks to relevant backstory or the generous use of slow motion and repetition. But it is also achieved through techniques unique to Japanese animation, such as the pausing of action—sometimes midstrike—to make time for commentary and reflection, either from onlookers or from the combatants themselves. Though Japanese manga and anime are known for drawing out climactic encounters, the point is not simply to defer resolution;[52] each interruption also helps to define the situation of play, to tease out the complexity of the melodramatic narrative's dialectic of pathos and action.[53] *Naruto* is rule-bound in the sense that it carefully establishes its agonistic situation and provides time for both participants and onlookers to process unexpected happenings and update their definitions of the situation. It sometimes goes as far as providing visual diagrams to instruct viewers about the rules governing specific elements of its fictional universe, such as the flow of bodily energy ("chakra"), which can be used to augment physical capacities (absorbing the force of a fall or clinging to the surface of water) as well as sensory abilities (chakra-infused eyes can improve sight or even hypnotize others). This is in sharp contrast with storytelling in American cinema and television, which often conspicuously avoids revealing specific details about the precise rules governing the interaction of bodies.

An example from the first season of *Naruto* demonstrates all these points. The episode "Gaara vs. Rock Lee: The Power of Youth Explodes!" takes place within the third and final stage of the "Chūnin Selection Exams," a rigorous screening process determining which ninja are promoted to the next rank. The setting of a competitive educational environment recurs across many anime and represents a familiar rite of passage: evaluation by powerful adults within an alienating institution. School settings facilitate a kind of fort-da game involving not just the presence and absence of protective authority figures but also a flirtation with the precarious boundaries separating students from the dangerous world beyond. Often, the unwelcome intrusion of a threatening Other (e.g., Orochimaru) from outside the institution halts the exam or contest, changes the stakes of the action, and forces students to act before they feel they are ready. Perhaps most importantly, a disciplinary setting is justification for the sustained scrutiny of bodies, personalities, and aptitude in a narrative of becoming—it is pretense for the moments of *recognition* at the heart of the fantasy of bodily transcendence (i.e., of special bodies exceeding expectations and overcoming anticipated limits).

In the final stage of *Naruto*'s Chūnin exam, the students must engage in direct, one-on-one, tournament-style combat: the fight ends when a fighter is incapacitated or killed. The episode in question takes place during this stage.[54] One of the series' main characters, Rock Lee (from the Hidden Leaf Village), faces off against a foreign combatant, Gaara (from the Village Hidden in the Sand). Prior to this sequence, Lee is portrayed as an honorable but naïve optimist specializing in hand-to-hand combat. He is fast and strong, and he adores and emulates his sensei, Might Guy: they share a green, full-body jumpsuit, a fervor for excessive physical training, and an optimistic worldview. By the time he is chosen to face Gaara, Lee's virtue is already clearly established in his apparent innocence, as well as in two prior occasions when he disregards his own well-being to help others in need. In contrast, Gaara is introduced through the cold-blooded killing of several competing shinobi during the second phase of the exam, when he goes far beyond what is necessary to collect the two scrolls needed to advance. His adolescent opponents surrender their scroll and beg for mercy as Gaara squashes them to death. Gaara carries a giant gourd on his back filled with sentient, chakra-infused sand, which moves autonomously to reflexively protect him from attacks, but which Gaara can also manipulate actively, shaping it into limbs and tendrils to snare, surround, and crush his victims.

Though spectators know well the mortal threat facing Rock Lee, Gaara's abilities are unknown to Lee and most of those observing from above the Chūnin exam arena. The agonistic situation that takes shape as the fight unfolds becomes increasingly ominous for Lee, whose attacks are automatically repelled by Gaara's living sand. The fight exemplifies one element of expressive amplification in particular—what Bordwell terms the "pause/burst/pause" rhythm, where intense flurries of action are interspersed with static moments that not only throw action into relief but also allow for a brief assessment of the situation generated with each attack and counterattack.[55] Bordwell conceives of the pause in purely formal terms—as a literal rhythm in the staging of action as well as in the montage itself. In addition, Gaara and Lee's fight draws on diegetic audiences (the fight's onlookers) to size up the situation during moments of pause in the action (e.g., Naruto: "So *that's* what he's got in that gourd"). Shino, upon seeing the sand, suffers traumatic repetition and can only mutter "that . . ." to a flashback of Gaara's recent slayings, which he had witnessed from a hidden vantage point. The pauses in the fight allow wider narrative material to enter the exchange as verbal interplay between characters and sometimes lengthy asides or flashbacks. In this way, the kinetic action becomes invested with meaning as it is stitched into overt questions about the identity of each combatant.

Reflective of action sequences in the series more generally, this fight's detailed animation and bodily kinetics are framed in medium-long and long shots that emphasize Rock Lee's fluid trajectories. Like *Hustle*, and like the globally circulating action genres influenced by Hong Kong aesthetics more generally, these sequences are carefully planned and organized; they progress through a series of complications and developments. However, in contrast with *Hustle*'s mostly nonverbal confrontations, the Gaara versus Rock Lee fight is advanced as much by its kinetic action as by the commentary of onlookers from the balcony (Sakura: "Even as fast as he is, Lee can't get anywhere close to him"). Such commentary highlights boundaries, guides expectations, and articulates the stakes of the fight as it unfolds, always clarifying and updating the situation for both diegetic and non-diegetic spectators. How diegetic spectators anticipate (and fail to anticipate) what will happen next is a key aspect of this mode of storytelling. For instance, Naruto comments that Gaara is using the sand as a shield, but he is corrected by Gaara's sibling, Kankurō, who introduces new information about the agonistic situation: "*He's* not doing it; the sand is protecting him of its own accord. It's almost like a living thing. It'll come to Gaara's defense without his doing anything. That's why Gaara's never been injured. No one can get at him. No one's ever even been able to touch him." This articulation reveals as much about Gaara as the fight's situation: Lee's intense physicality is mocked by Gaara's absolute stasis.

After several additional failed attempts to pierce Gaara's sand defense, the commentary that once again interrupts the fight not only reflects on the difficult situation Lee faces but also establishes crucial information for the *Naruto* world. Sakura states, "I don't get it. He's only using taijutsu. Can't he see that's never going to work? Why doesn't he get some distance and use ninjutsu?"

Ninjutsu is a kind of chakra manipulation, initiated by hand gestures, that projects force beyond the body in a variety of ways (e.g., breathing fire, extending one's shadow, imbuing a fist or blade with electricity, or producing a "shadow clone" or copy of oneself). Along with taijutsu (hand-to-hand martial arts combat) and genjutsu (or the use of chakra to hypnotize or control the thoughts and perceptions of others), ninjutsu comprises one of three basic types of ninja combat. Sakura's question at this moment is meant to reintroduce context necessary for following the fight, but at the same time it introduces new (clarifying) information about Rock Lee as well.

Lee's sensei, Might Guy, responds to Sakura with a confidence seemingly at odds with the situation: "That might be a good idea. That is, if he had any. Lee has no ninjutsu or genjutsu skills at all." Sakura is taken aback—as these skills are learned at a young age in ninja training. Guy continues, amused, "That's nothing. You should have seen how hopeless he was when I first met him. No talent whatsoever." At this point in the fight, Lee is tripped, and Gaara's sand looms overhead and splashes downward, apparently trapping Lee, causing shrieks and one onlooker to announce, "It's over." But Might Guy chuckles, amplifying a growing narrative tension, his conflicting definition of the situation of play. The next shot reveals Lee's flight (in a tightly held reverse summersault) into the vertical axis of the frame, where he perches atop a giant, ornamental statue of hands performing a ninjutsu sign. From atop the ninjutsu statue, at a safe distance from the sand, Lee's position reflects what Kristen Whissel has described as the spatial logic of "new verticality" in action cinema, where "struggles between protagonists and antagonists hinge on the degree to which each is able to defy or master the laws of physics making extreme vertical settings pervasive, almost regardless of genre."[56] The elision of Lee's actual escape from the sand prefigures the embodied action to come.

At this moment of pause in the fight, Guy sensei continues his verbal framing of the situation: "A ninja who can do neither ninjutsu nor genjutsu is certainly a rarity. Lee has only his taijutsu to rely on. Some might even consider that a disadvantage. But that's what makes him a winner." This explanation is meant as a provocation, fueling the tension that is building toward a bodily revelation. Guy addresses Lee from the balcony with a thumbs-up, shouting, "All right, Lee, take 'em off." Lee's surprise ("But, Guy sensei, you said that was only a last resort when the lives of very important people were at stake") both cements the impression that he and his sensei know something that others do not and helps reinforce Lee's virtue, his insistence on following rules set for him by his master even in trying situations. When Guy reassures Lee that this is an exception, Lee becomes elated, pulling back his socks and revealing training weights wrapped around his shins. The revelation prompts reaction shots from onlookers who set to work immediately reevaluating their understanding of the situation. However, the revelation is a one-two punch, so to speak, and its full implication is not yet appreciated. One of Lee's peers jeers, "How old-fashioned," and a fellow sensei remarks, "Leg weights? Basic training equipment." In fact, the information initially leads to a splintering of reactions ranging from Naruto's "Totally cool!" to Kankurō's "Totally dumb." Lee himself weighs in (unaware of the side-chatter): "That is better. Now I will be able to move freely." He holds the weights at his sides and then drops them to the ground. As they fall, Gaara's sister, Temari, remarks, "Come on. You really think you'll be able to get through Gaara's defenses just by dropping a couple of pounds of weight?" However, the weights hit the ground with such force that dust plumes are raised nearly the full height of the multistory ninjutsu hand statue, suggesting a heaviness beyond the scale of human corporeality. This moment of revelation uses an extreme height to unify spectators (as a literal distance for a dense and accelerating mass to generate a powerful moment of impact). This impact is pure agnition. Diegetic onlookers are uniformly stunned by the force the weights generate; they all recognize Lee as being more than had originally met the eye. Lee's arduous training is both temporally and spatially compressed into those extremely dense weights. The conflict between their volume (their apparent size) and the magnitude of their explosion repeats for emphasis the "impact" of Lee's bodily secret. This moment encapsulates how, in *Naruto*'s world, the body is capable of possessing latent potential that connects each person to the past and to one another in unexpected ways.

However, the moment of agnition is barely perceived when the action resumes: Lee leaps from the top of the statue at a speed that outstrips the eye's capacity to track motion (making Lee seem to disappear). Onlookers struggle to regain the power to speak (from stunned silence to "so fast" or "amazing") as Lee's blows begin—incredibly—to reach beyond Gaara's impenetrable sand barrier. At this moment comes another pause during which Might Guy introduces Lee's narrative of becoming. Because Lee had "no aptitude for ninjutsu or genjutsu," Guy reports having decided to direct Lee to instead focus entirely on his taijutsu. The result of years of intense training is that Lee has become "the world's greatest taijutsu specialist." It is at the delivery of this line, and the astonishment of the crowd, that Lee actually lands a direct hit on Gaara. Lee's fight with Gaara exemplifies a technique consistent in *Naruto* (and in Shōnen Jump manga-inspired anime more generally) that forges legibility from a combination of carefully constructed action sequences and verbal utterances that reflect upon and size up that action, clarifying and reinforcing its agonistic and narrative stakes. Moments of pause help emphasize the allegorical force of an image, such as Lee's perch atop the ninjutsu statue, which serves emblematically to challenge the assumed hierarchical position of ninjutsu. Such pauses also help articulate the moral and emotional significance of the action.

In a manner reminiscent of how *Hustle* weaves bodily revelations into plot at key turning points, it is subsequently revealed that there are unseen layers in Gaara's defense that thwart even Lee's amped up speed—literally, Gaara's sand has covered his skin in an imperceptible shell that has absorbed the force of Lee's

Perched above a giant ninjutsu statue, Rock Lee removes and drops his dense training weights. Images are from the *Naruto* (2002–2007) anime.

strikes. Gaara even escapes Lee's lethal "Primary Lotus" (a high-speed, multistory pile driver), the performance of which renders Lee unable to fight or even dodge for several minutes. As the fight unfolds, Guy elaborates on Lee's archetypally "hopeless" underdog status—how he was ridiculed and doubted by his peers, overlooked by potential mentors. Moments when flashbacks to Lee's ridicule at school are intercut with his being pummeled by Gaara's sand are infused with pathos. Guy, who narrates the flashback, does so with both love and faith that the fight's situation is not as grim as it seems. Guy recounts recognizing Lee's virtue when he once observed Lee at a secret, after-hours training session. Though Lee initially fails (even at his taijutsu) and doubts himself next to the "genius" or natural talent of his peers, Guy agrees to mentor Lee because of a different sort of gift Lee possesses: he is a genius of perseverance. Indeed, though Lee's body can move so quickly it appears to cheat the laws of time and space, Lee himself would never cheat, cut corners, or skip a single repetition in training—Lee cannot even use contractions when he speaks. Guy's narration cements Lee's virtue (success through hard work and perseverance in the face of overwhelming doubt). This narrative information is transmuted into pathos as Lee finally reveals his trump card, his "inner gates" technique—an even more drastic and destructive means of militaristic bodily deployment allowing Lee to dash through the air like a jet engine, a hyperactive motion that is again directly contrasted with Gaara's stasis (his sand fights for him).

Fellow sensei Kakashi's flash of anger upon learning Guy has taught this forbidden technique to his young pupil is pure intrigue for spectators sussing out the student-teacher dynamic in the shinobi world—the moment marks the first hint that Guy's love for his student, his embrace of Lee's dream to become a great ninja despite his deficiencies, has blinded Guy to concerns over Lee's safety. When Guy and Kakashi then explain the concept of the eight inner gates to Lee's peer, Sakura, one might expect the overly detailed explanation during a prolonged pause in the fight to undercut the pathos of this moment. However, as Kakashi explains the inner gates with the help of a literal diagram naming and locating each gate, the extended information has the effect of deepening engagement with the fight that then takes place. The revelation that Lee's Primary Lotus (the pile driver) had required opening the first chakra gate (the "Gate of Opening") demands a revision of the recent past, substantiating Kakashi's earlier description of the lotus as a double-edged sword that places tremendous strain on the body. Clarifying exactly what is at stake in the agonistic exchange—not only how it works and what its costs and limitations are but also why it evokes controversy—sets the stage for the pathos of the revelation that Guy supports Lee's dream of attaining greatness, even if it comes at the cost of Lee's life.

In the end, Gaara manages to survive the onslaught of Lee's inner gates, though both he and Lee are rendered too exhausted to move. The fight is far from a stalemate, however, as Gaara's sand remains alive and mobile—it creeps in and, following Gaara's command, crushes Lee's arm and foot. When the sand moves in once more (this time to kill Rock Lee), it is dramatically swept aside by Might Guy, who leaves the space of onlookers and intervenes in the contest at the last moment, ending the match and throwing the fight's moral contrast once more into especially stark terms. Guy's cold stare at Gaara as he stands in the arena between the two fighters and effortlessly displaces the sand collapses the fight's disparate layers (kinetic and moral, contestant and audience) and causes Gaara to experience a series of painful images from his past. While Might Guy behaves at this moment like a protective parent toward Lee, it is later revealed that Gaara is an orphan who is feared by all and loved by none. Because of the demonic sand that has protected him since infancy like an overbearing parent, killing both those who would harm him *and* those who might love him, Gaara has known neither ("no one's ever even been able to touch him").

Gaara wins—and Lee is maimed to such an extent that the on-site medics predict he will never fight again. Despite this, Lee (in what initially seems like one more reversal) climbs to his feet and adopts a fighter's stance, his body unwilling or unable to relent. In a moment my own students regularly identify as infused with pathos, Might Guy realizes that Lee, though standing, is actually unconscious. Guy embraces Lee and weeps. The tears express his love (which he struggles to convey with words) as well as his recognition of Lee as virtuous in the refusal to admit defeat, a refusal that originates beyond will, beyond consciousness, and that reflects something about Lee's identity that no utterance could. In Brooks's terms, once again, it is not an "intellectual" revelation, but rather a "dramatic finding-out from and on the body itself."[57]

It is important to emphasize that though each fighter's values are recognized immediately,[58] both are consistently misrecognized for what their bodies can do. Their bodies are written into narrative through a misrecognition that sets the stage for a dramatic finding-out that is, itself, also recognition of a virtue of sorts. Our understanding of what each fighter can do with their body evolves during the fight, necessitating frequent redefinitions of situation. It is as if the contest's rules shift during moments of peripety (such as when Lee removes his leg weights or Landlord hangs on the shoulders of the Harpist assassins). Such moments temporarily destabilize the clear articulation of action and cause the state of play to careen. The deliberate disruption to a spatiotemporal or agonistic order—along with the subsequent rush to reinstate comprehension—is the basic glue or suturing action for a narrative mode that anchors identity in spectacular bodies overcoming opposition. Our own bodies are mobilized as we watch these other, special bodies operate within clearly defined limits. Parsing the agonistic situation—processing it at the level of embodied meaning—directly involves our embodied understanding of events, tying our implicit hopes about recognition and overcoming restraints to a wider socioemotional framework. In addition to situation in the melodramatic sense, this mode of storytelling's use of peripety and agnition renders heroes' bodies the active focus of working memory and fantasy. The special body is the thing spectators (both in the arena and at home) must process throughout the entirety of an action sequence. As a serialized story's world becomes better established, the climactic fights tend to grow in scope and duration through a series of complications and developments, stretching across the entirety of multiple consecutive episodes, or even across entire seasons. In this way, a narrative mode predicated on the excluded middle (Manichaean conflict, moral polarization) comes to resemble gaming's looping, extended middles (the deferral of endings). Both between and within narrative episodes, spectators are held in suspense, left only with the special bodily capacities that take shape when everything is on the line.

The Kernel of Gamic Cinema

This chapter's discussion of bodies woven into the fabric of a story provides a small window into how narratives function as dynamic systems for supporting and extending a fantasy of bodily transcendence—a fantasy that represents a key point of contact between games, cinema, television, and comics. The focus on fantasy as the common term in convergence between games and narrative media provides an alternative to what sometimes seems like a *lowest-common-denominator* approach to isolating some formal system (or perhaps an overly broad definition of narrative) that is apparently shared by each convergent form. Fantasy accommodates asymmetry: it can connect a melodramatic narrative in a film with a game that has little or no narrative content without fundamentally shifting operative meanings of "narrative" from relevant disciplines (such as cinema studies) or requiring that the game also be thought of as a kind of melodrama.

There is one clear benefit to this approach. The melodramatic mode is popular and widespread, but it retains a degree of specificity in contrast with the broad, medium-independent definitions of narrative often employed in discussions of media convergence.[59] In a key example of the latter, Marie-Laure Ryan proposes a "logico-semantic" definition intended to help extend narrative analysis to digital games: "A narrative text is one that brings a world to the mind (setting) and populates it with intelligent agents (characters). These agents participate in actions and happenings (events, plot), which cause global changes in the narrative world. Narrative is thus a mental representation of causally connected states and events that captures a segment in the history of a world and of its members."[60] Ryan intends this definition of narrative to serve as a "cognitive universal" that is "flexible enough to tolerate a wide range of variations"—and, indeed, it is difficult to imagine a media object that does not satisfy its terms.[61] Nor is Ryan's the most capacious definition of narrative intended to also capture videogame play. Consider, for instance, Torben Grodal's approach, which conceives of narrative as more or less coterminous with all of lived, conscious experience, as "'cognitive-logical' patterns" or "story-mechanisms in the brain" that guide us whether we play a game, watch a movie, or shop for groceries.[62] By situating narrative in the mind of the reader/player, such theories attempt to bridge perceptibly distinct media objects through a live, internal, story-building process that is always operative. There is, of course, value to capacious definitions of narrative.[63] However, there is also value in maintaining a connection to the particular. By positioning fantasy as that bridging "mechanism in the brain," this chapter is able to draw on a definition of narrative that any reader will recognize in the commercial formats that populate everyday life. This allows for a stronger, more direct connection between two media that does not reduce either to the bits that both seem to share. The media objects in question do solicit embodied fantasy, but fantasy is also something brought to them.

As Freud suggests, fantasy can come "ready-made."[64] It can be embedded in a narrative—tied to each character, setting, and plot event—but it can also be evoked in an instant and without an otherwise coherent narrative scenario. The trope of the special body that is initially misrecognized is a well-established schema. Refused recognition produces a familiar tension that we have all seen released as agnition—in short, it inaugurates the fantasy of bodily transcendence, the wish for a leap (or other transcendent act) that affirms the body's specialness and stuns onlookers. This pattern transcends the boundaries of diegesis. Fans of Jean-Claude Van Damme need no narrative preamble when, in the very first scene of *The Quest* (1996), three young men attempt to rob a bar where Christopher Dubois (Van Damme made up to appear older) has just sat for a cup of coffee. The stage is set when Dubois asks the young men to leave and one responds, "What the hell are you going to do, old man—drool on me?" Audiences may not anticipate the exact way this "old man" will make use of his hook cane in the fight to come, but we know for certain that the younger men have badly misjudged the situation. In the aftermath, the bartender stares at Dubois in stunned recognition, pouring whiskey to the side of the coffee cup because his own routine is so disturbed. His question—"Where'd you learn to fight like that?"—inaugurates the film's story as a flashback. The initial scuffle in the bar takes place at the outer threshold of plot. We are launched into the film's narrative through a mode of embodied fantasy that in several ways exceeds the film's diegetic boundaries, drawing from extratextual sources such as familiarity with martial arts genres, Van Damme fandom, and a fantasy stretching across media about a belief in specialness that has been misrecognized. This pattern is the nucleus or kernel of action-body melodrama, and so too of gamic cinema—the dense cluster of body fantasy that itself occasions the telling of a story.

Insofar as a body fantasy that recurs can serve as Freud suggested fantasy often did in the formation of dreams, as a ready-made schema, then it can be understood as an anchor for identification and spectator participation in moments that conspicuously lack other orienting devices. Bodies that defy expectations in a story that has only just begun stymie the backward movement of additive comprehension (the reassessing backward glance). They pose questions that can be answered only by moving forward. Action sequences at the beginning of films such as *X2* (2003) and *The Matrix*, for example, use body fantasies to launch audiences expectantly into plot.

X2 opens with its most memorable action sequence: Nightcrawler's infiltration of the White House. Since no characters have yet been established, this sequence relies on an immediate identification with the special body. For even casual fans of the Marvel universe, Nightcrawler's ability to teleport short distances is already understood. However, making sense of what is at stake in this early moment in plot is primarily a matter of feeling the defenses of the invaded space: the White House is a charged cultural image and "protect the president" is a recurring narrative scenario in espionage novels and films, iterations of which appear in multiplayer first-person shooters, such as the "Pop a Cap" mode in *Perfect Dark* (2000). The moment when Nightcrawler can no longer remain hidden amid the White House tour group and is confronted by a guard quickly escalates into a revelation (that is also a leap) as the mutant sheds not just his overcoat but also the strictures of space and time. The erroneous report that there are multiple assailants represents a misrecognition of the situation. Like the unshackled Rock Lee, Nightcrawler begins a bodily motion in one place but completes it in another—a capacity ideally suited for infiltrating such a fortified and carefully surveilled space. Nightcrawler consumes the White House's inaccessibility—the lengthy corridors that frame and heighten the visibility of those who traverse them—and converts it into transcendence. Though the symbolic setting lends this introductory moment stakes of a sort, Nightcrawler's motives (like *X2*'s moral coordinates more generally) remain obscure at the outset. Thus, it seems, the sequence compensates for its moral opacity with an excess of kinetic legibility—a camera that emphasizes connectedness through a series of slow-motion pans while Nightcrawler's body renders space itself discontinuous.

Such excess is how one might best make sense of "bullet time," *The Matrix*'s famous visual effect. Bullet time's camera appears to defy space and time by roaming freely around a frozen profilmic scene. As scholars have noted,[65] even though bullet time is actually accomplished using an older technology, still photography, it seems to fulfill what Lev Manovich has described as computer software's "promise of new cinematic languages."[66] In particular, bullet time seems to exemplify the extension of new media logics to space itself: "For the first time, *space becomes a media type*" (and so it can be "transmitted, stored . . . compressed, reformatted," and so on).[67] Though there are several other instances of the effect in *The Matrix*, its initial appearance especially welcomes this sort of reading because it does not seem motivated by narrative context (which we lack at the film's outset) or by the specificity of the agonistic situation (e.g., slowing down time to trace the trajectory of bullets that narrowly miss their mark). Instead, the hacker Trinity jumps into the air for a kick and then hangs in suspense as the camera rotates 180 degrees to reframe the action, inverting the image's horizontal axis for a brief moment. That the next shot completes the kick from near the camera's *starting* position characterizes the effect as stylistic excess,[68] a gratuitous insert, or, perhaps, as an element of interface rather than plot: Bob Rehak is apt to refer to it as a "romanticization of the pause."[69]

Along similar lines, Alexander Galloway has identified bullet time as one of those "rare moments of cinematic illusion where the digital aesthetics of gaming actually penetrate and influence the aesthetics of film."[70] For Galloway, the effect exemplifies the tendency in "gamic vision" for "time and space" to become "mutable within the diegesis in ways unavailable before," since games themselves "pause, speed up, slow down, and restart often."[71] While Galloway's argument about gamic vision is compelling, one might also argue the opposite: that the need to respond in real time to the exigencies of situation requires strict spatial and temporal continuity freed from such intrusive manipulations. Insofar as it is even possible to do so, pausing a competitive videogame (or switching camera views) midaction would be disorienting, not to mention an unforgivable violation of protocol. Disruptions to the game can call its entire outcome into question. In other words, while bullet time may exemplify new media's logic of navigable 3-D space, its interruption of the situation midaction shares more in common with cinema's own temporal manipulations than with gaming's (especially if watching a movie from home).

Identifying bullet time as exemplary of gamic cinema (if not of games themselves) requires going beyond describing its formal grammars alone. The effect exemplifies game logics because it demonstrates an excess of kinetic legibility at a key moment in plot: the point of departure from the familiar world (and its spatiotemporal order). By framing a special moment from multiple points of view simultaneously, it dramatizes the time required to properly absorb the impact of our initial encounter with the surprising rules governing bodily kinetics in this world. In short, it reflects a wish for total-field awareness during an emotionally dense moment, like an instant replay in real time. The effect is not truly discontinuous with the narrative events that surround it. Rather than a pause to the action, it is best understood as part of the action in a broader "pause/burst/ pause pattern," such as the one David Bordwell identifies as a strategy Hong Kong action films employ for introducing beats that help organize frenzied action and clarify the affective stakes of the unfolding situation (in short, expressive amplification).[72]

As with the landlords in *Kung Fu Hustle*, Trinity is initially misrecognized in the film's opening sequence: a fully grown woman with transcendent power who is mistaken as "one little girl." It isn't that Trinity's outward appearance or her signifiers of gender are misleading to men with power; the problem (as well as the empowerment) lies with an error in the police's shared signified: the agonistic situation defined through their understanding of gender, body, size, and numerical superiority. In a nod perhaps to playful signifier/signified pairings within gaming—such as what Jesper Juul describes in fighting games as a "discrepancy between the outward appearance of the characters and the rules governing their behavior"[73]—*The Matrix* opens with a misrecognition; bullet time is the expressive undoing of this misrecognition. In other words, bullet time is pure agnition.

Moments prior, Agent Smith's lines to the commanding officer that instructions to wait "were for your protection" build toward strongly opposed perspectives: the officer's "I sent two units. They're bringing her down now" clashes ominously with "No, lieutenant, your men are already dead." When, in the next shot, an officer attempts to handcuff Trinity, it is clear that the men are not already dead; tension grows through a temporal contradiction. In this moment, the spectator's situational awareness is also divided: like Trinity, we are walled in by the fact that the film has just begun. Like the arresting officers, we fail to see the threat Trinity poses while alone, arms behind her head, flooded by light and approached from behind. When Trinity quickly disarms the nearest officer and then hangs in the air, bending the laws of physics (bullet time), the scene's multiple contradictions are released in a transcendent bodily display. Trinity runs up and down this "wall" at the start of the film that stymies backward movement.

It is no surprise that fantasy—as a dense, ready-made structure—might have a special role to play in a film's introductory moments before its central conflict has been established. However, the fantasy can take hold at any time in plot as an orienting pattern for moments when a narrative frame weakens and the film seems to transcend its own moral code. Consider the bloody free-for-all at the end of the second act of *Kingsman: The Secret Service* (2014), when a Kingsman agent is compelled (neurologically) to violently murder the congregation of a fundamentalist Kentucky church. The sequence is so gratuitous (and stunning for its fluid depiction of complex action) that it essentially halts narrative (the villain himself is disengaged, too squeamish to watch). In other words, story progression cedes the stage to body fantasy. However, there is still a relevant connection to the film's thematic concerns in that *Kingsman* ties misrecognition to its broader neoliberal message that success comes to those who earn it, regardless of one's socioeconomic background ("Manners maketh man").

The Kentucky free-for-all in *Kingsman* is evocative of the climax of *Serenity* (2005), when River Tam springs into action to save her brother by defeating an entire hoard of monstrous Reavers in hand-to-hand combat. In both cases, a moment of pure situation (in the melodramatic sense) unlocks some internal resistance or accrued tension, and a dormant or somehow inhibited body leaps into the fray, transcending not just the overwhelming force of villainy but the narrative's entire moral framework, at least for a moment. Consider one additional example of this pattern: *The Iron Giant* (1999). This film tells the story about a young boy (Hogarth Hughes) and his pet robot who fell from the sky (and so suffered an amnesia-inducing head injury represented by a dent in his metal skull). The giant behaves like a small child, mimicking Hogarth and practicing mastery not just of language but also fundamental concepts about the world: good versus evil, free choice, life and death, guns kill, and so on. There is a subplot where Hogarth, in his efforts to keep the giant, instills lessons in restraint and self-control; the giant must remain hidden, quiet, and master of both curiosity and hunger, if these feelings might bring him into populated spaces. The robot is gentle and virtuous in the melodramatic sense: innocent, childlike, and decidedly on the side of good, identifying with Superman, whom he glimpses on Hogarth's comic books, rather than the evil robot, Atomo. At a key moment near the film's climax, the subplot of self-restraint moves aggressively to the foreground in an inverted form as body fantasy.

This sequence—beginning when the giant and Hogarth are shot out of the sky by U.S. military jets—so thoroughly disrupts the progression of story, which seems prematurely truncated with Hogarth's apparent death, that it pulls the entire film into different generic terrain. The giant has little time to process the situation as he rises from the crash site and believes Hogarth (unconscious) to be dead. The army intrudes once more by shelling the giant with heavy munitions as he kneels over Hogarth's body. At this moment, the dent in the giant's head pops out and the film's message of self-control collapses into unrestrained vocalization and force: the giant transforms into a towering arsenal of alien weaponry replete with glowing compartments and appendages all previously hidden by his placid exterior. Whereas the giant's body had once matched the tones of his surroundings, he now serves as the source of bright explosions that wipe out military artillery on a death march away from Hogarth. Insofar as spectators have felt the gradual accumulation of restraint upon the giant's motility and self-expression (inhibited transcendence) alongside moments of genuine bonding and play with Hogarth, they are carried on the force of the limit's release into an identification with the giant as the invader from outer space (Atomo, after all).

Moments when body fantasy predominates may be stitched into plot even though agnition may be so potent that much of a film's narrative framework fades into the background, and a subplot of bodily restraint (for example) comes to the foreground as a violent letting loose of every internalized tension. The fantasy sticks out, stands apart from plot even while remaining part of it. On the other hand, our encounter with the kernel of the fantasy in narrative can be brief, and we might not even consciously process its presence. We may, nevertheless, find ourselves struck at the level of body memory by a provocative gesture that represents a compromise between two or more (often opposed) objectives—such as when Inspector Lee (Jackie Chan) must battle opponents while simultaneously protecting precious heirlooms in the climax of *Rush Hour* (1998) or when Evelyn Wang (Michelle Yeoh) must fight while satisfying a litany of arbitrary conditions to disturb her timeline and "verse-jump" with another version of herself in *Everything Everywhere All at Once* (2022). Somehow, the single move that satisfies both conditions seems to stick in memory, to recur as fantasy, and to evoke the aesthetics of videogames. Each such gesture carries with it an impression of the special body exceeding expectations, fusing the social and the kinetic in one cleanly articulated gesture.

The next chapter considers a distinct fantasy tradition—the tether fantasy—which, in terms employed in the first two chapters, might also be thought of as an *immediately graspable embodied experience*. Core body schema that we regularly employ to make sense of the world and our place in it—such as the experience of encapsulation, the difference between being inside or outside, sheltered or exposed—pertain directly to the experience of a tether, which is a pleasurable though sometimes tense encounter with vulnerability and safety. Tethers can operate in the background as a secondary narrative to plot, a narrative that suddenly intrudes into and disrupts foreground concerns. When this happens, especially in games, we might be called upon to fight, to reach for the protection afforded by a certain skill or competency—we might attempt to *close the open loop* in a favorable manner. But with tether play, the sudden appearance of a threat often overwhelms our capacity to respond, and all we can do is flee for safety.

3

The Tether Fantasy

• • • • • • • • • • • • • • • • • • •

Imagination about travel corresponds in Verne to an exploration of closure, and the compatibility between Verne and childhood does not stem from a banal mystique of adventure, but on the contrary from a common delight in the finite, which one also finds in children's passion for huts and tents: to enclose oneself and to settle, such is the existential dream of childhood and Verne. The archetype of this dream is this almost perfect novel: *L'Ile mystérieuse*, in which the manchild re-invents the world, fills it, closes it, shuts himself up in it, and crowns this encyclopedic effort with the bourgeois posture of appropriation: slippers, pipe and fireside, while outside the storm, that is, the infinite, rages in vain.
—Roland Barthes, "The *Nautilus* and the Drunken Boat"[1]

For Heidegger, the house is understood "as the most primitive drawing of a line that produces an inside opposed to an

> outside." The debate as to whether this
> line is (or should be) rigid and unsurpass-
> able, or indeed, as to whether it should
> exist at all, also goes back to antiquity.
> —Maria Kaika, "Interrogating the
> Geographies of the Familiar"[2]

To Shiver from Well-Being

I often recall a game I played before sleep as a child on cold Michigan winter nights. The game consisted of pulling my blanket up over my head and imagining I was safe and warm in a shell or fort. I would stretch one arm or leg out into the dark and leave it there. The cold on my exposed limb would aid in imaginatively restaging dramas of exploring the unknown. I would sometimes imagine Luke Skywalker's run-in with the snow beast (wampa) on the surface of Hoth in *The Empire Strikes Back* (1980), which I had watched on television. I would picture Luke stuck in the wampa's cave, unable to return to the safety of the rebel base. I would resist the urge to pull my arm or leg back for warmth, forcing myself to endure exposure just as Han Solo had—Han was told it was not possible to survive a night in Hoth's deadly climate and that when he left, the base's ramparts would close behind him until morning. Nevertheless, Han set out in search of his friend who had not returned. My game would conclude in a burst of warmth when I finally recalled the cold limb. I would pull my arm or leg tightly into the blanket and wrap myself around it, as if my entire body were rushing to embrace the cold and share in the thrill of exposure.

It is perhaps because I played this bedtime game as a child that I was especially struck by a passage in Sigmund Freud's *Civilization and Its Discontents* in which he briefly mentions the "cheap enjoyment . . . obtained by putting a bare leg from under the bedclothes on a cold winter night and drawing it in again."[3] Admittedly, this passage is at best a tangent. Freud himself mentions the game only by way of analogy, in order to pooh-pooh the idea that modern civilization (and attendant technological advances) adds genuine happiness to the world, such as with the telephone's power to relay the voice of a loved one across a great distance. The game played by Freud's bedclothed bourgeoisie is meant to illustrate how modern technology offers only a "cheap" pleasure when fulfilling a social need, since technology creates that need in the first place:[4] "If there had been no railway to conquer distances, my child would never have left his native town and I should need no telephone to hear his voice; if travelling across the ocean by ship had not been introduced, my friend would not have embarked on his sea-voyage and I should not need a cable to relieve my anxiety about him, [and so on]."[5] Technology both creates and bridges distance.

At issue in Freud's anecdote is the reason for the extension. One may look forward to a warm bed on a cold winter night or a radiant fireplace after a ride through snowy woods. But when already warm in bed, it is a "cheap enjoyment" to opt to extend one's leg into the cold air simply for the pleasure of disrupting and restoring thermal equilibrium. In this sense, the game I played as a child could also be understood as a "cheap" pleasure, though undoubtedly one in search of enrichment. The snowy fantasy scenarios that I grafted onto the pattern of exposure and recovery promised a story, some contrivance locking me into a state of exposure (the rebel base shut tight). By identifying a game of thermal equilibrium, calling into question the motivation for leaving warmth and safety and extending into the cold, and tying this process to themes of communication and transportation technology, Freud offers us the contours of a fantasy process: a pleasure in imagining a need to depart (or to withdraw) that intersects with the banal, lived experience of daily life.[6]

Freud's game of thermal equilibrium may even anticipate what Francis Spufford describes as "a tingling disruption of the domestic realm": the way the British avidly consumed news of failed early twentieth-century polar expeditions.[7] Spufford refers to the pleasure of consuming this news as "armchair travel to the far North," a form of schadenfreude (pleasure taken in the misfortune of others) from the safety and comfort of home. By extension, Freud also predicts Jenny Turner's identification of a patterned oscillation between exposure and recovery in the fiction of J. R. R. Tolkien as well as in adventure stories writ large: "Scary, safe again. And so to sleep. This rhythm is also fundamental to the pleasures of adventure stories—explorers' tragedies, Westerns, space operas like *Star Trek*— in which it is amplified by the pleasures of schadenfreude. There they are freezing on the ice, dying of thirst, infested by aliens on a leaky spaceship; here I am on my cozy sofa, about to have my snooze."[8]

Though both seem similar to Freud's bedclothes game (imagined travel and the recovery to warmth and safety), it must be granted that in Spufford and Turner's examples there is anxious enjoyment both in the separation (when brave explorers—almost always men—travel to far-off places) and in the news of a brush with death. Schadenfreude and "armchair travel to the far North" are both cheap pleasures, perhaps even deserving of scorn. There is also more than a hint of cheapness in the culturally devalued fictional genres that have begun to accrue in these examples. Andrew Burn and Diane Carr even trace Turner's "scary, safe again" pattern to the still-undervalued cultural domain of digital games in their analysis of *Baldur's Gate* (1998). They identify a tension between the game's live-action moments (scary) and the pause menu (safe again)—a regular oscillation in play they then connect with two basic references: Tolkien and Freud's notion of the "death instinct" ("the desire to be free of all tension for ever").[9]

In fact, the basic pattern that Burn and Carr identify has broad applicability to a range of digital games. Establishing and discussing this pattern in the context of contemporary entertainment media is one major goal of this chapter. Such a goal also requires demonstrating that the cultural influences informing this pattern are much wider than is suggested by the standard lineage traced from

Tolkien to the genre of the role-playing game (RPG) by way of the table-top game *Dungeons & Dragons* (1974).[10] It is also important to demonstrate that the theoretical basis Burn and Carr (and Turner) provide by way of Freud's "death instinct" (more commonly referred to as the "death drive") is, itself, also too narrow, and perhaps premature as well.

That Burn, Carr, and Turner link their examples back to Freud—to his 1920 essay, *Beyond the Pleasure Principle*, in particular—is not surprising. Readers of the present chapter who have encountered Freud's work before may in fact have already remarked to themselves how similar the bedclothes game is to the more famous game Freud analyzes in that essay: "fort-da." In fort-da, a child (Freud's grandson) throws a thread reel attached to a string over the edge of his crib (uttering "o-o-o-o," which Freud takes to mean the German word "fort" or "gone"). Then, in the second part of the game, the child pulls the reel back into view accompanied by "da'" or "there."[11] In Freud's interpretation, the child repeats in play what in firsthand experience had been traumatic (the departure and continued unavailability of the parental figure) because doing so allows him to achieve an active role in his parents' comings and goings. This apparently simple game carries much theoretical weight.[12]

That this chapter begins with the "cheap" example of the bedclothes game instead of the theoretically rich one (fort-da) reflects an effort on my part to resist the temptation to read each of the above examples—the bedclothes game; armchair travel to the north; and scary, safe again in adventure novels, television, cinema, and videogames—as repetition compulsion and death drive. Each example demonstrates both the avoidance of a premature death and an embrace of mortality, of life. They share a profound perturbation, a jolt that destroys the steady quiescence of the death instinct, and a complication that defers narrative resolution. More importantly, even if one were somehow limited to psychoanalysis as a framework, there are better psychoanalytic models for understanding play in these examples than id psychology's theory of instinctual drives.

I draw from contemporary clinical psychoanalysis in referring to each of these above examples as a *tether fantasy*. For the sake of a definition, the tether fantasy, and the play that reciprocally enacts it, involves pleasure in imagining exposure and the recovery to safety. It can also be thought of as the pleasure of dwelling on the transition between those two states (safe and exposed), including the boundaries that allow those two states to remain separate but also related to one another. The metaphor of a tether—a rope, string, or perhaps umbilical cord—ties these states together and captures something of their spatial dynamics, such as radial orbiting or what Jacques Lacan terms a "centrifugal tracing" around a central anchoring point.[13]

The tether fantasy seems to capture aspects of Otto Rank's womb fantasy, which expresses the literal wish to return to the womb. Rank sees this wish symbolically expressed in examples ranging from yonic apertures in architecture (halls, doorways, arches, etc.) to the pleasure of driving in cars, the relaxation of taking baths and even the ritual of sleep—insofar as this ritual entails dark, quiet rooms, soft beds, heavy blankets, and the withdrawal of consciousness from the outside world.[14] One could update Rank's list by adding the cellular phone, with its umbilical charging cable. In fact, Sherry Turkle argues that as we venture out into the world, cellular phones keep us tethered at all times to points of security (parents, friends, etc.), preventing us from feeling alone. Rather than identifying timeless or essential drives, however, Turkle's framework emphasizes the developmental impact of a new communications technology on a person's most meaningful life relationships. In other words, Turkle follows in the tradition of object relations theory, a more recent school of thought within psychoanalysis which—along with much of clinical psychoanalysis—has shifted emphasis away from instinctual drives (be they Eros or Thanatos, libido or mortido) and toward the "objects" of these drives—the people who have played a meaningful role in an individual's development. Object relations is interested in how a patient's earliest attachments establish basic emotional dynamics that persist through life.

There is a theory within object-relations psychoanalysis called "separation-individuation" that focuses on how a child comes to develop an autonomous sense of self by exploring the world with the parent as anchor—sometimes losing sight of the parent before anxiously returning to them again. Working within this separation-individuation subfield, psychotherapist Salman Akhtar offers the term "fantasy of a tether" (or, more simply, "tether fantasy") for the "ubiquitous" if "largely subterranean" notion that "a rope or chain keeps one bound to a central reference point and thus assures one's staying within certain bounds."[15] In the pathological cases Akhtar reports, imagining a tether serves as a way to "minimize the anxiety of separation" while, at the same time, allowing "autonomous functioning."[16] Whether refusing to move too far from home while jogging or fearing that reading fiction might absorb and carry them away, Akhtar's patients share a "concern about distance, literal or figurative, from an anchoring person or environment"—in short, they feel "confined to an orbit" with the need to "return to the secure base" in order to "refuel" once they feel they have "stretched [their] mental tether to the limit."[17] Such severe disturbances to the process of separation-individuation are rare.

Far commoner are banal reverberations or tether fantasies that populate everyday experience. Akhtar identifies themes "of losing and regaining safety" in the games that delight children—Peekaboo is the "universal" example Akhtar offers readers, but fort-da is also included. Such themes extend into the tether play of later childhood as well as adulthood (e.g., thrill seeking and trips to amusement parks): "All these games involve leaving a zone of safety, courting danger more or less voluntarily, and returning to the secure zone (almost always called 'home'). Attempts at mastering separation anxiety are clearly evident here. At the same time, these games permit the player, rather like the rapprochement-phase toddler,[18] the vicarious enjoyment of both merger and separateness from the 'home base,' that is, mother."[19]

The application of these dynamics to the structure of videogame play is too tempting. In fact, in a sense, it is surprising that this framework has not generally been applied to games by psychoanalysts who engage with digital technologies, such as Sherry Turkle.[20] The general omission of digital games from discussions of this developmental period is even more surprising when it is considered that (nondigital) games themselves are frequently referenced in such discussions. Consider the following description of "attachment theory" (separation-individuation's counterpart in the more empirical-observational field of behavioral psychology) from the late 1970s, which reads almost like a scenario from the *Call of Duty* franchise (2003–present) of popular wargames:

> The safety of an army in the field depends both on its defense against attack and on maintaining a line of communications with its base. Should the field commander judge that retreat is the best tactic, it is essential that the base be available to him, that he not be cut off from it, and that the commander in charge of the base be trusted to maintain the base and the support implicit in it. By analogy, the young child may be afraid of the threat implicit in the clues to danger he perceives in a situation, but he may also be afraid if he doubts the accessibility of his "base"—his attachment figure.[21]

Attachment theory addresses the same developmental phenomena as separation-individuation and its studies arrive at similar conclusions despite different theoretical frameworks.[22] Its early experimental research seeks to explain how a young child "uses the mother as a 'secure base' from which to explore the environment during times of safety and from which to seek comfort and security at times of stress."[23] Early life experiences establish what precisely gives one a sense of security. However, in contrast with the psychoanalytic model, attachment theory also postulates that this point of security is never truly outgrown. Rather, it is internalized (the internal secure base) and must be actively sustained and fostered thereafter.

As Jeremy Holmes puts it, there is a "continuity of attachment needs throughout the life cycle, even into adulthood."[24] Even those adults who seem entirely autonomous nevertheless rely on "an *internal* SB [secure base] zone—which can also be conceptualized as a schema or object relationship—to which they turn when needed, especially as part of affect regulation."[25] Holmes reports a range of objects and interpersonal connections that research subjects have identified as helping to activate secure base experiences, regulate affect, and achieve the "desired state of calmness": they mention "partners, pets, family and close friends" as well as "quasi-transitional object-type resources such as hot baths, duvets, photograph albums, being in touch with nature, favourite books and music."[26] They even "describe the reassurance of a sense of self—of knowing who one is, where one came from and where one is going to."[27]

Digital games provide the best examples of affect regulation and self-soothing through secure-base objects because of their capacity to sustain all three basic elements of the secure-base experience: "(1) a set of behaviours activated by threat; (2) a response to those behaviours by the caregiver; and (3) a psychophysiological state that is the end result of those behaviours."[28] These different stages of the "secure-base cycle" are interconnected, so games that emphasize the threat can also nevertheless generate a feeling of contentedness regardless of whether a secure base (a literal safe space in the game, or a protective other) intercedes. The notion of tether fantasy (nearly synonymous with attachment theory's secure base experience) helps conceive of videogame play as a dynamic activity meaningfully structured by developmental phenomena we never quite outgrow, as reverberations of separation-individuation or activations of an internalized secure base.

However, despite the application of object-relational and behavioral psychologies to digital games, this chapter does not cede the full power of explanation to such theories. As explanatory frameworks, neither is well equipped to speak to historically and culturally specific manifestations of tether play: the meanings of terms such as "comfort," "home," "family," and "security" vary by place, culture, and time. Any analysis of games or the people who play them would require greater historical and cultural specificity than can be provided through attachment theory's evolutionary scope alone. The term "tether fantasy" may originate in psychological theories, but in this book it stands for the wider set of associations that this chapter traverses. The notion of a tether is enriched by coming into contact with historical and cultural differences as well as differences in how we think and write about media.

In addition to "cheap" pleasures in adventure and pulp novels, tethers abound in experimental architecture and poetry. Robert Frost's "Stopping by Woods on a Snowy Evening," for instance, is rife with tether imagery:

Whose woods these are I think I know.
His house is in the village though;
He will not see me stopping here
To watch his woods fill up with snow.

My little horse must think it queer
To stop without a farmhouse near
Between the woods and frozen lake
The darkest evening of the year.

He gives his harness bells a shake
To ask if there is some mistake.
The only other sound's the sweep
Of easy wind and downy flake.

The woods are lovely, dark and deep,
But I have promises to keep,

And miles to go before I sleep,
And miles to go before I sleep.[29]

Frost's poem reflects on the act of stopping midway between origin and destination, dwelling on exposure, coldness, darkness—pausing at a moment when the tether is most extended on the "darkest evening of the year." The tension between safety and exposure is made especially overt by the fact that these snow-filled woods belong to someone else—someone who, like the poem's reader, is probably safe and warm in a house in the village. The poem's oft-acknowledged metaphorical treatment of the deferral of death ("But I have promises to keep, / And miles to go before I sleep") is cast as a spatial tension—the allure of a journey's midpoint. To dwell on the tether in this poem is to find beauty in an inhospitable in-between space on the threshold of an abyss ("lovely, dark and deep"). Its narrator stares into the abyss, and may seem weary at the path ahead. But the suspension of a journey at its midpoint, like the limb left exposed in Freud's bedclothes game, speaks to life, to tension, to difficulty—far from the easing of all tensions in the Freudian death drive.

Wherever it occurs, tether imagery seems to weave together two opposed states that cut across the grain of the death drive. Consider, for instance, the binaries that animate a number of resonant passages in Gaston Bachelard's *Poetics of Space*—the way (to keep with the theme of winter) he suggests "we feel warm *because* it is cold out-of-doors," how "Behind dark curtains, snow seems to be whiter," or how "A reminder of winter strengthens the happiness of inhabiting" by making our nests (quoting Baudelaire) "all the warmer, all the downier, all the better loved."[30] In his pursuit of the "roots of the function of inhabiting," Bachelard quotes a passage from Henri Bachelin's book *Le Serviteur*, in which a character relays a childhood daydream about being isolated in a hut with his parents:

> I felt very strongly . . . that we were cut off from the little town, from the rest of France, and from the entire world. I delighted in imagining (although I kept my feelings to myself) that we were living in the heart of the woods, in the well-heated hut of charcoal burners; I even hoped to hear wolves sharpening their claws on the heavy granite slab that formed our doorstep. But our house replaced the hut for me, it sheltered me from hunger and cold; and if I shivered, it was merely from well-being.[31]

This passage's rich tether imagery invents a scenario of proximity to parents while holding the threat of fusing with them at bay ("I kept my feelings to myself"). It imagines the wider world as tonally opposed to the self-reliant home (and family); this world's function is to move dangerously inward, to enclose the home—now a vital, life-preserving membrane—and then to scratch at the doorstep. Bachelin is what Bachelard terms "a dreamer of refuges," a person who "dreams of a hut, of a nest, or of nooks and corners in which he would like to hide away, like an animal in its hole."[32] To a greater or lesser extent, we are all dreamers of refuges.

Tether imagery abounds in representational media. Turner's examples ("scary, safe again" in explorers' tragedies, Westerns, and space operas) speak to some the tether's breadth. As a reader, you might have already begun your own list of popular tether narratives: forays into the unknown, temporarily away from the armored vessel of space operas (e.g., *Star Wars*, *Star Trek*, *Battlestar Galactica*); the improvised fortification in the zombie apocalypse (e.g., *The Walking Dead*, *I Am Legend*); maritime survival stories about braving the depths or sheltering from the storm (e.g., *Twenty Thousand Leagues under the Sea*, *Treasure Island*, *Robinson Crusoe*); or siege narratives that dwell on the protective barrier and its breach, from the *Iliad* to *The Lord of the Rings* (1954–1955).

Tethers even play a role in nightly news stories about a turbulent world that sometimes punctures the sanctified bubble of the suburban, bourgeois home. ABC News, in a 2006 story about constructing makeshift panic rooms from bedroom closets, articulates a detailed fantasy scenario of home invasion: "By spending a few bucks on a dead bolt lock, some different hinges and a jam lock, and by storing your cell phone there at night, you can hide and keep your assailant at bay for a long time—time he doesn't have. While he's thinking, you can call 911, and by keeping a list of neighbors' phone numbers there as well, you can call reinforcements for help, too."[33] Under the auspices of planning for the worst come instructions for playfully imagining a domestic space of fortification. While an actual home invasion would be traumatic, the presence of a safe room (even if just in imagination) enables the pleasurable experience of moving away from and toward that secure space in one's daily routine. Lying awake at night, dwelling on the space between one's bed and a panic room becomes an imagined flirtation with danger.

The idea of the private shelter offers a secure base experience whether you've built one or not. Even though very few were ever made, backyard bomb shelters were ubiquitous in advertising imagery and governmental messaging in the 1960s. They served a symbolic function in the American popular imagination by emphasizing "family security and togetherness in the face of a frightening world."[34] That these shelters doubled as a safe place to store food or where children might play reflects attachment theory's affirmation of Maslow's hierarchy of needs—the idea that our capacity for higher-order psychological phenomena (such as the ability to learn or play) depends on more fundamental needs, such as feeling secure. In this case, the secure base (the shelter-cum-pantry) is both a place one might seek in an emergency and a place where one anchors food security (a stockpile). If, like me, your grandparent or great-grandparent survived the Great Depression, you likely know such a space from childhood memories.

In American suburbia, the private shelter has become a home entertainment fortress. So argues Barbara Klinger, who acknowledges a resonance between Cold

War anxiety and post-9/11 cocooning in the American suburb. In both its media content and its design, the post-9/11 home theater expresses a wish to be "armored by technology, controlling the ebb and flow of media within the comforts of a self-defined refuge."[35] It isn't simply in entertainment media that viewers entertain the fantasy of "seek[ing] shelter from dangerous, invasive forces," but also in the home entertainment "fortress" itself, which popular media (e.g., *Panic Room* [2002]) have increasingly imagined as an "inner sanctum," a fortress that is also "equipped to bring the world to the home viewer."[36] A tether fantasy has taken hold in the American suburban home, framing what Klinger terms the "interrelationship of sanctuary and hardware" there—an analogy that casts domestic infrastructure itself as a medium through which entertainment contents flow.[37] Klinger notes the "architectural plans that wire every room in the house for multimedia," as well as the "potentially infinite regression of minifortresses enabled by personal technologies (e.g., the Walkman, the PlayStation, and the Game Boy) that allow individuals to sequester themselves additionally within the household."[38]

Today, suburban Americans live out Bachelard's dream of the refuge, with so many more "minifortresses" (tethers nested inside tethers) than Klinger might have imagined: personal devices, smart appliances, Apple HomeKits, and immersive media rooms with dynamic LED lighting. Americans may not have their own term for feeling cozy during the dark days of winter like the Norwegian word *koselig*,[39] but of non-Scandinavian nations, it is difficult to out-cozy the masters of suburban sprawl, "bunkering the house," and "post-9/11 cocooning,"[40] not to mention the inventors of the Snuggy sleeved blanket, originally marketed as the Freedom Blanket. Klinger's study deserves an updated, post-COVID-19 edition in order to attend to the pandemic's restructuring of daily patterns involving the consumption of media and the boundaries of public and private spaces.

During the early months of the 2020 pandemic, demand for home-delivered groceries and other consumer goods skyrocketed along with the use of media streaming services such as Netflix and Disney+. Friendship circles became "COVID bubbles" of coinhabitants who spent the first year together while socially distancing from others. And indeed videogames played a big role in COVID bunkering—the videogame industry enjoyed record-breaking sales of $57 billion that year (a 27 percent increase from the previous year) according to the NPD Group (a marketing information firm). Data also show increased play time in 2020. As Activision CEO Bobby Kotick recently acknowledged, this increase was visible across every player demographic, a fact he makes sense of in terms of bunkering (i.e., playing games "helped keep people safe at home").[41] Survey research bears out this claim. In fact, Matthew Barr and Alicia Copeland-Stewart's study finds that videogames helped many cope with the COVID-19 lockdown by allowing for affect regulation (as a response to anxiety), a sense of normalcy (habit, pattern), cognitive stimulation, the experience of agency, and a means of socializing. The pandemic even changed the *sorts* of games people played—for instance, many found space in their day for "longer or more involved games"; one respondent notes, "I started playing some games that required more time investment such as *Dark Souls*."[42] Several others reported an increased use of their Nintendo Switch, a home videogame console that can be played on a large screen or as a portable handheld device.

The Switch seems especially suited to moving through repurposed domestic spaces during a lockdown since, at times, it serves a shared, social function, and at other times can be brought somewhere more private—a bedroom or nook: infinite regress into the minifortress while, outside, there is chaos and unrest. It is not surprising to learn that videogames helped many cope with the pandemic. Games have long served affect regulation in domestic space—and one of the key ways they do this is by providing especially active secure-base experiences. In action RPGs such as *Dark Souls* (2011), players move from safe place (bonfire) into danger and back to safety again. In *Valheim* (2021)—a pandemic-era update to the popular *Minecraft* (2011)—players gather materials in order to design and then defend their own secure base, a miniature utopia.

Although Klinger is careful not to romanticize home as an uncomplicated space of respite, a "presumed sanctuary from the working, public world," the media experiences she describes nevertheless attest to a certain amount of privilege.[43] Tether play is most available to those who feel secure, who not only possess their own minifortresses but also have a safe and comfortable place from which to visit them. As Turner puts it (once more), "There they are freezing on the ice, dying of thirst, infested by aliens on a leaky spaceship; here I am on my cozy sofa, about to have my snooze":[44] to shiver from well-being, indeed. The following section discusses how tether fantasies are inextricably knotted up not only with home spaces but also with issues of identity and privilege that have been studied in relation to home. The tether fantasy can itself be thought of as a string connecting entertainment media to (and anchoring them within) the spaces where they are consumed. Like these spaces, tethers have a history.

Home as a Contested Domain

In her discussion of television's entry into the 1950s American suburban home, *Make Room for TV*, Lynn Spigel highlights a cartoon from *Better Homes and Gardens* in which a husband returns home from work bundled up under snowfall. Glimpsing his wife setting the dinner table through the window, the husband imagines a leisurely evening indoors smoking a pipe and watching a boxing match on TV. At the same moment his wife, who has presumably spent the majority of her day working at home, imagines dressing up and spending an evening out with her husband at the cinema. The cartoon pokes fun at the patriarchal doctrine of separate spheres: a masculine public sphere and a feminine domestic one. For Spigel, the cartoon helps emphasize how emerging communication technologies (such as television) become caught up in a gendered division of space when they enter the home. However, the cartoon also illustrates a conflict of gender through the lens of a tether fantasy, one caught between titillating departures from and warming returns to a domestic interior in the dead of winter. Put more succinctly, the cartoon illustrates how tether fantasies can become bound up in distinct ways with gender, with domestic space, and with issues of class as well.

This claim may seem counterintuitive since, for starters, separation-individuation is supposedly a process all infants undergo before adopting a gender identity (it is "pre-Oedipal"). Attachment theory's empirical research on infant attachments shows no measurable difference in attachment styles by sex; feeling secure from threats is necessary for everyone's emotional well-being, though there are different cultural expressions for feeling secure in different parts of the world.[45] Even the cartoon in Spigel's study softens its gender-based conflict by suggesting that husband and wife do not have fundamentally opposed wishes; the pleasures of leaving and returning home are, rather, out of sync (even if perpetually so).

However, the cartoon may well mark a deeper gender disparity, at least insofar as it evokes popular and romantic conceptions of home as a fortress or a space one returns to for respite after work or travel. For J. Douglas Porteous, this meaning is timeless and essential: as an "emotional minimum," if nothing else, "home is simply a sure refuge between journeys"; home "cannot be understood except in terms of journey"; and home is "a fortress from which to essay raid and foray, an embattled position behind whose walls one may retire to lick wounds and plan fresh journeys to farther horizons."[46]

Such an image of home is not universal. Even if only socioeconomically privileged homeowners were considered, Porteous's view would still reflect a masculine cultural attitude. As Janet Wolff puts it, "heroes of modernity"—from the intrepid traveler to the flâneur—are all *men*, and the public sphere has tended to cater to "men's experience."[47] Women, who have historically been more constrained and confined to home—where they often undertake unending, unpaid, and unacknowledged labor—must maintain a more complicated, ambivalent image of home. As Doreen Massey argues, it is "culturally masculine" to view home as containing a singular and fixed meaning (a fortress, a nest, etc.)—impervious to time as well as other flows that connect home to the rest of the world and therefore change its meanings. Massey suggests that notions of home as an uncomplicated space of security extend from a culturally masculine overemphasis on boundaries and "a defensive and counterpositional definition of identity."[48]

Psychoanalysis itself may impose a masculine worldview on its subject matter, in that it "emphasizes difference over sameness, boundaries over fluidity" and "conceives of polarity and opposition, rather than mutuality and interdependence, as vehicles of growth"—so argues Jessica Benjamin.[49] Even the theory of separation-individuation, by emphasizing the child's separation from the parent, evinces male rationality. For the male child, a repudiation of the mother as *not-me* models masculine responses to otherness throughout life. From its inception, then, it can be argued that the tether fantasy—a reverberation of unresolved separation-individuation—embodies the male rationality that feminist scholars such as Benjamin and Massey critique in psychoanalytic thinking more generally.

The tether fantasy and a masculine cultural attitude are inseparable from popular conceptions of home as a timeless space of protection to which one returns after venturing into the wider world. When Bachelard declares that the "house shelters daydreaming," that it "protects the dreamer" and "allows one to dream in peace," he attributes to home the status of a happy secure base.[50] His poetics of space builds outward from this idea, which he returns to repeatedly in metaphors of corners, nests, shells, or the romantic image of the hut in the middle of the woods in "owl-and-wolf-infested lands."[51] Similarly, the dueling fantasies of the *Better Homes and Gardens* cartoon are anchored in a middle-class image of well-being—a set table, a single-family home, and money for leisure activities. And of course Freud's limb-extending game requires the luxury of a warm bed at night; Turner's schadenfreude rests upon a cozy sofa. If you, the reader, are reading this book from home, then your home likely offers you some basic sense of comfort and security—not to mention the requisite space and quiet to read, to study, and to think. And yet, perhaps not. Perhaps this book is being read under headphones in a library or café. The privileged bourgeois attitudes of some philosophies of home space exclude the experience of close, multigenerational living arrangements experienced by many people in America, Europe, and around the globe.

It is no coincidence that tether imagery often populates descriptions of "good homes." For example, Jacobson, Silverstein, and Winslow suggest that beyond merely providing the bare necessity of refuge, good homes also serve the psychological need for "prospect, for a view out, overlooking the wider world beyond . . . from a protected position of advantage and safety."[52] Moreover, "good homes" offer plenty of experiences with "in-between spaces": the pleasure of being near the fireplace while listening to rain on the roof, sitting under a covered porch and watching life on the street from a safe distance, or reading in a bay window.[53] The tether fantasy tends to speak to wellness, even when it involves an imagined temptation with disaster.[54] However, insofar as it evokes apparently timeless discourses about the good home, it can also be employed as critique.

Such a critique is contained in Bong Joon Ho's Academy Award–winning film *Parasite* (2019), which has resonated with American audiences.[55] The first half of the film approaches poverty through a lighthearted tale of upward mobility. However, a major thunderstorm in the second half abruptly shifts focus to matters of class disparity. The film's slow, dramatic rise during this storm is built around dueling tether fantasies—one for each of its two families. For the wealthy Parks, the storm is a reason to call off a camping trip and return to their beautiful and spacious home atop a hill: a position that renders the weather event a quaint tableau to be viewed through a panoramic living room window (a *pro-tected position of advantage and safety*). The wealthy family's young son, unwilling to forego the camping adventure, pitches a tent in the yard, tethered to his parents via handheld radio as well as the overlooking window. For the Parks, the storm speaks to comfort and well-being.

At the same time, expecting their employers to remain away for the duration of the camping trip, the working-class Kim family squats in the wealthy home and overindulges in luxuries (bubble baths, pricey alcohol, sweets, etc.), which they lack in their own lives and which, for them, exemplify secure base experiences. The audacious exploitation of their employers is at its maximum point of advancement when, sprawled and covered in the mess of their own excess (a tether stretched too far), they learn that their hosts have canceled the camping trip due to the weather and are nearly already home. The Kims must scramble to hide evidence of their exploitation, but this task leaves no time for escape; they are forced to hide under furniture with the hope of slinking away in the dark after the Parks are asleep. However, the Kims' uncomfortable stay is extended when the Parks decide to sleep on their downstairs sofa and keep watch over their son's tent in the yard. As the wealthy husband and wife begin sexual contact, titillated and comforted by their view of the yard and the (easily managed) thrill of getting caught by their son, the working-class family is stuck in a horrible, anxious tether, frozen, partially exposed, and unable to flee.

When, finally, the Kims can recover to their own cramped and musty basement apartment in the city, they find it flooded with sewage from the storm and must spend the evening in a disaster relief camp. Before the displaced Kims can begin processing their loss the following morning, the Parks call them in to help host a lavish birthday party on their freshly watered lawn; the storm has only enriched the lives of the wealthy. The Parks' one-of-a-kind home exemplifies Bachelard's spatial poetics by giving solace during a raging storm. But the film's stark message about class offers an especially clear example of the unacknowledged socioeconomic disparities underlying much romantic imagery of happy homes and domestic tethers.

Home—either materially or symbolically—looms large in our storehouse of secure-base imagery as what shelters us, anchors us to the past, to loved ones, and allows us to continue on. But just as not every attachment is secure,[56] and not every connection to a parent or family member is based in love, so too can home be fraught with ambivalence. Even though Bachelard presents his happy image of home as cosmic truth, he is certainly not describing an experience of home that can be universally shared. Rather than some hallowed realm, it would be more precise to describe home as Karen Fog-Olwig does: as a "contested domain: an arena where differing interests struggle to define their own spaces."[57] As David Morley's review of critical literature about the home puts it, home is always "a locus of power relations."[58] And the families that dwell within are "sites of egocentric, strategic and instrumental calculation as well as sites of usually exploitative exchange of services, labor, cash and sex, not to mention, frequently, sites of coercion and violence."[59]

American homeownership remains one of the key levers of power in racist and discriminatory "redlining" policies that have led to enforced segregation, denial of health care, and the emergence of food deserts. At the same time, homes are also sites of resistance. Consider, for instance, what bell hooks describes as "homeplace," or the basic security created and maintained for Black families by the sacrifice of primarily Black women working within the context of white supremacist and sexist domination. She tells the story of women who work long hours serving white families for very little pay, who then muster further strength and energy to provide a homeplace for their own family, "however fragile and tenuous."[60] Homeplace serves as "the one site where one could freely confront the issue of humanization, where one could resist."[61]

As cultural objects, representational texts, and interactive systems, videogames are complexly imbricated with the questions of identity and power that scholars of domesticity have long engaged. This imbrication is expressed in any game concerned with security, threat, exposure, and recovery, even when that game does not explicitly represent domestic space. As Lynn Spigel demonstrates with television, the question of how entertainment media fit inside the home always has a double meaning. The first pertains to where media are located: in which room and in relation to which media devices already present there (e.g., a basement, a bedroom, or at the center of the family circle). The answer to this question also speaks to that technology's social function—the second sense of where media fit into our homes (and our lives). Sheila Murphy, Raiford Guins, and Michael Newman have all built upon Spigel's work on the history of television and the gender politics of domestic spaces by addressing the historical question of what it has meant for games to move inside the home. A tether fantasy allows us to ask what it means for notions of home to move inside games—a question with its own historical continuities and ruptures.

In game studies scholarship, there are at least two clearly established ways to approach the question of where videogames fit into our homes—and, not surprisingly, tethers play a role in both. There is, first, the notion that games enter the home in order to bring the wider world within. Henry Jenkins makes this case when arguing that videogames in the 1990s offered virtual worlds as compensation for shrinking access to real-world spaces outside the home (especially those beyond adult supervision) due to urban sprawl and cultural anxiety about children being outdoors unsupervised. As Jenkins argues, this is not a genderneutral phenomenon. Boys and girls have not enjoyed equal access to spaces outside the home—historically, boys have been far freer to leave. So, specifically, digital games brought *boy culture*—with all its corporeality, violence, and profanity—into the home, where it then conflicted with genteel feminine domesticity and led to efforts to regulate videogame content. Jenkins's transhistorical analogy between adventure novels for boys such as *Treasure Island* (1883) and action-adventure videogames such as *Adventure Island* (1986) provides a basic set of tools for exploring questions of gender in popular game mechanics: regardless of the identity of their protagonists, there is a masculine structure inherent to games about leaving home, venturing into dangerous and exotic environments, facing threats and mastering them, often violently. Jenkins's essay anticipates games such as *Minecraft*, which offer especially direct expression to imagined departures from "home base"—or "the world which is secure and familiar"—and into a digital "home region," which is "an area undergoing active exploration."[62]

Mary Flanagan provides a second approach to the question of how games fit into the home: by reflecting home space in their design and content. Flanagan places perhaps just as much emphasis on socioeconomic status as on gender when comparing post–World War II suburban development in Europe and America to *The Sims* videogame series (2000–2020). Flanagan argues that suburbs—whether real or virtual—"embody particular kinds of architectural values and ideas about access."[63] These values are built directly into the architecture and embody "a growing U.S. trend to move to controllable spaces."[64] In Flanagan's terms, the American home "has shifted from being a place of comfort to a site for defense," with particular emphasis on "the idea of 'safety,'" which even extends to suburban vehicles, such as the SUV.[65] The scope of Flanagan's analysis is deliberately narrow—her argument about games played in suburban spaces speaks to *The Sims* as "dollhouse" games that directly mimic external reality (i.e., they are games about pretending to live in the suburbs). However, the comparison she draws between digital games and "an almost infinite set of grandiose suburban control fantasies" likely has a much broader application.[66]

The connection between games and the home spaces where they are often played is core to much of our affective investment in the medium. The tether fantasy flows through games, narrative media, and domestic architecture, operative at all times in culturally shared notions of comfort and security, refuge and prospect. Keeping tethers in mind helps anchor digital games to the home by way of the security our home base provides. In turn, this connection between games and the home offers a new point of entry for thinking about games in relation to the dynamics of gender, race, and socioeconomic status in such spaces. A videogame set in a familiar, suburban environment may explicitly thematize home spaces in its representational content (e.g., *The Sims*). A game may even ask players to make sure their avatar is comfortable: properly clothed or able to rest in a warm place (e.g., *The Legend of Zelda: Breath of the Wild* [2017] or *The Long Dark* [2017]). However, given the polarized extremes characteristic of the grammars of action in most commercial videogames, if players must secure shelter, it is more likely to be from deadly "razorhail" (*Gears of War 2* [2008]) or caustic atmosphere that corrodes armor (*Metroid Prime 2: Echoes* [2004]). When shelter does find its way into a game's core algorithmic loops, it tends to protect against the undead or infected, which descend upon home base in hordes. Most tether games emphasize the extension into the unknown, leaving the safety of a home base well behind. In every case, tethers help communicate the necessity of interrogating not only home's sheltering function but also how home becomes a contested domain.

Tethers in Games and Media

When used for the regulation of affect, digital games and entertainment media are much like the other "quasi-transitional object-type resources" we might seek out after a long day, "such as hot baths, duvets, photograph albums," and so on.[67] Turning to these resources when we wish for contact with our secure base produces a feeling of calmness and the sense that "all's well with the world."[68] The particular qualities or contents of such resources matter less, perhaps, than their position in the rhythms and spaces of daily life. But what does it mean for the secure base object to reflect the structure of security seeking in its very form? This is a question that can be posed to any of Holmes's domestic examples, which provide feelings of weightlessness (soft cushions), womb-like enclosure (hot baths), and boundedness and encapsulation (books and photo albums). But there is more than a quantitative distinction at stake when we turn to tethers embedded in narrative media. Adventure novels, for instance, are secure base experiences par excellence. The oscillation of *scary, safe again* in novels such as *The Swiss Family Robinson* (1812) or *The Lord of the Rings* reflects the affective posture of the reader, bringing us back and forth across the boundaries of the text to our secure corner of the sofa, to our liminal window nook or, as with Henry Jenkins's childhood example, up into the treehouse during a thunderstorm.

There is an especially strong affinity between tether fantasies and videogames, which often explicitly and repeatedly stage the extension and retraction of a tether to safety. That games offer such active tether dynamics likely means they represent particularly deep and complex secure base experiences. At the same time, games are a flexible medium and one can never be certain a player will entertain a fantasy while playing—especially in games where the tether's role is subtle. Some games, however, are so thoroughly structured by tethers that it is impossible to overlook them in the game's wider systems of meaning making. This chapter breaks such videogames into three distinct subcategories. The following sections introduce *lifeline tethers*, *home base tethers*, and *perpetuum mobile tethers*, which refer (respectively) to tether fantasies built around linear excursions from a secure point of origin, oscillating departures from (and returns to) a secure central hub, and permutations of exposure and recovery with a hub that itself goes along for the ride.

Lifeline Tethers

Videogames have long facilitated "lifeline" tether fantasies, which involve departing one safe space, exploring a hostile world that exhausts resources, and searching for the next space where energy can be replenished and progress saved. There
may be no better visualization of this pattern than Nintendo's *Chibi-Robo! Plug
into Adventure!* (2006), a game about a tiny robot who perpetually tidies a clut-
tered suburban home. In the game, Chibi's battery is depleted as he moves and
must be recharged frequently. To do so, players insert the black electrical plug
that always trails behind the robot into one of the home's many open power out-
lets. With the battery nearly empty, the home's open, three-dimensional space
contracts into a linear and single-minded need to find and connect with the nearest outlet. Once charged, the game's virtual environment opens up again as a
renewed horizon of possibility. *Chibi-Robo!*'s lifeline tether divides the game into
ebbs and flows, tying a rhythmic pattern to spatial coordinates and investing
domestic space with the potential to stage dramas of tense overextension and
nick-of-time recovery.

Despite its pervasive umbilical imagery—the literal and prominent tether
Chibi carries with him at all times—*Chibi-Robo!* is admittedly an imperfect
example. Players are only mildly inconvenienced (forced to endure a cutscene)
when their battery runs dry. In most progression-based games, there is something
more at stake when resources are depleted. For games where progress since the
last save is lost upon death, a great deal of player time and energy are on the
line in those moments just before a new checkpoint is reached. Lifeline tethers
are an example of what Wardrip-Fruin calls an "operational logic," or a common
pattern of meaning built into the algorithmic functions of computational media.
A weak or shallow version of a lifeline tether exists in most progression-based
games in the sense that actions undertaken just before reaching a benchmark are
filled with a tension that was not necessarily present in those same actions at the
outset. All that invested time and energy leading to the checkpoint are weigh-
ing on those final few tasks. There is a special sting in missing the last jump in
an arduous platforming stage or dying when a frustrating boss is on its last leg.
So too is there a diminution of tension upon finally reaching the goal and securing one's progress. Once a checkpoint is reached, players can orient themselves
to the next task from a point of security, unless of course the game cannot be
saved or failure is irreversible, a mechanic playfully termed "permadeath."[69]

I characterize the broad relation of progression mechanics to a lifeline tether
fantasy as weak because, although these mechanics may (or may not) occasion
tether play, this play has not been meaningfully built into the game's algorithmic infrastructure. Some players may reflect upon flirtations with disaster and
momentary recoveries to safety at the end of a section of play, but others may
focus on pragmatics, viewing the threat of loss merely in terms of its inconve-
nience, the time wasted. Some may embrace loss as an opportunity to tend to

other matters (e.g., a trip to the restroom). Skilled players will serve as their own secure base, tethered to their mastery of the game. High levels of skill can render in-game checkpoints less meaningful. In an extreme example, speedrunners often skip save points altogether since saving game adds time to their playthrough or "run." Speedrunners play a different metagame, largely shifting the terms of tension and relief onto the broader time frame of their entire run; the record time, once set, is secure (until beaten).[70]

There is a genre of progression games called "Metroidvania" that build the lifeline tether's pattern of risk and recovery directly into their core grammars by casting it in spatial terms and making it a regular part of play's unfolding. Metroidvania is a portmanteau of *Metroid* and *Castlevania*, two game series that have popularized the genre. Examples include *Super Metroid* (1994), *Castlevania: Symphony of the Night* (1997), *Shantae* (2002), *Ori and the Blind Forest* (2015), *The Mummy Demastered* (2017), and *Timespinner* (2018). Metroidvania games are often structured as two-dimensional side scrollers with elements of action genres such as platforming built in. Players typically explore large, interconnected maps while gradually acquiring abilities that allow them to reach previously inaccessible areas. As players discover new paths, challenges, and enemies—taking the lumps that come with first-time encounters—they become exhausted of vital resources: health, energy, ammunition, and so forth. Finding safe points to secure progress and save their game is an important early objective whenever players venture into unexplored places. "Tethering" one's way from safe zone to safe zone in these games has a meaning similar to the term's use in rock climbing, where a climber clips a tether to anchors in the rock face as they ascend, securing their safety by limiting the potential distance of a fall. Instead of anchors in a rock face, Metroidvania players discover and then tether themselves to save rooms with futuristic energy pods (*Super Metroid*) or plush coffins (*Symphony of the Night*). By positioning narrative events, puzzles, and encounters with difficult enemies near these safe zones, Metroidvania games can either dramatize the challenge of reaching the next safe point or else encourage players to face a difficult opponent with the confidence of a nearby point of security.

To an extent, each Metroidvania game permits players to progress at a preferred rate, either advancing with haste or securing each new area slowly and with care. Players can choose to press onward into the unknown with only a sliver of health remaining, or they can defer progress and turn back toward safety.[71] What is thrilling for one player may induce anxiety in another. Along these lines, Metroidvania games offer players enough latitude to locate and maintain their own "optimal distance" from a point of security (to use psychoanalytic terminology for describing the pursuit of a middle ground between stifling proximity to and anxious separation from the anchoring parental connection).[72]

Metroidvania games might be considered a subset of RPGs—a broadly defined genre that includes traditional Japanese RPGs (JRPGs), such as *Final Fantasy* (1987), *Earthbound* (1994), *Paper Mario* (2001), and *Dragon Quest XI* (2018);

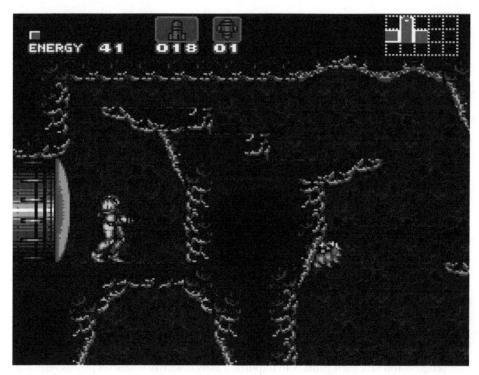

Samus overextends her tether in *Super Metroid* (1994). The subterranean lava flow in this area is too hot and she must turn back for now.

tactical RPGs such as *Fire Emblem: Shadow Dragon and the Blade of Light* (1990), *Shining Force: The Legacy of Great Intention* (1993), and *Final Fantasy Tactics Advance* (2003); action RPGs, such as *The Elder Scrolls V: Skyrim* (2011), *Dragon Age: Inquisition* (2014), and the *Dark Souls* series (2011, 2014, 2016); dungeon crawlers, such as *Diablo II* (2000) and *Minecraft Dungeons* (2020); massively multiplayer online RPGs (MMORPGs) such as *EverQuest* (1999–present) and *World of Warcraft* (2004–present); and multiplayer online battle arenas (MOBAs) such as *Defense of the Ancients* (*DotA 2*) (2013–present) and *League of Legends* (2009–present). While a lifeline tether fantasy operates differently in each of these RPG subgenres, what they generally share in common is a pattern of progressing as far as possible into hostile terrain before withdrawing in order to recuperate, restore health and other resources, upgrade abilities, and acquire new equipment so that, on the next outing, play may progress further and with more confidence.

JRPGs and MMORPGs emphasize spatial navigation and offer the clearest RPG examples of moving between safe and dangerous spaces in play. Players often set out from idyllic, sunny villages and encounter monsters or enemies in fields, caves, or darkened woods before reaching the next town, with its shops and inns. In contrast, it is often the case in tactical RPGs and MOBAs that player characters are tethered to *one another* as points of security. Terrain may affect fights in tactical RPGs (e.g., movement penalties through swamps, high-ground bonus damages, fog of war, choke points, etc.), but space in these games is best understood in relational terms. One's party forms a frontline (of "tanky" fighters to draw enemy attention) and a backline (of mages and marksmen who skip defensive gear to focus on dealing big damage). These specialized lines interlock and reinforce one another—but they also depend on one another for survival.[73]

In general, RPGs are an especially story-driven game genre.[74] In most RPGs, a lifeline tether is couched in the quest's theme of leaving home—a safe, idyllic place—for a dangerous and uncertain world beyond. Turner has remarked upon this tether pattern in adventure novels and Burn and Carr have extended it to *Baldur's Gate* and so to RPGs as a genre. How a tether in a game's narrative intersects with the one in its core gameplay loop varies by game. It is rare for any narrative tether to be foregrounded in an active and anxious manner. More often, the tether is a tension looming in the background, on the fringe of attention, captured largely in tone (e.g., darkening skies, cobwebbed woods, etc.). However, regardless of medium, a tether has the tendency to move abruptly from background to foreground (from the fringe to the focus of attention).

Lifeline tethers can connect a game's narrative frame with its gameplay. For instance, when I first played the JRPG *Earthbound* in the 1990s, I was caught off guard by the game's third major area, Threed. After the generally sunny and uplifting Onett and Twoson (the game's first two towns), Threed's sudden shift in tone tightened my lifeline tether, rendering my play style slow and hesitant. Players can reach Threed only by riding a bus that promptly leaves the player stranded in the middle of a dimly lit, foreboding, zombie- and ghost-filled circus town. The path back is blocked. Aided by an unsettling musical score and the sense that one is traveling quite far from home without the possibility of return, this moment in the game represents the introduction of a tether into setting.

The game's RPG lifeline tether play resumes as players explore the graveyard and woods, encountering enemies that inflict the player's party with strange new status effects. However, not far into Threed, setting intrudes into play, suspending and transforming it. The game's protagonists follow a strange woman into Threed's hotel, which is typically a safe space to recuperate and save game. There, they are ambushed by a mob of the undead. When they wake up, they find themselves buried alive underneath Threed's graveyard. Unable to escape, the player's party dispatches a telepathic message across a great distance to a stranger—a young inventor fated to become the third party member. The young man is asleep in a cozy bed at the Snow Wood Boarding House in the northern land of Winters when he is suddenly tethered to the party as their "one and only hope." Play resumes with this new character who seeks a way to reach those calling for help in the night. Split apart, uncertain how these distal spaces (Threed and

Winters) connect to one another, the fate of the game's protagonists is held in complete suspense: tether upon tether. And then one more: the young inventor sets out into the unknown (alone on a cold winter night) with level 1 stats.

The twining of tethers in this example—when gameplay patterns collide with similar patterns in plot and setting—represents a special interplay between rules and fictions. It is as if the tether fantasy's fluid transition across narrative and mechanical systems were capable of hiding the seams where a game's world stitches image and setting to mechanics. Consider in any tether game the image of a setting sun, the ominous sound of a zombie on the other side of a door, or the plot device where a member of the player's party is taken and must be rescued. Each example pertains to a game's representational or narrative systems. And yet it might be difficult to think of them apart from rules (which underlie and reinforce the meaning of each) if, when the sun sets, dangerous monsters emerge (*Minecraft*); if the zombie outside your home cannot open doors until a "blood moon" rises (*Terraria*); or if, when your party member is suddenly taken hostage in a lavish department store (*Earthbound* again), you must rescue them without access to their items or abilities. In each case, a narrative event presents play with a new situation; focus may shift, but in a way that *galvanizes* play. Rather than noting how story and play interrupt one another and conceiving of games as heterogeneous objects (story and play), it is helpful to emphasize how the tether fantasy is assembled simultaneously from both sides of the much-debated onto-logical divide: from both story and play, fiction and rules, setting and situation.

Lifeline tethers are the most common and general category of tethers. They are not, for that reason, any less interesting or innovative than home base or per-petuum mobile tethers. The popular *Dark Souls* games comprise some of the most compelling experiments with lifeline tether play. The games divide their Lovecraftian worlds into a number of resting points—bonfires—where players restore resources, level up (by spending the "souls" they have acquired), and plot a course to their next objective. However, most enemies are also reset upon rest-ing. Gameplay entails traversing dangerous, monster-filled spaces in search of that next bonfire before resources are exhausted or weapons break. Upon death, all carried souls are dropped on the spot. Players must return and reclaim this vital currency before dying again, or else it is irretrievably lost. Returning to the site of one's recent death requires extra caution (at least more than was previously exercised). Players must, the second time around, repeat all prior successes while also overcoming whatever difficulty led to their fall. Imagine if a tightrope walker had fallen in their first attempt to navigate an elevated obstacle course and was then forced to repeat the challenge, this time with no safety net. At a macro level, the *Souls* games can be understood as efforts to map lifelines across (and so safely manage) a frightening, hostile environment; at a micro level, the point seems to be to carefully extend one's lifeline tether to its breaking point (again and again). As implied in the name for the *Dark Souls* "Prepare to Die" edition, player-character death and catastrophic loss are expected to occur often.

It is helpful, while on the topic of *Dark Souls*, to briefly comment on masochism in tether play. While there is clearly no shortage of sadism in the *Souls* games, it has become a cliché to say these games will serve up stinging defeat. The tether is clearly adjacent to masochism, whether considering what Francis Spufford describes as a cultural fascination with narratives featuring a "sublime of defeat" ("a dreamed-of conquest *by* raging elements") or what John Kucich says of masochism's power to evoke "a powerful or punitive other" (summoning absent parents in order to "overcome separation anxiety").[75] The prominence of a lifeline tether fantasy in commercial videogames helps frame failing, dying, and losing in games as empowering experiences.[76]

Home Base Tethers

A home base tether fantasy is similar to a lifeline tether with the important difference that it transforms the lifeline's linear and progressive pattern into a radial one by situating home base at a fixed, central point. Play still progresses, and progression is still contingent upon journeying away from home. But home base is not left behind. It retains a special significance in play and is transformed by the player's many comings and goings, their centrifugal tracing of the surrounding world—its threats, its treasures. The home base tether is encapsulated in the image Gaston Bachelard provides of the well-heated hut of charcoal burners in the woods: it is a shelter, a pocket of light in a world of darkness. Home base opens onto that darkness while keeping it at bay, offering a special vantage from which to safely view the wider world and its dangers. Its protective boundaries introduce a fundamental differentiation of space between an interior and exterior world, serving as both a conceptual and a sensory threshold between what is safe and dangerous, light and dark, known and unknown. This threshold serves as a point of orientation for home base tether play, which involves fluidly negotiating the terms of home's borders, including what passes through them and what does not.

Home is a common starting point for adventure games and RPGs modeled after the archetypal hero's quest or the melodramatic tradition of beginning and wanting to end in a space of innocence.[77] For instance, *The Legend of Zelda: A Link to the Past* (1991) begins in a cozy domestic interior as rain falls outside. However, as is often the case in these games, events compel the protagonist to quickly depart home. *Earthbound*, part of the *Mother* RPG series known for its suburban settings, provides one of the more thoughtful uses of home as a point of origin, allowing players several dry rehearsals before finally requiring that they change out of their "jammies" one last time and leave. Metroidvania games such as *Shantae* or *Guacamelee!* (2013) regularly involve returning to centralized safe rooms or hubs, which assume a degree of familiarity over the course of the game. Players may even fantasize about the hub *as if* it were a home base, a place where they might dwell. As presented, sprawling Metroidvania hubs are separated from the wider world and yet offer no clear sense of boundedness.[78] Sometimes, a game's villain may lay siege to a point of origin or hub town (e.g., *Dragon Quest XI*), but such events indicate narrative progress more than a wish to protect (or be protected by) home base. To see one's home in ruin means there is no going back—only forward.

The subcategory of home base tethers would seem unjustified if the above were its only examples. After all, it is possible to play through each without taking the additional voluntary step of graphing the fantasy onto game mechanics. In a sense, there is nothing surprising about the fact that few games have built their systems around the pattern of remaining within the environs of a static home base.[79] That adventurers leave home behind is one of gaming's unspoken assumptions, perhaps even a compensatory device for the player's own general immobility while playing. A home base tether embedded in a game's algorithmic systems—made into a core principle of play—is a recent and restricted historical phenomenon largely tied to a specific popular game: *Minecraft* (2011).[80]

Minecraft presents a pastoral world that can be broken apart and reassembled block by block. When released, the game represented a significant reimagining of three-dimensional game space. For most three-dimensional videogames, in-game objects and spaces possess only a polygonal aggregate, a mesh surface. In contrast, players can analyze any space in *Minecraft* into individual building blocks. Rather than concentrating its visual processing power on the verisimilitude of the surface of things, *Minecraft* organizes its world in depth as a "voxel" system (think pixel, but with the emphasis on volume). This system stores data about its virtual terrain on a three-dimensional grid, where each point corresponds to a square block. In effect, there is a deep and complex world beneath the grass you see under your feet.

It is beyond the scope of this book to tease out the full consequences of *Minecraft*'s design of game space.[81] When playing, however, one grasps its fantasy potential almost immediately. If players dig beneath a grassy hill with a shovel, they will find blocks of dirt and maybe clay or gravel; under those is more dirt or stone; then, perhaps a pocket of coal or iron ore. The deeper one digs, the less the sun lights the way. Nearly every location in the game has the potential to disclose something interesting at a certain depth: players might stumble upon a buried dungeon with treasure chests or drop into a cave spotted with precious metals and lit by flowing lava. After digging a long path, players who turn back will realize that while focusing on the blocks ahead, they have cut a channel through the earth. Whether by design or chance, players seamlessly change the world as they explore it.

Minecraft is often understood as a massive sandbox game in that it supports non-goal-directed play. However, the terms of progression in its default Survival Mode urge players to design a centralized home base where they withdraw for safety, stock taking, and storing collected materials.[82] By way of a few simple rules that encourage players to tend to their gardens, *Minecraft*'s world is divided

between inside and outside, near and far, light and dark, and safe and dangerous. The borders of home base orient all subsequent tether play, whether that
entails designing or policing those borders, venturing beyond them, or returning within.

In Survival Mode, players begin empty-handed in the middle of a procedurally generated world configured as a wilderness.[83] Survival and progression require
actively modifying the game's environments to extract resources, neutralize
threats, and establish settlement. Players must build or find shelter before
night falls because monsters (i.e., zombies, skeleton archers, giant spiders, and
creepers—all colloquially known as "mobs," meaning mobile objects) are spawned
near the player wherever there is darkness. The simple rule that mobs emerge in
darkened spaces makes the game's diurnal cycling more than an accessory to play.
For play to continue after sunset, players must work on home base by expanding
its size, controlling its points of ingress and egress, lighting it with torches, and
outfitting it with the necessary accoutrements (e.g., chests, ovens, crafting tables,
and so on). With the sun above, players can venture outside in search of food or
wood for crafting. However, even in daylight, players must remain tethered to
home in the sense that they must always be able to find their way back before
nightfall. More than spawning dangerous mobs, darkness also inhibits navigation. Losing one's way after dark, amid roaming mobs, entails the serious risk of
dying and mislaying all those carefully gathered materials (not to mention any
equipped gear or armor). Dropped items are lost (*despawned*) after five minutes.

For *Minecraft*, world modification is tied to a logic of spatial and temporal
continuity. The game eschews discontinuities that are conventional in many other
games, such as cutscenes and loading screens between different in-game areas.
For instance, nightfall in a game such as *Pikmin* (2001) is represented by a
cutscene that interrupts play's activity, breaking its gameplay into daily segments.
Night is only implied at the level of fiction. The pervasive industry convention
of loading indoor and outdoor spaces separately, such as in *The Legend of
Zelda: The Wind Waker* (2002), renders those spaces infinitely remote from one
another, connected only symbolically, through montage. *Minecraft*, on the other
hand, presents a world fluidly and spatially connected throughout play's duration. Every present moment in play builds directly upon a past moment, and
every interior space fluidly communicates with an exterior space through soft or
porous boundaries that both separate and connect these spaces.[84]

We immediately grasp the significance of spatial continuity when, after
becoming disoriented near nightfall, we find our way back by the twinkle of interior light spilling through the windows of home base. Our built fortification
both separates and connects us to the zombies and skeletons that hunt us: we
are able to look through windows and doors and see these mobs wandering,
lurking, and sometimes peering back. We hear their groans and creaky bones
through the walls, just as we hear the sound of a gentle rainfall on the roof. Bachelard frequently circles back to the point that home's protective function is

most pronounced in these moments when its boundaries register the world outside, representing and communicating directly to us the spatial tensions that they hold precariously in place.

Home base tether play's affinity for spatiotemporal continuity is most apparent during a game's many transitional moments (e.g., the flow of diurnal patterns or the fluidity of movement between interior and exterior spaces). But in a game such as *Minecraft*, this affinity is also expressed on a grander scale in how a home base becomes a palimpsest for play that registers traces of significant play events from even the earliest decisions (such as where to begin building). For instance, shortly after beginning my most recent *Minecraft* world map, I discovered a tunnel that ran through a hill. After collecting building materials, I decided to wall up each end of the tunnel with dirt blocks, creating a protected tube in the hillside (like a hobbit home) for surviving the first night. The sun began to set just as I finished blocking one end of the tunnel. Before I could turn to the other side, however, a creeper (a mostly silent mob that sneaks up and explodes) entered through the tunnel's other side behind me and detonated. The explosion opened a hole in the base's floor, dropping me into a stream of water that had been softly flowing through a lower part of the hill from a nearby lake. Very near death (less than one heart remaining), I climbed out of the water, plugged the hole, and survived night one. The next day, I laid stairs to that subterranean stream so that if I ever found myself outside in the lake fishing at sunset, I could simply float into the darkened cavity and climb into my base from below. The creeper's first-night attack became memorialized in my home base's design. The built fortification in *Minecraft* is itself a kind of additive secretion, a fantasy of security seeking concretized in play. After not playing for some time, one can return to an old *Minecraft* map and encounter the remnants of this fantasy's activity as one finds an empty shell on the beach.

Minecraft's defensive structures emerge from play and so index a compromise between players' plans, the geographic and spatial qualities of the surrounding world, the rules and procedures governing all actions, and play's contingent happenings over time. This does not mean that player-built fortifications in *Minecraft* are themselves procedurally generated (i.e., assembled from preformed patterns according to specific rules or algorithms and random number generation). Player-built fortifications are generated through fantasy, and so they reflect a player's habits, knowledge, and ambition: the memories and hopes of bases past and future. They can also express the longing to dwell. Procedural generation alone cannot (yet) replicate these sorts of spaces.

For instance, in the same *Minecraft* playthrough, I later discovered an abandoned fortress of dark, crenellated brick across a stretch of water near my hillside base. This was the first time I had ever encountered such a procedurally generated structure in *Minecraft*, so I was eager to explore it. After rowing a boat to the shore and climbing to its outer wall, I cut a hole inside and assessed its design. I even briefly considered relocating my own base. However, the found

A hillside base in *Minecraft* (2011) featuring a lit interior visible through water flow.

fortress's layout made little sense. It clearly did not emerge from efforts to resist a hostile world, nor from an interest in settling a home. Its interior was cramped and stuttered, lacking throughflow: there were stairs and hallways that led nowhere. The fortress was born without an entrance. Moreover, external points of vulnerability—where mobs could approach from the darkness—were not rendered visible in the views the fortress offered of the outside world; its framing of this world was incomplete. Its spaces were entirely unlit. In short, the fortress felt unsafe and un-home-like.

The game's procedural architects were, however, successful in at least one aspect of their plans: I experienced the thrill of discovering a single chest in the fortress's lowest level, guarded by tripwire traps. The chest contained valuable, late-game materials, which I could only barely fit in my inventory. And though the procedurally generated fortress failed as a substitute home base, its discovery inaugurated a home base tether fantasy that depended on its fluid spatiotemporal relation with my own home base, which awaited my return, across the water, as the sun began to set. On the way out from the fortress, I collected the tripwires so I might install them in my own base.

When I emerged, pockets full, I found that night had already fallen. As quickly as I could, I found my boat in the dark and rowed off. Over the sound of rain that began to fall, I could hear but not see the zombies gathering on nearby shores. Finally, I caught sight of my base. Slightly disoriented, I landed my boat further inland than intended but managed to climb the uneven terrain unharmed and slip in through my hillside base's rear entrance as zombies searched for me on the shore. Once inside with door closed, I felt safe—and the tone of the rainstorm shifted, held at bay by my base's warming interior. As I organized my inventory into chests, I was surprised to not see the tripwires there. I mined them in the fortress but my inventory must have already been full, meaning I did not collect them.

All at once, I was transported in my spatial memory to the tripwires' position in one continuous arc that led through the rain and darkness, across the lake with its lurking zombies, and up the hill to the fort, down the winding stairs into the stronghold and around the corner: there they must be, on the floor, where they fell when plucked off the wall. In my cozy home, spoils in hand, I was like Llewelyn Moss in *No Country for Old Men* (2007), who stumbled on the aftermath of a cartel shootout and left with the cash. Though safe and at home, Llewelyn could not resist the call to return to the scene with water for a wounded survivor, so he might learn what had happened. The path I traced in my spatial recall was like a lure. If only the game could contrive some reason for me to risk returning to the fortress right then, in the middle of the storm.

Home base tether play longs for titillating departures from the world that is safe and secure. Both departing and returning help give home meaning by situating it in a reciprocal relationship with the world outside. *Minecraft*'s survival mode ensures that this relationship alternates between times that encourage a relaxation of borders, an openness, and times that call for a tensing and closing up. Our own homes where we play games are also flexible membranes whose boundaries are never stuck in too open or too closed a state. As Orrin Klapp emphasizes of systems theory, there is "homeostasis in all living systems, as a balance between intake and outgo."[85] *Minecraft* is about finding this balance, which involves an especially "sensitive alternation of openness and closure."[86] At any moment and at any locality within home base's assembled structures, openings can be walled off and barriers can rupture.

Terraria (2011) may even better illustrate the principle of opening and closing in home base tether play. As a side-scrolling game, *Terraria* presents a procedurally generated world of blocks in two dimensions. The game is distinct from *Minecraft* in its optics, movement mechanics, tone, and even its style of progression. Despite this, the game is frequently regarded as a "2D Minecraft." Anyone who plays both games quickly intuits the *fantasy* they share in common. More precisely, they share a core set of mechanics that facilitate home base tether play: dynamic lighting, terrain modification, enemies spawned on a diurnal cycle, themes of mining and crafting, and the development of specialized tools and objects intended for creating a dwelling place (e.g., lights, doors, furniture, chests, etc.). Early in *Terraria*, home base tether play is especially pronounced: at any moment, players behold the entirety of their base in a single image from the side, like an open dollhouse. Home's spatial relation to the wider world is immediately graspable. The game's restriction to two dimensions—which introduces distance between the virtual camera and the optical point of view of the player character—may seem to pose a challenge to the perception of enclosure and encapsulation. This would be only partially compensated for by *Terraria*'s dynamic lighting system, which helps align what is seen by the player with the player character's assumed visual field.[87] However, in practice, the perception of enclosure is pronounced (made especially legible) by the game's diagrammatic presentation of the world.

What weakens *Terraria*'s home base tether is not its visual style, but its structure of progression. As players explore dungeons and encounter bosses, they craft powerful weapons and gear that render home's protective function meaningless (nocturnal enemies on the surface no longer pose a threat). Before long, players are attached to home base only as a familiar place for storing/retrieving gathered materials and housing nonplayer characters. Perhaps sensing a need for the home base tether play to continue, *Terraria* features special invasion events ("Blood Moon," a "Goblin Invasion," and, eventually, a "Pirate Invasion").[88] Announcing each event in advance provides time for a return journey and so interrupts any ongoing exploration by tugging at that lifeline tether, recalling attention to the secure base that now needs *your* protection.

Not all of *Terraria* is as tense as during its invasion events. In the sunshine, harmless woodland creatures replace the zombies. Players can walk in the open and explore at their own pace, stopping to pick flowers or chop trees. So too is much of *Minecraft*'s play undertaken in a sunny environment where home's borders can relax. Players can leave during the day without needing to close the door behind them. The game's bifurcated world slackens in the sunlight, when—not coincidentally—distant hills on the horizon seem within reach. The security that home provides is extended by the warm sunlight that spreads across all that is seen, enabling exploration. As the sun sets, these distant spaces suddenly feel very far off. Even at night, however, home base connects players to the wider virtual world through busy activity in anticipation of exploratory play to come. Since one cannot safely venture too far from home at night in *Minecraft* (or early in *Terraria*), one instead makes plans (journeying in imagination). This dynamic presents a sanitized image of home as a safe, clearly bounded, and recuperative space. Of course, in these games, such an image is won only through a brutal enforcement of home's boundaries. Play's respirational expansions and contractions rely on a sense of free mobility, on an image of the domestic hearth that is inviting but not stifling—a home, not a prison.

To the cynic, home base tethers may seem narcissistic in the apocalyptic wish they express to wipe all humanity from the world. The apocalypse sanitizes the symbolic order, leaving behind only a simplistic binary of "us" and "them" split along the boundary of the home-entertainment fortress. This sort of worldview is captured in the architectural logics of expensive getaway lodgings for the wealthy: mountain chalets or one-of-a-kind fly fishing cabins on the river.[89] But in home base tether narratives, the luxury home often gives way to the militarized compound. And in tether games, the threat of rising river water is usually replaced with hordes of zombies. Home base tether games like *Minecraft* and *Terraria* harken to feudal times, when life and livelihood depended on the integrity of the walled defense—ignoring, of course, the historical fact that boundaries of private and public were drawn very differently in such times. Many home base tether games may be best understood as taking place at the end of human history, or simply outside of time. After all, built structures in *Minecraft* also exemplify postmodern pastiche: in a few simulated days, or about an hour of gameplay, players can retrace an abbreviated history of architectural achievement from mud huts to stone fortresses, log cabins, and even modern ferrovitreous (iron and glass) designs that resolve the historical conflict between structure and light. Above all, the home that is also a castle represents a frame of mind. Home base tether games anticipate a preoccupation with security in their players, but also a certain degree of privilege and stability, as well as a penchant for spending an evening at home, indoors, rather than out.

Minecraft's Survival Mode does not speak for the full range of potential meanings in tether play. The wish for solitude expressed in a home base tether game such as *Gone Home* (2013), or a lifeline tether game such as *The Long Dark* (2014), orient play differently. Though these games mostly present tether dynamics in their fictions, not in the design of their interactive elements, they point the way for alternative thematic couplings of security and home. *Gone Home* is a first-person-point-of-view game where players explore an eerily empty house that shelters them during a thunderstorm. Using simple sound cues to register off-screen space, visual motifs (e.g., an abandoned pillow fort), and a theme of discovery (with secret passages hidden in the walls), *Gone Home* troubles the fantasy of dwelling. Its home may have been warm and inviting at one time, but the lights have since gone out, and its darkened spaces are haunted by its family's conspicuous absence. In *The Long Dark*, an independently designed game made in part with public funding from the Canadian government, players wander a postapocalyptic snow world in search of temporary shelter to recover some body heat and avoid predators, prolonging the inevitable moment when they finally succumb to the elements. Like *Gone Home*, *The Long Dark* employs tethers in its narrative frame to encourage players to reflect on the impulse to become entrenched in home base. Home—and the human relations contained within—is not simply a protected space that must be maintained and defended in these games, nor is it simply left behind at the outset, as in many lifeline tether games. Rather, it is let go reluctantly, painfully. It is mourned.

In the next section, where home base goes along for the ride, it is helpful to keep in mind that even journeys beyond the edge of the galaxy are inevitably freighted with a set of culturally and historically inscribed notions of what a home is or ought to be.

Perpetuum Mobile Tethers

A perpetuum mobile tether fantasy imagines extending the shelf life of a home base tether by mobilizing the home, bringing it along for the journey, and putting it in dialog with a range of new situations. Because the mobile home fortress can be departed at any point in play, perpetuum mobile tethers might be framed as the imagined potential for an unending series of home base and lifeline tethers staged across an unpredictable variety of spaces and circumstances. Home moves *through* the storm that rages outside, adopting its own ceaseless motion against the backdrop of the void, the infinite. Conceptually, the uprooting of home allows for playful juxtapositions between it and frontier space, opening the domestic to new meanings while reorganizing its dynamics of gender, the shape of family, and the boundaries of private and public space.

The term "perpetuum mobile" is drawn from Otto Rank's discussion of a womb fantasy, or the wish to return to a uterine state where all needs are met. Our separation from the womb is, for Rank, the original and most severe of all traumas. This trauma's residual presence as a wish to return to the womb supposedly finds a variety of everyday expressions, from the pleasure of riding in cars to the feeling of relaxation when climbing into a comfortable bed in a dark room at night. Specifically, for Rank, "perpetuum mobile" describes a "mania to invent," to devise some machine or other solution to "the problem of permanently dwelling in and fitting into the mother's womb."[90] "Perpetuum mobile" literally means perpetual motion, typically in reference to pieces of music played with a continuous stream of notes. But in Rank's sense the term relates more to "the motion of a hypothetical machine which, once activated, would run forever unless subject to an external force or to wear."[91] Such a machine would be a closed and entirely self-sufficient circuit, generally considered impossible (a fantasy). This makes it an apt metaphor for a womb-like enclosure through which we might more confidently encounter new worlds.

Rank's discussion offers up the charged imagery of the zeppelin, a fortress floating on the wind. But there are examples in popular fiction that better realize the fantasy, such as Captain Nemo's fantastic *Nautilus* from *Twenty Thousand Leagues under the Sea* (1870); the implacable *Starship Enterprise* from the *Star Trek* universe; the rugged but reliable *Millennium Falcon* from *Star Wars* films; the paradoxical TARDIS from *Doctor Who* (1963–present); the *Thousand Sunny* from *One Piece* (1997–present); the eponymous starship from *Battlestar Galactica* (2004–2009); and the mobile fortress from *Howl's Moving Castle* (2004). Each example imagines a self-sustaining vessel that carries its passengers through both safe and dangerous times, always to the uterine hum of an eternal engine.[92] Even when inhabitants must leave its confines and face danger on their own, the perpetuum mobile vessel enables bravery by offering a way back to safety (a lifeline). The fantasy of a perpetuum mobile vehicle has exerted its own influence on the structure of these narratives, pushing them into the perpetual motion of serialized and episodic formats that, were they ever to end, would be carried forward by fans who have come to inhabit the fantasy—who have, in other words, imagined life aboard the perpetual motion vessel.

Passengers on a perpetuum mobile (hereafter PM) vessel vary in their occupation and motivation for seeking the frontier: they often tend to be explorers, scientists, soldiers, or wanderers. They may hope to encounter the new or return to the past. What is consistent is how PM narratives position their characters in the midst of the direst imaginable circumstances: the vacuum of space, crushing ocean depths, or a war-torn countryside. The harshness of surrounding conditions justifies and motivates the unprecedented protective function of the vessel itself, which is initially experienced as a womb-like quiescence or calmness despite the danger beyond. Nevertheless, as latent tether dynamics move to the foreground and demand attention, this calmness is punctured—often violently and with little warning.

PM plotlines devise some need to depart the safety of the vessel: a mission to gather resources, a diplomatic dinner invitation, a rescue attempt, and so on. With clear Oedipal overtones, the tether's spatial dynamics reverberate up the chain of command by introducing divisions within the social unit: away teams detached from a central authority test hierarchies while providing an occasion for steely rhetoric about duty to the mission, so often undercut by the refusal to leave someone behind. Bonds between crewmates serve as lifeline tethers when those who are separated and dispersed across dangerous spaces opt to risk their lives for one another. A PM tether often frames its lifelines against the backdrop of impending doom—a volcano about to blow, a star about to go supernova— which imbues spatial separation with an urgency verging on separation anxiety.

With home base tethers, the tension of exposure is typically relaxed at the moment when one returns safely, indoors. However, returning to home base is rarely the final step in the heightened stakes of a PM tether's chain of imbricated lifelines, such as when one member of a crew is somehow delayed in their return to the PM vessel, which then must decide how long to wait before fleeing the solar system (or ocean port) where a star is about to explode (or the villainous World Government's navy is closing in). While one group races back to the vessel, those already aboard are suspended, hand on throttle. Like Freud's bedclothed bourgeoisie with outstretched limb, PM tether scenarios contrive to prolong the vessel's exposure for as long as possible before turning toward safety in unison (usually with everyone back aboard). These narratives tend to dwell on the moment of separation and exposure, so that those who choose to wait for the return of an away team come under attack while doing so, amplifying the tension of their PM tether with slow-motion cinematography, shaky cameras, and pyrotechnics.

Many PM tether narratives exemplify what Paul Edwards describes as the "shell-game strategy characteristic of closed-world discourse" during the Cold War: "When one enclosure is punctured, the strategist or theorist immediately retreats to another, each more baroque and at the same time more abject than the last."[93] Edwards argues that closed-world aesthetics in popular culture, which were often permeated by a metaphor of containment ("with its image of an enclosed space surrounded and sealed by American power"), reflected a confluence of historical phenomena: the threat of nuclear holocaust, a worldview increasingly characterized as a binary rivalry between two superpowers, and the first successful ventures into outer space.[94] Key for Edwards's discussion of closed-world aesthetics in popular culture is the recurring image of a white, nuclear family undertaking "ordinary daily activities" within these artificial spaces ("bubble-like shells") that are set in the midst of "hostile environments."[95] The survival of the American family despite the destruction of the world is a powerful ideological device centering the family unit and naturalizing its reproductive function.

On the other hand, the temptation to characterize PM tether aesthetics as somehow inherently "closed world" must be resisted. PM can also be found in what Edwards contrasts with closed-world aesthetics: the "green world," or "an unbounded natural setting such as a forest, meadow, or glade," where "action moves in an uninhibited flow between natural, urban, and other locations and centers around magical, natural forces—mystical powers, animals, or natural cataclysms."[96] One would be hard-pressed to find a better example of the green world's penchant for thematizing "the restoration of community and cosmic order through the transcendence of rationality, authority, convention, and technology" than Hayao Miyazaki's *Howl's Moving Castle* (2004).[97] Nickelodeon's *Avatar: The Last Airbender* (2005–2008) is also a popular green-world narrative with PM elements, such as the heroes' relationship with the giant flying bison, Appa. The anime *One Piece* is yet another green-world PM narrative. In it, characters regularly spend entire story arcs split up from their crew mates and the PM vessel, the *Thousand Sunny*. The Cold War's influence on the American imaginary that Edwards tracks does seem to speak to apparently culturally specific tendencies, such as the American emphasis on space-themed science fiction (e.g., *Star Trek, Star Wars, Battlestar Galactica, Lost in Space* [1965–1968; 2018–2021], *The Expanse* [2015–2022], etc.) in contrast with the green-world anime and manga produced in Japan (or with clear Japanese influences). But exceptions can be as meaningful as the rule. Note, for instance, a more recent Japanese anime, *Attack on Titan* (2009–present), which is suffused with dark tether imagery (lifeline, home base, and PM) in an apocalyptic setting that blends closed- and green-world aesthetics.

From a different historical vantage, PM tethers in contemporary narrative media often resemble the nick-of-time rescues from transitional-era American silent cinema (1907–1915). In a striking number of early American narrative films, a sanctified, feminine domestic space is threatened by the intrusion of a dangerous external world that is coded masculine. These two spheres appear to approach one another through the narrative technique of parallel action (cross-cutting back and forth between two different spaces in order to imply simultaneous lines of action). Given the many examples of home invasion, these "parallel" lines of action are actually convergent trajectories. PM tethers can also be understood as a dangerous convergence of disparate spaces (a domestic bubble and the threatening world beyond). However, PM tether narratives are also distinct in that their mobile home bases often trouble rather than merely reinforce the culturally established spatial and social coordinates of domesticity. Their principal avatars are often brave women who explore frontier spaces, such as Maureen Robinson, Michael Burnham, Philippa Georgiou, River Tam, Toph Beifong, Leia Organa, Capt. Kathryn Janeway, and Lt. Kara "Starbuck" Thrace. And rather than presenting the mobile home base as a sanctified space, the PM tether's interest in vital boundaries has generated a series of creative scenarios about failing to manage distance, proximity, safety, and threat.

Star Wars: The Empire Strikes Back offers a familiar example when Han Solo's ship, the *Millennium Falcon*, hides in a cave on an asteroid from an Imperial fleet (whose bombs can still be heard above). When Solo and Princess Leia venture outside the idle ship to remove parasites from its hull, they are especially vulnerable, equipped only with oxygen masks and a blaster—but the *Falcon* itself, along with the droids who remain on board, is also vulnerable without its captain and crew. As the ground sways, Han recognizes the situation for what it is (later stating the obvious: "This is no cave"), and he and Leia rush back aboard. The *Falcon* lifts off and accelerates toward the "cave's" closing mouth, gliding through a gap in the teeth of the giant space slug (Exogorth) they had unwittingly hidden inside. Though evocative of the biblical parable of Jonah and the whale, the *Falcon* in the Exogorth's only clear moral lesson is that it is necessary to venture beyond the protection of one's mobile home base—that otherwise a hiding place may entomb you (a womb fantasy gone amiss). This sequence supports a fantasy about the perpetual motion vehicle: about the ability to alight on any surface, about the delightful instability of the ground under foot, and about outer space as a frontier and a dynamic backdrop for an unending series of encounters between the unexpected and a familiar home space.

As with the parallel action of D. W. Griffith's crosscutting films, the nick-of-time rescue (or escape) is a mainstay of the PM genre. *Battlestar Galactica* employs the device many times throughout its serialized narrative. The large military vessel "battlestar" *Galactica* has the power to "jump" instantaneously to another point in space: a dramatic discontinuity that concludes the tether's play. However, before jumping, the ship's jump drive must be charged ("spooled up"). Even when not malfunctioning, jump drives are devices evoking vulnerability and justifying a rise in tension. To protect the fleet as jump drives are prepared, *Galactica* launches smaller, single-pilot fighters that must take care not to venture beyond the *recovery line* (their tether's limit) because once *Galactica* is prepared to jump, the fighters risk being left behind. If William Adama, paternal captain of *Galactica*, waits too long for any errant fighters to return to the launch bay, the ark-like vessel might be lost, along with what remains of humanity. The last fighter returning to the base ship often executes a *combat landing* to signal that the maximum safe exposure to threat has been endured—and *Galactica* can finally blink away. The PM tether's last-second recovery becomes correlated with the wish for perpetual repetition. In other words, nick-of-time recoveries in space operas like *Galactica* and *Star Trek: Discovery* (2017–present) do not resolve narrative tension once and for all, such as with the PM ending of *The Matrix* (1999).[98] The tether's contraction in the narrow escape forms part of a broader pattern encountered early and often within each narrative universe.

The promise of this pattern's indefinite extension is a point of congruence between serialized PM narratives and digital games. This section's discussion has not yet explicitly included digital games despite their interest in PM tethers from their earliest days.[99] In truth, though many commercial games evoke PM tethers in their thematic and narrative frames, relatively few have built this fantasy into their mechanical systems. Nintendo's *Super Metroid* (1994), which owes an obvious debt to the closed-world aesthetics of *Star Wars* and *Aliens* (1986), offers a familiar example of a PM tether in a game's narrative frame. Once at the game's outset and again at its conclusion—both times while protagonist Samus Aran is maximally distant from her mobile gunship—a clash with a powerful opponent triggers a self-destruct sequence that requires Samus to race back to her ship within a set period of time (one minute and three minutes, respectively). The return trip is marked with a special urgency (a tether stretched too far) not just by a countdown timer, but also by flashing lights, sirens, and ground that tilts underfoot. If players return to Samus's ship in time, a cinematic cutscene portrays the ship's subsequent departure as a narrow escape (regardless of how many seconds actually remain). From the perspective of a PM fantasy, little has changed in the *Metroid* series since 1994. The Nintendo Wii title *Metroid Prime 3: Corruption* (2007) contains several moments clearly intended to incorporate Samus's gunship into fantasy play, but these moments are still pre-scripted and confined to the game's narrative frame.

The *Metroid* series headlines a group of games featuring PM tethers in their stories but not necessarily in their gameplay. Such a grouping includes games set in fictional universes marked by PM tethers that do not contain any tethers whatsoever in play—for example, the action platformer *Super Star Wars* (1992). Players may or may not project tethers onto gameplay developed from arcade-style action and platformer game genres. This PM grouping also includes games that, like *Super Metroid*, do incorporate lifeline and home base tether fantasies in their play, but that relegate PM tethers to the fictional frame, such as the *Pikmin* series (2001, 2004, 2013) and independently produced titles such as *FTL: Faster than Light* (2012), *Starbound* (2016), *Pyre* (2017), and *Haven* (2020). In *Haven*—a survival/exploration game about a couple that crash-lands on an alien planet—play switches back and forth between exploration outside the PM vessel (appropriately named Nest) and domestic life within. Even though exterior and interior space are mainly related at the level of fiction, narrative events during exploration (e.g., an earthquake) affect the domestic interior in thoughtful ways (e.g., the Nest tumbles down a hill, its tidy contents spilling everywhere).

There is a second group of games with PM fantasies built into gameplay, such as *Blaster Master* (1988), *Solar Jetman: Hunt for the Golden Warpship* (1990), *Dragon Quest Heroes: Rocket Slime* (2006), *Lovers in a Dangerous Spacetime* (2015), *Titanfall 2* (2016), *Gato Roboto* (2019), and *Astroneer* (2019). Beyond merely thematizing vehicular transportation, these games also include lifeline tether play (experiences of exposure and recovery) that is somehow anchored in a protective vessel. In *Blaster Master*, a side-scrolling Metroidvania game for the Nintendo Entertainment System, players explore an underground world in a mobile tank (named SOPHIA III). At any moment, players may opt to exit the tank and explore on foot as the tank's pilot, Jason. Remarkably, the tank waits obediently where it is left. The option to depart the PM vessel sets *Blaster Master* apart from games developed with far greater computational resources decades later. As when Samus returns to her gunship in *Super Metroid*, entering *Blaster Master*'s tank restores the health of its pilot. Unlike *Super Metroid*, however, Jason and SOPHIA III (hereafter SOPHIA) go most places together as a dual avatar, generally separating only for specific tasks.

Besides differences in size and appearance, SOPHIA and Jason are also differentiated in simple mechanical ways that help the game weave a PM fantasy into its gameplay. Stepping out of the tank renders players much more vulnerable to attack, as Jason's firepower, mobility, and defenses are greatly exceeded by SOPHIA's. While the tank can drop safely from any height, Jason suffers damage or can die falling even short distances. Nevertheless, there are some tasks better suited to Jason—in fact, there are areas in the game that can be accessed only on foot. However, more significant from the perspective of a PM fantasy are moments when a player might be encouraged to depart the tank but ultimately is given some latitude to choose. For example, some enemies are too low to the ground for the tank to target. These can simply be avoided. However, opting to step out and face them as Jason, who stands at their height, allows for easy targeting. Doing so inaugurates a PM tether and is reminiscent of Han and Leia clearing parasites from the *Millennium Falcon*. Late in the game, Jason must separate from SOPHIA for an especially long time, traversing a maze-like underwater chasm full of dangerous enemies, completing a dungeon, and then navigating back. Though not the conclusion of the game, this is perhaps the apogee of *Blaster Master*'s PM play.

The reward for the prolonged separation is a SOPHIA upgrade that enables underwater tank navigation. Players can finally pilot SOPHIA across the precarious stretch of water Jason just traversed, and water will never again require that Jason and SOPHIA separate. In other words, the upgrade permanently shifts the terms of the game's PM tether play. Like many Metroidvania games, *Blaster Master*'s late-game tether play cedes ground to a different fantasy process. In contrast, one of the game's spiritual successors, the monochromatic *Gato Roboto* (2019), opts to keep its focus on PM tether play throughout. Its protagonist—a small cat named Kiki—dies in one hit if caught exploring outside her mobile mech suit. As the game progresses, the suit becomes stronger, but Kiki does not—and the game invents many clever excuses for their separation. That a relatively small-scale, independent production such as *Gato Roboto* can connect with and extend the fantasy framework from a thirty-year-old game helps emphasize how fantasy does not develop at the same pace as the technology that supports it.

There is no Moore's law for fantasy, even though fantasy traditions do change over time.[100] A game's formal systems and the fantasies they instantiate recipro-cally inform one another. But each moves independently as well. For instance, the Nintendo DS's dual-screen hardware anchors and reinforces *Rocket Slime*'s (2006) PM tether play, but not *Metroid Prime Hunters* (2006). While *Metroid Prime Hunter*'s touchscreen displays an interactive menu during play, *Rocket Slime* evokes encapsulation by devoting both the system's built-in screens to depicting a massive PM vessel (the Schleiman Tank) from inside and outside simultaneously. Moreover, despite the loose sense of continuity between *Rocket Slime*'s interior and exterior spaces, its tether play resonates in part because the Nintendo DS's clamshell design itself evokes PM tether play. It is reminiscent of miniature dollhouse toys such as Polly Pocket, which appropriately fit into pockets when clasped and, when taken out and opened, reveal hidden worlds.[101] Polly Pocket was apparently inspired by a makeup powder compact that a father refashioned into a small house with miniature dolls for his daughter. As Susan Stewart says of dollhouses, and one might say of Polly Pocket and the Nintendo DS as well, the "aptest analogy is the locket or the secret recesses of the heart: center within center, within within within. The dollhouse is a materialized secret; what we look for is the dollhouse within the dollhouse and its promise of an infinitely profound interiority."[102] Both the Nintendo DS and Polly Pocket com-bine enclosure with portability, exemplifying what Barbara Klinger describes as the "potentially infinite regression of minifortresses enabled by personal technologies" in the home.[103] And yet this experience of nesting (center within center) is even better illustrated by a more recent game played on a standard, widescreen television.

In *Lovers in a Dangerous Spacetime* (hereafter *Lovers*), players control tiny, Polly Pocket–like avatars who pilot a round, pink ship (the Gumball Zero) as it fends off enemies and explores asteroid fields, planetoids, and caves. As with the depiction of home base in *Terraria*, *Lovers'* mobile vessel is sliced and open to view from the side, like a rounded dollhouse. Its diagrammatic side view (in con-trast with *Rocket Slime*'s isometric perspective) allows the interior of the ship to share continuous screen space with what is seen outside—an apparent continu-ity that benefits from the prevalence of high-definition, widescreen televisions in the 2010s. As a PM game, it is significant that the Gumball Zero's major systems (weapons, navigation, etc.) must be accessed by eight corresponding

The pink Gumball Zero, a perpetuum mobile vessel from *Lovers in a Dangerous Spacetime* (2015).

terminals spread across the vessel. This spatial situation is an arbitrary compli-cation of control, a contrivance that requires the ship's tiny operators to fre-quently crisscross the vessel's interior and that encourages players to consider their tiny avatar's position *within* the vessel in relation to what is happening outside.

By joining an interior and exterior space, *Lovers* approaches a third and final category of PM tethers. This category is reserved for games with significant home base tether systems (including boundary porosity and secure-base play) that have been rendered mobile. And this category is still waiting for its *Minecraft* moment. Despite steep learning curves, space-themed voxel-style sandbox games such as *StarMade* (2012) and *Space Engineers* (2016) are among the most interesting recent efforts. Regardless of whether *StarMade* players understand how to opti-mize the design of their ship's reactor, they will easily be able to construct a small fuselage, block by block, with a cockpit, windshield, and entrance—and they will experience something like a home base tether the moment they view this entry-way as a threshold to the dangerous vacuum of space.

Unlike *StarMade*, where players begin by crafting their own PM vessel, early play in *Space Engineers* more closely resembles survival-crafting games. The PM tether play that does emerge only slowly crystallizes atop lifeline and home base tethers. This makes *Space Engineers* somewhat like other prominent examples, such as *No Man's Sky* (2016), *Subnautica* (2018), and *Astroneer* (2019). Each game begins with the equivalent of a stranding. Early play entails getting one's bearing, exploring, extracting resources, and crafting structures (solar panels, turbines, drills, etc.). Eventually, players can build land rovers (*Astroneer*) or ocean gliders

(*Subnautica*) to explore more distant surroundings. In *Astroneer*, players can eventually construct rocket ships to blast into space and explore different planets. However, in these examples, movement into and out of the PM vessel tends to be truncated rather than fluid and continuous (*Subnautica* is the exception), and play prioritizes tethering to home base over PM play: *Astroneer*'s interplanetary rocket is largely a means to establishing new outposts elsewhere.[104]

In *Subnautica*, players explore the ocean around their floating life pod, gradually extending their tether's reach (e.g., with batteries, oxygen tanks, or an underwater glider). The game is depicted in a first-person point of view, and movement across any barriers (including the spatial barrier of ocean water itself) is apparently continuous. Eventually, exploration allows for the crafting of larger and more versatile PM watercrafts, such as the small, single-seat Seamoth or the massive Cyclops (so named for the rounded glass dome at its fore). When this glass shield crests above the waves, it provides players a composite view of the bright world above the water and the murky space beneath, helping evoke the ocean's surface as not just a conceptual threshold but a sensory one as well. As the submarine dives toward an underwater trench, it supports PM play, serving as a mobile home base players may position as they like before deploying from its belly a smaller, more versatile vessel, such as the mechanical Prawn Suit (reminiscent of the Power Loader Ripley pilots in her fight with the Xenomorph Queen in *Aliens*). Players may, in turn, exit the Prawn Suit to gather materials more efficiently by hand. But they must do so while keeping an eye (and ear) open for dangerous ocean creatures. Should one appear, players will need to return to the Prawn Suit, then to the Cyclops sub, before fleeing the area. The game enacts Paul Edwards's shell-game strategy—shells within shells (*within within within*) for braving the inhospitable depths.

PM vehicles in *Subnautica* are crafted but not designed by players. In *Space Engineers*, by contrast, players must design every structure and vehicle block by block, keeping in mind how power is generated and routed toward productive ends (through thrusters, shields, drills, wheels, etc.). Players must attend to physics as well, as the center of gravity, torque, turn radius, and weight will affect how a vehicle handles. A rover may be controlled well on the way *to* a mineral deposit, but heavy ores will change the center of gravity and could complicate the return trip. Becoming caught in the midst of a return—needing to recalibrate a transport system on the fly, as the sun sets, cut off from the home base awaiting your return—is an emergent PM tether scenario to rival any other. As with *Minecraft* and home base tethers, designing the mobile fortress serves as an occasion for sustained focus on its protective function. Every mechanical element of the vessel is put into dialog with this function: fast thrusters enable evading threats; lights help avoid collisions; strong shields allow time to react to danger; if all else fails, life support systems enable respawning nearby. *Space Engineers* helps render visible a wider lesson about PM tether play: whether simply responding in the *environs of a breach* or building a new vessel from scratch, a PM tether game is an excuse for focusing attention on the systems that shield us from the world's overwhelming stimuli as we move through it.

Accretions or Sticky Tethers

This chapter began with Freud's game of extending a leg from under the covers and drawing it in again on a cold winter night (a "cheap enjoyment").[105] It concludes with another Freudian analogy that exhibits the same pattern of stretching out and withdrawing but with nearly the opposite implication. The analogy (which appears in several of Freud's essays) draws on the imagery of an amoeba that feeds by extending tendrils (pseudopodia) outward and withdrawing them into its body again.[106] The pseudopodia analogy illustrates Freud's notion of the ego as a reservoir for the libido, which flows outward from the ego to objects and must sometimes be drawn in again. In general terms, when a special object of our affection (a loved one) is lost and we acknowledge this loss (when we mourn), our love for that person is being drawn back in from the world. When our love comes back to us, though, it is changed by its close attachment to the lost loved one. And, as a result of drawing that love back in, *we* become transformed in the process (by our own investment, we become more like what we loved). In other words, Freud's libido amoeba does not risk extension into a dangerous world for the thrill of exposure alone. It reaches out in search of enrichment.

Likewise, the player in most tether-based videogames does not venture into the world for the mere thrill of exposure. Rather, stretching out is most often tied to some sort of reward, something that changes us in our capacity to reach out once more. In the dragon's stomach, in the deepest recesses of the troll's cave, in the castle's well-guarded treasure room—once the tether has been stretched to its farthest point without snapping—exposure is rewarded with invaluable new *accretions*, things gathered from a game's environment that correct a perceived limitation or weakness. Recall the apogee of *Blaster Master*'s PM tether play—the lengthy underwater passage Jason must navigate without the help of his tank, SOPHIA. At the end, players are rewarded with an upgrade that makes underwater tank navigation possible. This accretion is symbolically imbued with the longed-for reunion with a secure base following such a stressful separation. Its accrual permanently shifts the need for (and the meaning of) separation from the PM vessel by eroding one of the last advantages Jason holds over the tank, underwater mobility. The newly acquired accretion augments and extends the tether's reach, pushing the game's collection quest one step closer to realizing that wish to permanently dwell inside the womb-like vessel. And the process of gradually progressing by upgrade toward permanent encapsulation, insulation, or *quiescence* (a freedom from shocks or other strong sensations) expresses a *fantasy of accretions*, which is the focus of the next chapter. In truth, there are few tethers in videogames that do not intersect with and find renewal and enrichment in a fantasy of accretions.

4

The Fantasy of Accretions

• •

In his study of fairy tales, Bruno Bettelheim notes how children make special use of villains by projecting their "badness" onto them.[1] Children see in the Big Bad Wolf, for instance, their own "wish to devour," as well as its inverse, the fear of being eaten.[2] As clinical psychologist Phebe Cramer puts it, projection protects us "by attributing unacceptable feelings, wishes, and impulses to someone else; the disturbing thoughts are placed outside the self—'ejected' into the external world and attached to some other object," where they can be managed more safely and constructively.[3] It is along these lines that a more contemporary Big Bad Wolf—*Naruto*'s (2002–2007) immortal, serpentine villain Orochimaru— can be said to court the projection of a troubling wish: to avoid death by embracing it.

Orochimaru embodies the dark side of a fantasy about collecting things— he collects knowledge, ability, and people (both living and dead). He has even collected his own soul, or at least a forbidden technique that allows him to preserve his soul safely in the body of another (and so avoid death). He ruminates on his special predilection shortly after slithering from the mouth of his own corpse, reborn after being cut to pieces by the young ninja he hopes to collect next, Kabuto Yakushi. Kabuto, stunned at the spectacle of rebirth, listens with rapt attention as Orochimaru speaks: "If you're not satisfied with what you've had so far. . . . Just find other things and add them to yourself, one by one. I also want to know who or what I am. And I've been collecting all sorts of things."[4] Orochimaru's Promethean quest to acquire all knowledge about the shinobi world makes him a pariah to the Hidden Leaf Village, and so he cuts ties with the village just as he has learned to sever the mortal bond between body and soul.

But if he lives forever, this is avowedly only so that *collecting can continue without interruption.*

Orochimaru is like a negative mirror image of the series' principal character, Naruto Uzumaki—an orphaned boy who is perhaps just as eager as his adversary to collect things from the world. However, in contrast with the villain, Naruto's collection quest emphasizes growth and change rather than the maintenance of a status quo. The entire series and its sequel, *Naruto: Shippûden* (2007–2017), follow Naruto as he seeks expert training, practices ambitious abilities, and forges bonds with nearly everyone he meets, slowly winning all to his side. Naruto sheds much blood in pursuit of his dream to become Hokage (leader and protector of the Hidden Leaf Village). But every experience enriches him, and across the series' more than seven hundred episodes, Naruto never stops gathering wisdom and strength.

Naruto's narrative universe is stitched together by the logic of accrual. This is a quality *Naruto* and *Naruto: Shippûden* share with other Shōnen manga and anime such as *One Piece* (1999–present), *Hunter × Hunter* (2011–2014), and *My Hero Academia* (2014–present).[5] Like many heroic tales, these stories focus on growth in a narrative of becoming. But these Shōnen series are also unique because they do not compress this growth in an isolated training montage, as happens for instance in *Rocky* (1976), *The Karate Kid* (1984), *Dark City* (1998), *Mulan* (1998), *Kill Bill: Vol. 2* (2004), and *Batman Begins* (2005). Instead, they make the slow and arduous process of accrual a core part of their serialized narrative formats throughout, from beginning to end, and both in the background of other matters and as a dramatic focal point of its own.

This distinction also marks a key point of convergence between videogames and these principally narrative media. The experience of growth through accrual is a core logic of games, no matter the genre. For dozens or hundreds of hours per game, players scour their surroundings, defeat enemies and collect loot, peruse shops for new spells and magical trinkets, plunder treasure chests, toss Poké Balls at wild Pokémon, and, in so many other ways, gradually draw the world and its experiences inward, toward some perceived weakness or deficiency in the self. With the things they collect, players gain access to new places or improve their means of overcoming opposition so that collecting may persist unhindered. In the end, there is no place out of reach and no foe the player's party cannot handle. The promise of new discoveries orients play to the horizon, toward the next challenge, which hails players even when they aren't playing the game. After something especially useful has been acquired, there is a renewed confidence in the self, even if the next encounter had once seemed foreboding or hopeless.

I term the pursuit of such a pattern of experience through imagination and play a *fantasy of accretions*. To accrete is to grow by accumulation or coalescence. As a kind of coalescence, the term "accretion" evokes the imagery of many disparate things coming together to form one apparent whole. The fantasy of accretions is a wished-for wholeness that is staged by gathering separate things from the world into one place: the self, which seems to be unified in the process. While many different types of gathering would satisfy this broad description, I reserve the term "accretion" for what seems to fundamentally and permanently alter the self, changing some aspect of the process of accrual. The many hours of play motivated by this pattern of gathering is termed an "accretions project." This project is core to the role-playing game (RPG) and has become increasingly significant across every major game genre in recent years, from first-person shooters to strategy games, puzzle games, sports games, and even so-called casual games that are free to play.

Often, accretions projects mediate our first encounter with virtual characters and spaces, which can initially seem enchanted with possibility until emptied of their collectible contents, at which time they can seem depleted, meaningless, or merely material (polygonal). Accretions are also at the center of significant conversations about the cultural status of games—especially regarding questions about their relation to gambling, since accretions are part of a game's reward system, how it *motivates* playing by promising a burst of dopamine at the end of the maze or trial. Questions of motivation have always mattered for game design but are centrally important to free-to-play profit models that depend on a large player base's regular, daily engagement. In short, gaming has become a locus of intense interest for a fantasy of accretions.

In games with narrative progression, the accretions project is the province of heroes who, as Nintendo's Shigeru Miyamoto puts it, begin inauspiciously, "bound" and weak, but who gradually experience happiness and freedom (they "come untied") by leveling up, earning gold, and collecting items from the game's world.[6] Accretions fit well in narratives of becoming, which feature heroes of generally humble origins—youth interrupted. This is reflected in level 1 stats, mostly empty inventory screens, and the weakest items and equipment in the game. While there are always one or two enemies weaker than the level 1 hero, the world is big, and nearly everything is stronger.

It is a trope in such games for a premature encounter with a powerful villain to inaugurate the accretions project.[7] The fight the player cannot hope to win at (or near) the game's outset creates a kind of narcissistic scar in the Freudian sense, following the loss of one's perceived omnipotence. The sting from this moment orients play toward the imperative of shoring up weakness. By seeking manageable challenges, by exploring the wider world and connecting to its figures and spaces, by gathering what is good and storing it in the self, players prepare for *a trauma that has already come*.[8] In effect, becoming more powerful, more mobile, or less vulnerable—this gradual and nearly imperceptible process of becoming—is an overarching, long-term goal that fractures into dozens of more immediate goals, each of which can become connected to an array of granular, specific tasks, such as chopping blades of grass, opening chests, looting abandoned buildings, defeating enemies, mining ore, bombing weak points in walls, crafting items, spending gold at a shop, and so on. In the clearest possible application of goal-setting theory,[9]

You got the Super Hammer!
The attack Power of
Mario's Hammer increases!

Mario finds the Super Hammer upgrade in *Paper Mario* (2000). Not only will hammer attacks now do more damage, but Mario can also break stone blocks like the one currently obstructing the room's exit.

these small, specific, and concrete tasks can be resolved for immediate feedback. Small tasks come and go in a cascade of busy activity on the way to satisfying more abstract goals: the wider process of becoming that resists closure across the entire game.[10] Over and over, players traverse a circuitous path of expenditure, renewal, conflict, and accrual. We are caught up in a figurative loop—or, in the case of *Loop Hero* (2021), a literal one.

"Grip and Grind": Accretions as Game Design

Accretions projects in games take many forms that vary in the timing and predictability of their reward schedule as well as the nature of the reward. Traditional Japanese-style role-playing games (JRPG), such as Nintendo and Square's *Super Mario RPG* (1996), are linear and scripted.[11] In such games, players accrue more valuable items and gear as they progress further in the game's narrative. By contrast, "rogue-lite" games such as *Dead Cells* (2018), *Wizard of Legend* (2018), *Hades* (2020), or *Loop Hero* feature procedurally generated challenges and upgrade options that are determined largely by random number generation (RNG).[12] These games are meant to be played recursively, dozens or hundreds of times—each "run" will feel unique. Like rogue-lites, multiplayer online battle arena (MOBA) games like *League of Legends* (2009–present) are also iterative, so players begin their accretions quest anew each round of play. MOBAs are like JRPGs in that they offer accretions at regular intervals. *League of Legends* players can predict when they will level up and know in advance which upgrades they will purchase with accrued gold. In contrast, the Metroidvania-style game *Castlevania: Aria of Sorrow* (2003) utilizes variable reward ratios determined by RNG in the form of rare, special "drops" that emerge from defeated enemies a small percentage of the times they are defeated. For instance, in addition to contributing a bit of experience toward the next level-up, the common zombie enemy in *Aria of Sorrow* drops a cloth tunic about 3 percent of the times it is defeated. It drops a rarer dagger about 0.7 percent of the time. And the game's protagonist, Soma Cruz, can collect the enemy's soul 0.27 percent of the time he defeats it (Soma gains new abilities and becomes more powerful with each accrued soul).[13]

In the iOS action RPG *Mage Gauntlet* (2011), the accretions project may help motivate play, but each accretion's miniscule stat boost only marginally influences play's situation. Conversely, a minimalist, web-browser "idle clicker" game such as *Cookie Clicker* (2013) is little more than the process of accrual itself. *Cookie Clicker*'s core mechanic is attaining more cookies, which is achieved by simply clicking on an image of said baked good. One's accrued cookies can also be invested in upgrades that, in turn, generate larger numbers of cookies automatically (e.g., hiring grandmas who bake them in batches). Idle clickers have no explicit story and no clear spatial coordinates. They don't even really require a player. In fact, Jesper Juul has referred to these games as "zero-player games," which operate ambiently in the background without active player involvement.[14] Idle clicker games are accretions projects in the most abstracted and yet most direct sense. Everything is stripped away except the numbers—which unambiguously define the situation of play—and the experience they provide of expanding rates of accrual. The sense of reinforced expansion is apparently satisfying in its own right, regardless of genre, regardless of whatever other forms of motivation are present, regardless of whether the player is actively involved or just periodically checking in, and regardless of whether the game has complex graphical systems or is text based.

In game design terms, most accretions projects employ a one-sided, positive feedback loop. A positive loop is something that reinforces what's already happening: the more one gathers from the game in terms of gold, items, abilities, and so on, the better one will become at gathering. And the loop is one-sided in most single-player games because only success, not failure, is reinforced.[15] In other words, accretions projects impart optimism over the possibility of player success. Because they reinforce accrual itself, accretions are "intrinsically" motivating: they are their own reward. This also means that the accretion's value is confined to the space of the game and its systems, which invest it with a very specific, contextual meaning.[16] Because "extrinsic rewards" such as unlocking an achievement on one's PlayStation account do not affect the player's ability to accrue (they do not enter into a reinforcing loop), they are not included under the accretions heading, even though they may also motivate play (e.g., by providing social rewards or bragging rights).

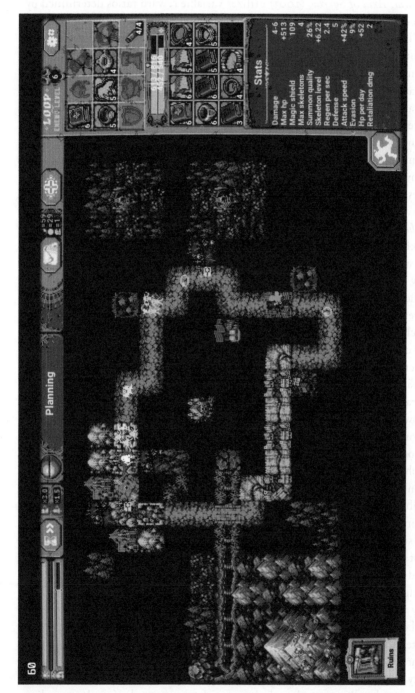

Self-reflexively traversing the loop in *Loop Hero* (2021). Rather than exploring new spaces, players accrue gear and fill in tiles around a circuitous path.

The fundamental optimism of an accretions project's one-sided, positive feedback loop seems rooted in tabletop wargame simulations. Jon Peterson's term for the process of becoming more powerful in tabletop role-playing is "stratified progression": "We say that systems that distinguish the relative power of units by assigning a hierarchical value like 'level' have the property of *stratification*, and that systems that allow units to advance in power exhibit the property of *progression*."[17] Perhaps most significant is Peterson's claim that in early wargames, circumstantial modifiers (such as progression) originally took the form of decay or debilitation: "Troops became shaken or surprised or tired as a consequence of combat," and so "armies grew weaker through fighting, rather than stronger, and the use of military power extracted an enormous cost even from the victor."[18] However, a contrasting perspective emerged in wargaming that drew on Napoleon's Imperial Guard, known as "les Grognards" or "the Grumblers" ("those so deep in Napoleon's counsel they could 'grumble' to the Emperor without fear of reprisal").[19] The idea that the Grognards' "experience as veterans made them more effective in combat than unseasoned units" is connected with a quote often attributed to Napoleon himself: that "moral power is to physical power in war as three parts out of four."[20] Along these lines, Peterson even evokes Nietzsche's famous assertion that "what does not overcome me makes me stronger."[21]

Peterson seems to view wargames as simulations for actual warfare, which limits the meanings attributed to circumstantial modifiers such as stratified progression. However, he does concede that these systems might go beyond mere correspondence with simulated phenomena; in addition, they may express distinct worldviews. For instance, he notes that systems of decay encapsulate a pacifist perspective by emphasizing war's debilitating effects.[22] Further, his reference to the Grognards suggests that progression might romanticize not only war but imperialist conquest as well. Indeed, Peterson quotes *Dungeons & Dragons* creator Gary Gygax at length for how the famed designer characterizes progression in terms of conquest. In the passage, Gygax praises a tabletop wargame from the 1960s whose "system of plundering and expending credits in an economy of ongoing conquest is a good example of progression: a system where repeated success in a game grants a player incremental bonuses that assist in achieving future victories against more formidable foes."[23] And despite the existence of historical alternatives in tabletop wargaming, digital games seem to have mostly inherited tabletop gaming's systems of plundering and economies of ongoing conquest.

As Alenda Chang points out, there have been very few experiments with decay (such as "de-leveling") in commercial digital games. Instead, digital games have tended to prefer one-way progression, "consequence-free play," and in the end have seemed complicit in the "mega-growth fantasies perpetuated on Wall Street at quarterly stockholder meetings, and in the councils of transnational trade organizations, not to mention the grocery store and the mall."[24] In other words, games still exemplify the "principle of unlimited good in American culture" that Gary Alan Fine has observed in the tendency of 1980s tabletop RPGs to endlessly restock dungeons with treasure so each adventurer's interest could be maintained.[25] Games have an established history, then, of extending what Žižek terms the "sociopolitical fantasy *par excellence*": "the myth of 'primordial accumulation'" or "the narrative of the two workers, one lazy and free-spending, the other diligent and enterprising, accumulating and investing, which provides the myth of the 'origins of capitalism,' obfuscating the violence of its actual genealogy."[26] There is a lot at stake in the observation that gaming's systems of one-way progression might help perpetuate a mythological view of the world as infinitely abundant and accommodating (to those who work at it). And by terming gaming's operative mind-set a *mega-growth fantasy*, Chang foregrounds commercial gaming's preference for wish fulfillment over direct depictions (simulations) of real-world phenomena.

While Chang's ecological approach to games problematizes the mega-growth wish, proponents of "gamification" have instead sought to preserve some version of this wish for its motivational power in other contexts, such as business and education (e.g., reframing banal tasks as games by building in points, badges, and achievements).[27] Gaming's power to motivate has long interested researchers, who have discovered that games usually offer multiple, overlapping motivations in game design—a "kitchen sink" approach.[28] Psychological studies of game motivation have applied frameworks such as self-determination theory,[29] Maslow's hierarchy of needs,[30] and Skinner's reinforcement theory to the problem. Burrhus Skinner has been especially relevant to research on the structure of rewards—whether, for instance, rewards come at fixed and predictable intervals, or else are variable (determined randomly) as with slot machine payouts. Indeed, when viewed strictly in terms of the neurotransmitter, dopamine— which is understood to be the chemical basis of motivational salience for nearly any pleasurable activity—digital games and slot machines are indistinguishable because the nature of the reward matters less than the timing and the manner in which it is doled out.

The conventional wisdom in the literature on psychology and games is that variable ratio reinforcements are the most motivating because the uncertainty of the payout creates a situation where the player is always on the verge of winning.[31] However, as Chris Bateman points out, before resorting to variable reward ratios, most accretions videogames are like animal trainers in that they first employ "escalating ratio schedules" where, for instance, the number of experience points required for a level-up steadily increases between each level.[32] Bateman refers to the anticipation of a reward like a level-up as "grip," and the tedious and repetitive activity the grip motivates as "grind." He acknowledges that videogames have long employed "grip and grind" to "directly target their players' reward centers" and that even by 2011 this had transcended major game genres.[33]

Viewing one-sided positive feedback loops as grip and grind shifts the apparent meaning in accretions games of the pursuit of mega-growth fantasies. Although games about gathering resources are usually set in naturalistic worlds (terrestrial or otherwise), they are perhaps more about *stimulating* than *simulating* (more about reward centers than mapping real-world ecologies). Put differently, the trope of unchecked growth seems to be a side effect of the need for progression, for perpetual activity, for the continuous activation of reward centers. For designers, the salient issue is not growth, realism, or ethical responsibility—it is the perpetuation of play. From the point of view of a designer like John Hopson, for instance, the problem with the continuous growth of fixed-ratio reward schedules (e.g., level-ups that occur on regular, predictable intervals) is simply that they introduce a "pause" in the flow of play's motivation. After attaining the level-up, the knowledge that the next payout is a long way off serves as a stopping point. Hopson's game design ethos seeks to introduce "other, less rewarding activities" during these pauses, encouraging players "to test a new tactic or try out different aspects of the game" instead of putting the controller down. In this way, games perpetually deny closure.[34] Hopson even advocates for games to encourage players to temporarily forget about the game's core motivational structure (the next big level-up) in order to simply remain somewhere (anywhere) within the game's overlapping patterns of reinforcement. Once one task is completed, two more open.

In this way, contemporary games are very aware of the tensions that players maintain and carry with them throughout play. Games epitomize the "Zeigarnik effect," which refers to the phenomenon where we tend to better recall details related to tasks when they remain incomplete—and that we tend to quickly forget or let go of these details once tasks are considered resolved. Jamie Madigan has applied this idea to quest structures in RPGs, and the "'just one more turn' effect where we can't seem to stop taking tiny, incremental steps toward completing some kind of structure, upgrade, technology, or conquest that we started 30 turns ago."[35] Free-to-play games often build delay mechanics into their design, denying the possibility of closing down core tasks for long periods of time (e.g., twenty-four hours). They might be thought of as a kind of dopamine ransom system that throttles a key resource unless the player opts for an in-game purchase.

Reward structures in games are tied to real economic relations in another way as well. Although Madigan's discussion of the Zeigarnik effect describes how game systems perpetually deny closure, every player has likely encountered a moment when the loops fail—when, as Bateman puts it, the "grip" loosens and the "grind" is revealed in its full tedium and pointlessness.[36] Rather than critique such moments as poor game design for allowing us to escape a game's sticky hooks (as game makers like Hopson or Bateman might), humanistic scholars have instead targeted such moments for revealing gaming's underlying ethos of exploitative labor practices, what Joyce Goggins terms "playbour" and Nick Yee a game's "labor of fun."[37] Yee notes the tendency of games, in their extreme repetition, to collapse apparent binaries between work and play. Similarly, Scott Rettberg has argued that the quest structures in games such as *World of*

Warcraft exemplify "the contemporary world's most popular ideology, market capitalism."[38]

As Alharthi and colleagues argue, idle-clicker or zero-player games such as *Cookie Clicker* seem to undermine the playbour argument by sidelining the corporeal hinge of the work-play analogy: the player's own body.[39] A game's reinforcing loops, its stratified progression, and its grip and grind seize us whether we play or others do, and whether human agency is on display or AI bots square off in the periphery of our attention. Grip and grind operate even in a nearly brainless state where agency has been overtly supplanted by sheer repetition. As the IGN *Nintendo Voice Chat* podcast puts it in a description of *Castlevania: Aria of Sorrow*, a game with a strong accretions system (featuring both stratified progression and variable ratio reinforcements), "If you've got that sort of brain-dead part at the back of your head that can run in and out of a room for a half an hour, while you're listening to a podcast, like this one, and slash bats or fight a mummy until he drops a card . . . , you'll love this game."[40] Running in and out of a room for thirty minutes for a rare drop is not *flow* play—it does not balance skill and challenge.[41] It is pure tedium. But it does not feel that way. Grinding is not alienating in a Marxist sense either. It is almost meditative, a form of concentration and harmony with the body, even if the task is not challenging in a technical or mechanical sense. One can so optimize the dance of in-and-out-of-room movement that, if not careful, it is possible to miss the rare drop when it does finally occur by reflexively exiting the room to reset the spawn once again.

What a motivations-based approach to game design helps clarify is that repetitious grinding in a game—an activity intimately related to reward ratios and schedules of reinforcement—seems better compared to casino gambling than office work. The point is not the production of a good that somehow holds some objective, independent value. Rather, what is generated each time the mere potential for reward is evoked is raw pleasure (dopamine)—and the player, the one eagerly undertaking the repetitive task, immediately consumes this pleasure. Though accretions play's mind-numbing repetition may resemble Fordist factory labor, its product is not capable of abstraction from the "labor" that has generated it. When the reward (accretion) finally comes in the form of that rare drop, it is intrinsically meaningful only in terms of the effort to win it. The accretion directly impinges upon and somehow modifies the terms of player efforts (e.g., by extending the capacity to move through space and transcend opposition—capacities the player hones while seeking accretions).

Certainly, the time involved in pursuing an accretions quest also holds extrinsic value as well. And so what is leisure for one can be another's work. There exist exploitative labor relations such as gold farming in online games like *World of Warcraft* where accretions are treated as goods for exchange in real-world economies.[42] Buying into the game in this manner might be criticized as missing the point of accretions play. Short-circuiting the accretions project by beginning with an end-game character would mean playing some other game, one that is especially socially mediated. In the game's own terms, hundreds of play hours purchased are not tantamount to the sum total of the enjoyment that might have been had in that play, as if it were directly transferrable through the things that play produced.

It is likely that thinking about accretions projects as a fantasy loop orients one away from both the work-play analogy and bare-bones neurobiological explanations as well.[43] Such approaches are helpful in their own way, but they tend to ignore videogame textuality—the key contexts of character, setting, theme, and even game genre that frame and intersect with any videogame's reward schedules. An accretions fantasy solders the rewards schedule to the rest of the game's world. In effect, the "brain-dead" lever pulling of accretions games is only half of a dual fantasy process. On one hand, players can participate even when reduced to *zero*, when the game plays itself. We share in the evacuation of tension, in the pleasure of acquiring an upgrade and crossing it off our list. In this sense, the fantasy of accretions is similar to Freud's notion of death drive, a push toward closure and the release of all tension. On the other hand, accretions play entails constant interruption and the avoidance of closure. Its to-do lists are endlessly repopulated by the allure of the *next* accretion in an extended process of becoming.[44] Of course, this accretion is hidden somewhere remote and dangerous, but we pursue it with optimism and secure it with elation. Accretions play is a whirlwind of busy activity that covers over and disavows the gradual pursuit of stability or quiescence—an inorganic state where nothing can harm us. This observation is key to thinking of accretions as a core fantasy opening onto a range of questions about videogame textuality, including how accretions intersect with other play fantasies in games as well as how they might be thought to connect with other media.

"What Is Dead May Never Die": The Body Displaced by Arms (and Shadows of Growth)

Accretions quests seem to exemplify the Freudian notion of the "Nirvana principle," the term, as Laplanche and Pontalis put it, Freud uses "to denote the tendency of the psychical apparatus to reduce the quantity of excitation in itself, whether of internal or of external origin, to zero—or, failing that, to as low a level as possible."[45] Freud equates the Nirvana principle with the "principle of constancy," which also seeks to maintain homeostasis, but with the key difference that the Nirvana principle is more closely tied to the death drive by preferring where possible to "reduce excitation to zero-point."[46] The connections games share with the principle of constancy are perhaps more clearly perceived than those shared with the ominous death drive. Laplanche and Pontalis identify three distinct ways constancy is achieved in Freud's energic model of the psychic apparatus: "through *discharge* of the energy already present" in a system, "by *avoidance* of whatever might increase the quantity of excitation and *defence* against any such increase that does occur."[47] Discussions of this model often draw the clearest examples from reflexive corporeal responses to external and internal stimuli: if the sun is bright, we shield our eyes; if there is an itch, we scratch it.

One could just as easily imagine its application to an accretions-based game such as *Valheim* (2021), a recent, Nordic-themed survival game where players gather materials from the environment and craft protective armor and weapons so they may venture into more dangerous places (where valuable crafting materials lie in wait). *Valheim*'s geographic regions or "biomes" are procedurally situated at the start of play, but progression through each follows a predetermined path. Thus, while exploring, players will encounter dangerous places before they are prepared. They may wander into the swamp and become disoriented by its dark and foggy atmosphere or stuck and poisoned in its soggy terrain; they may sustain continuous frost damage by climbing into the frigid mountain biome without fur-lined armor; or they may suffer a "deathsquito" bite (which is instantly lethal) if they are unlucky enough to cross into the plains biome without silver-plated armor. Dying in *Valheim* means losing a portion of core stats (de-leveling), dropping all equipped gear and accrued materials on the spot, and respawning back in home base; as with *Dark Souls*, dying introduces a new tension to play: the need to return to that dangerous place where one fell. Unlike *Dark Souls*, players must make this return trip without the supplies, gear, and weapons dropped in death. In other words, in death, a tether fantasy temporarily interrupts the game's accretions project. In terms of the Freudian principle of constancy, retrieving one's gear after death would exemplify a *discharge* of tensions already present. Of course, *avoidance* would have been preferred: players likely hope to keep a healthy distance from swamp, mountain, and plains biomes until they can mount a proper *defense* (a strong shield can absorb a head-on death-squito strike, strong armor can help survive a back-stab). Playing *Valheim* means seeking in the most dangerous places the precious metals used to build protective gear and weapons—risking life and limb while chipping, gathering, and then carrying this booty across the ocean, beset by sea monsters that threaten to send your entire haul to the murky depths. If successful, the next outing will be that much more assured, the monster's bite less harsh.

Accretions serve a homeostatic function by rendering the player's character less susceptible to shocks. They permanently reduce in piecemeal fashion the strength of whatever *quantity of excitation* crops up in play: whatever threatens, inhibits, or stands in the way. The difficult enemy, the dangerous biome, and the inaccessible but visible passageway: each produces a tension that players must carry along until the moment of accretion that permits release. Usually bit by bit, but sometimes all at once, those tensions are irreversibly "mastered" or "bound," to use Freud's language, stripped once and for all of their power to affect the player.[48] The accretion may mean dealing a bit more or suffering a bit less damage per attack, or else may provide additional options for responding to threats. A change of a couple of points of damage per attack in an RPG may seem negligible, but, in frequently repeated encounters, small differences add up. Learning a new skill such as Healing β in *Earthbound* (which heals the same status afflictions as a Refreshing Herb, but without occupying limited inventory space) means exploration can continue apace even when multiple party members suffer the poison status effect far from a town or hospital. Accretions change how players encounter and move through space—especially spaces that are dangerous or unknown. In other words, accretions *consume* tethers. They are won by casting light on the darkness and clearing it of threats. By armoring the body, it is as if the hero has become their own secure base. Late in many accretions projects, if players must return to an area from the start of the game, standard foes and obstacles that had once slowed the player or posed a challenge can usually be cut through in an instant; if the enemies do manage to land an attack, it will rebound off the hero's diamond-plated skin.

As the trope of armoring the body in RPGs makes explicit, accretions offer a glimpse of the fabled return to an inorganic state, to what Catherine Malabou describes as "the nonliving and the nondying" that temporally surrounds life as "its past and its future, its before and its after."[49] Malabou is referencing Freud's notion of conservative instincts that labor to restore "an earlier state of things."[50] Freud imagines a fragile organism that would "from its very beginning have had no wish to change," but which would have been forced to adapt to its environment for survival.[51] Harsh external stimuli would cause the organism's outer shell to become hardened, "baked through," forming a "protective shield against stimuli."[52] A stimulus shield would help sustain life by protecting the organism from the trauma of external intrusions—"By its death, the outer layer has saved all the deeper ones from a similar fate."[53] However, with each such adaptive modification, Freud's imagined organism would retain the same "conservative" wish to "return to the inanimate state" before life had begun and before all those difficult modifications became necessary.[54] For Freud, this wish expresses the trend of the death instincts, "whose aim is to conduct the restlessness of life into the stability of the inorganic state."[55] The inorganic represents life material emptied of all its tensions. One might imagine, for instance, the continuation of that external layer's *baking through* until no living, vulnerable interior remained.

When acted out, the accretions fantasy concretizes Freud's death instinct. This does not necessarily mean the person playing an accretions game—or even the person who plays such games on a daily basis—wishes for death. By always extending and complicating this return to the stability of inorganic matter, accretions play also seems to function as the opposite of a death wish, as death's forestallment. It pursues many "detours" en route to its conclusion, much as Freud suggests each organism prefers "to die only in its own fashion."[56] Slavoj Žižek captures this accretions dynamic most fully when he discusses a "precipitous identification" with the *symbol of death*, something that represents death but also *outlives* it: "By assuming a symbolic identity, i.e., by identifying myself with a symbol which is potentially my epitaph, I as it were 'outpass myself into death.'

However, this precipitation toward death at the same time functions as its oppo-site; it is designed to forestall death, to assure my posthumous life in the sym-bolic tradition which will outlive my death—an obsessive strategy, if there ever was one: in an act of precipitous identification *I hasten to assume death in order to avoid it.*"[57]

Some games explicitly position their accretions play as a conservative wish to return to a prior state. For example, consider the trope of heroes who lose their armor and abilities at the game's outset. When a fiery blast knocks Samus Aran's systems offline in *Metroid Prime* (2002) or when Death confiscates Alucard's belongings near the start of *Castlevania: Symphony of the Night* (1997), both heroes must venture into a dangerous world underprepared. As if split in half by Zeus himself, the heroes of these games must search for special objects that promise to restore an idealized, prior self.[58] Indeed, as with Lacan's mirror stage, the initial taste of power at the game's outset—before the armor was stripped way—is akin to a misrecognition that creates a gap between an idealized memory and a difficult reality. Closing this gap motivates play. But if Samus Aran's shiny armor is like a mirror (in the Lacanian sense), it does not simply reflect an ideal-ized image of the player. Rather, it captures the entire virtual world Samus tra-verses. This world defines her through opposition. The self that is gradually rebuilt in accretions play enjoys a harmonious relationship with the world. Its pieces (the accretions) are situated at the world's farthest reaches and must be gradually drawn inward. And reconstituting this self means negating this world's tensions and inhibitions, realizing how Samus and the world fit together as one.

While picturing the threshold to life itself leads Freud to the image of micro-scopic organisms with stimulus shields, Otto Rank's modified death drive (the compulsion to return to the womb) refers to something more directly accessible to perception. Like with Samus's armor in the beginning of *Metroid Prime*, Rank situates the experience of Nirvana not in an imagined state before and after life but rather as something we supposedly experience (in the womb) and then spend our lives imaginatively recapturing. Rank's theories about womb imagery tie the Freudian death drive to a charged set of images, to themes of "heroic *invulnerabil-ity*" in fiction or mythology that evoke "a kind of permanent uterus, which the hero brings with him into the world as armour, horny skin or helmet (magic hood), but which still betrays in the single mortal place, as, for example, Achilles' heel, how strongly even the hero was once purely physically attached to the mother."[59]

Rank would likely see accretions games as a means of reassembling the womb armor, piece by piece, working in imagination to negate or cover up that "single mortal place," which is also the place that marks our attachment to (or depen-dence upon) others. And yet, even for Rank, the trope of armoring is tinged with death's imagery. Rank begins his book with an epigraph that evokes the tempo-rality of the nonliving and nondying: the story of when King Midas asks the wise Silenus "What is the very best and the most preferable thing for Man?" and

Death takes Alucard's gear at the entrance to Dracula's castle in *Castlevania: Symphony of the Night* (1997), inaugurating the game's accretions project.

Silenus responds that as a "miserable, ephemeral species, children of chance and of hardship," the "very best is quite unattainable . . . it is not to be born, not to exist, to be Nothing," and "the next best for you is—to die soon."[60] The passage, from Nietzsche, is ostensibly about the hardships of living,[61] but its meaning for Rank speaks more directly to the womb's maintenance of excitation at a "zero-point"—a state awaiting us after death as well (the coffin is like a womb too). Rank's use seems echoed in George R. R. Martin's *A Clash of Kings* (1999), the second novel in his epic fantasy series that inspired HBO's *Game of Thrones* (2011–2019), when the ironborn (of the Iron Islands) honor the Drowned God and repeat, "What is dead may never die—but rises again, harder and stronger"—a sentiment accompanying the severe religious rite of a baptism in which the servant is held underwater until they drown and is then reborn stronger and fearless ("with salt," "with stone," "with steel") if they revive on the shore.[62] Such imagery would repeat for Rank the trauma of birth—a trauma that exceeds all others. Life in this sense is a disruption of what Zygmunt Bauman terms death's "eternal suspension."[63] Bauman views death as a "perverse victory over bankruptcy," as a way to help preserve ("cryonize") certain hopes against reality.[64]

The preceding discussion of the death that is in life has subtly shifted the meaning of a fantasy of accretions. At first, death was located *behind* the wish to reduce excitation to a zero-point—Žižek's precipitous identification (to *hasten to assume death in order to avoid it*). But Bauman's notion of *eternal suspension* moves closer to something like André Bazin's *mummy complex*, the wish to preserve life from death such as by recording it on film or, more recently, in fantasies about downloading consciousness into a computer. Like with the ancient Egyptians, death's imagery gathers around the wish to preserve life.

An accretion in a digital game moves us closer to that reconstituted womb armor, and at the same time it assumes the qualities of eternal suspension. In this way, the fantasy speaks less to temporary power-ups, such as those in *Super Mario Bros.* games, than to items that, once gathered, remain always in the player's possession. A temporary power-up (e.g., the Starman) is an additional tension: we must enact new rules while also remembering the old ones, anticipating the moment when the status quo resumes (and we are no longer invulnerable). Each accretion, on the other hand, is a permanent discharge of tension for the game's duration. Once players acquire the Leap Stone in *Castlevania: Symphony of the Night*, they will subsequently *always* be able to double-jump and so better outmaneuver enemies as well as reach some previously inaccessible areas on the map. Once it becomes our own, we can feel confident in this power, in its preservation—safe enough to install it in muscle memory as a new manner of moving through game space. At the same time, we can let go of the old way of moving, as well as the memory of all those barely unreachable ledges we had carried with us—once we finally reach them, they become like *any other ledge*. For the armored and well-equipped hero, the world's spatial tensions and hardships begin to relent. We no longer need to recall an enemy's attack pattern when we can bowl them over without thinking.

The pervasive videogame trope of wearing armor, weapons, or other gear gathered from a game's virtual spaces can also be productively tied to Hal Foster's historically and culturally specific study of the "(proto)fascist ideal, forged in the aftermath of World War I, of the male body become weapon"—the "soldierly body."[65] Foster pathologizes the fascist "obsession with the body as armor" where armor serves as a prosthesis "to shore up a disrupted body image or to support a ruined ego construction."[66] This characterization draws on Klaus Theweleit's argument that proto-fascists have not developed a stable ego in the Freudian sense (built from the inside out), but have instead been forced to "'grow' a functioning and controlling body armor, and a body capable of seamless fusion into larger formations with armorlike peripheries."[67] Theweleit considers whether "the armor of these men may be seen as constituting their ego" due to the effects of a "society that replaces the experiences of pleasure in the body with its experience of pain": "Drill and torture . . . I feel pain, therefore I am."[68] Foster riffs on the word "hypertrophy," as in the overdeveloped, muscular male body—noting that the first definition of "trophy" is "arms etc. of a vanquished enemy" and that "in the trophy the body is displaced by arms; death renders it so much armor."[69] There may be no more apt description for most accretions projects in digital games than as the vanquishing of enemies for trophies, for arms (the body rendered armor by death), which the player then stores and equips as their sense of self also becomes hypertrophied and, like Foster's masculine ego, is gradually replaced by armor.

Foster's argument about the hypertrophied masculine ego (replaced by armor) is provocative and seemingly appropriate for a discussion of a masculinized gamer culture and its "dreamt-of metalization of the human body."[70] However, the historical and cultural specificity of this work limits its applicability to contemporary digital games.[71] Moreover, it is important to resist reflexively pathologizing accretions play. On its own, seeking out accretions is not equivalent to using armor as Foster says, "in lieu of a formed ego"—even if we imagine games to be a key contemporary formation of this process.[72]

Contra the ego that is shattered and will never develop, accretions games might find a better analogy in the temporal delay inherent to the ego that is *not quite formed yet*. Roger Caillois frames such an image in terms of the childhood game of accruing and hiding secret "treasures": odds and ends gathered from the peripheries of the adult world (e.g., pieces of foil, glass stoppers, old coins, etc.). As Caillois observes, these objects enable their collectors to imagine going "beyond what is normally possible: . . . to disappear at will, to paralyze from a distance, to subdue without a struggle, to read thoughts, and to be carried in an instant wherever you want to go."[73] Caillois imagines children projecting their egos into these hidden treasures and then stowing them away safely (e.g., in a cavity behind the wallpaper, or "behind three, or even four, false fronts"), a game aiding the fantasy that "the life, the power, and the courage of the hero is fastened to an external and material soul: a weapon or a mirror, a feather or an egg; to some magnificent or humble but always fragile object, guarded in the crook of a tree or locked in a sunken vessel, in a place not easy to recognize or reach."[74]

In a formulation that feels especially appropriate for the scalar fluctuations of accretions play, Caillois situates accrued treasures as "intermediaries" for the child's ego, which may not yet feel itself "on the same scale as [the] environing world."[75] The adult world's mysterious and harsh approbations present their own tensions (wounds to omnipotence) which children at play may wish to discharge or defend against. In Caillois's sense, at least, this is less a drive toward constancy than a wish to grow up. By hiding treasured objects away, the child "tempers his spirit and is enabled to safeguard, with a little secret, the source and warrant of his future strength."[76] In Caillois's sense, then, accretions would be like a child's treasured objects—"sudden bursts of splendor" that are "brilliant, rare, difficult to acquire," and that ameliorate the feeling of not being at scale with one's environing world.[77] In this model, one invests a piece of oneself in an accrued object, which then assumes a magical aura like a talisman. Rather than covering the body with armor, what is vulnerable is projected outward and then hidden away, cached.

One can detect echoes of Caillois's formulation in perhaps the most famous narrative accretions quest: Voldemort's "horcruxes" (magical objects that house part of his soul) from the *Harry Potter* book series (1997–2000, 2003, 2005, 2007). In plot, the horcruxes—which can prevent Voldemort from dying—represent a reverse-accretions quest; the heroes' desperate task is to undo Voldemort's accrual by seeking and destroying each magical object. Whether intentionally or not, it is likely that both Caillois and J. K. Rowling draw from the same Norwegian fairy tale, "The Giant Who Had No Heart in His Body," about a giant who could not be killed because his only vulnerability (his heart) was hidden inside a duck egg, which was, itself, hidden within layers of obfuscation, depending on the version of the story: for example, in a nest, which is in a church on an island, in the middle of a lake. The hero finds the egg and bargains with the giant to release those he has trapped. The giant complies, but the hero still crushes the egg, killing the giant. Phebe Cramer discusses this story as an example of the concept of projection or "placing parts of oneself within another . . . demonstrated when the attack on the duck results in pain to the giant."[78] Perhaps the impulse to gather a treasured object and stow it away so that it protects one from harm has become an archetypal pattern repeated in fables and popular fiction.[79]

Like Caillois's hidden treasure play, the fantasy of accretions in digital games is driven by the *warrant of future strength*. Delay is a central rather than incidental part of this drive. Accretions play is about growing stronger, but never about *being* powerful—it is an activity always oriented toward the *next* accretion. The fantasy cannot conceive of endings (there is no final accretion), only suspensions and repetitions (e.g., beginning a new round or a new game). This is explicitly reflected in the looping, recursive structure, and thematic interest in escaping death and rebirth cycles in rogue-lite games such as *Dead Cells* and *Hades*. As these examples attest, growth through accretions play is a shadow of growth. It is *queer* growth—the sort that Kathryn Bond Stockton connects to childhood because children are not permitted to *grow up* until adults say so (instead, they grow *sideways*). Stockton draws on Derrida's notion of the delay built into the act of reading in order to think about the future orientation of a child's identity, "where meaning is delayed, deferred, exactly because we read in sequence, go forward in a sentence, not yet knowing what words are ahead of us, while we must take the words we have passed with us as we go, making meaning wide and hung in suspense."[80] Contra Freud, Stockton sees the death drive as a sort of "negative capability," as the *maintenance* of tension, not its evacuation—as long as this tension is not reproductive (not based in Freud's notion of Eros).[81] Children exemplify this sort of queer death drive for Stockton. They are "moving suspensions and shadows of growth" who "[locate] energy, pleasure, vitality, and (e)motion in the back-and-forth connections and extensions that are not reproductive."[82]

This is perhaps the most apt expression for accretions play: a precipitous identification with a symbol of death (the body become armor) that is suspended across dozens of hours of unexpected encounters, detours, and side quests—the asymptotic process of *becoming*. To play an accretions game is to play in sequence, go forward on a virtual path, not yet knowing what challenges lie ahead, while needing to take past experiences and the treasures we have won with us as we go, making play (and its meanings) "wide and hung in suspense." Accretions games may make us feel especially useful, offering a glimpse of what it will mean to grow up to full stature, all the while experiencing the "blissful productivity" that Jane McGonigal identifies in digital games ("the sense of being deeply immersed in work that produces immediate and obvious results").[83] However, there is generally nothing gained from that final, Oedipal encounter with the game's central antagonist. Players do not generally *become* the villains they unseat. There is no ending to an accretions project—just new beginnings, new games, new tensions to sustain.

Identification in Accretions Games

Each chapter in this book considers distinct approaches to the question of identification in games and related narrative media. Its fantasy traditions both draw from but also offer new formulations of Laplanche and Pontalis' notion of fantasy as a "scenario with multiple entries" (i.e., fantasy's peculiar "absence of subjectivization").[84] Fantasy is flexible enough to capture a range of positions media consumers may adopt in relation to a text—it can accommodate some of the instability, for instance, that Adrienne Shaw sees in a player's relationship to textual "identifiers" (e.g., gender, sexuality, racial identity, and so on).[85] Fantasy normalizes the idea that a reader, spectator, or player may adopt multiple, contradictory subject positions at once. Corollary to this is the notion that any part of the text may serve as a point of entry—a videogame's avatar is just one term among many. The fantasy of accretions at times involves becoming invested in the powerful image of the avatar herself (e.g., Samus Aran's shiny, phallic armor so clearly intended as a fetishistic object of contemplation); at other times, accretions games minimize focus on the avatar, if one exists at all (e.g., *Sword & Poker*, *Slay* [1995]); and the fantasy seems capable of operating even without the player's own active participation (e.g., *Cookie Clicker*, or "afk" activities players can automate, such as fishing or traveling to a distant vendor in *Black Desert Online* [2015–present]).

As the term implies, "zero-player games" such as *Progress Quest* (2002) are often understood to cut the player entirely out of the gameplay process—or to at least minimize player involvement by operating autonomously in the background of other activities. But if accretions games are understood to give expression to a Freudian death drive, then it might be more precise to say that what they obviate is the player's *ego*, their sense of self. Freud's understanding of the vicissitudes of psychic life affords little space for our fragile egos, which are assailed on one side by intense drives (or representations of bodily needs) and on the other by the superego, that agent of guilt and conscience cobbled together from internalized authority figures. If we break off the most vulnerable part of our ego and project it into an external object (e.g., a treasure we stow away in an accretions game), then are we not necessarily split apart as a result? Does such a game situate us in the position of the invulnerable protector of that special cache, or else as the frail thing that gets hidden away—the thing writhing on the ground that Harry Potter and his own internalized authority figure (Dumbledore) pity near the end of *Harry Potter and the Deathly Hallows* (2007)?

The two halves of accretions play's split or ambivalent identification seem captured in the helpful distinction Kaja Silverman emphasizes between "idiopathic" (or "interiorizing") and "heteropathic" (or "exteriorizing") identification. In the former, one controls and draws an identification inward: the object of identification is consumed (incorporated, but also destroyed), its otherness and our relation to it through identification are both disavowed; in the latter, one's own sense of self is exteriorized, "overwhelmed and hypnotically bound and fettered by the other," an ecstatic (masochistic) loss of self.[86] In the accretions fantasy, it seems that the avatar-player relationship could be "heteropathic," on the model of the giant's heart hidden in the duck's egg. In this sense, playing an accretions game would mean exteriorizing feelings of vulnerability or anxiety in an external object—either the avatar, or else an empty inventory screen—and then working to shore up this weakness through play. The avatar may be a potent signifier of accrued powers, as the place where accretions are assembled (interiorized), but the marginal changes each accretion introduces take effect at the avatar's own margins, at their interface with the world. Accretions are felt when enacted. And so our interest is anchored in these moments that put into play some piecemeal improvement, the source of which is usually anchored elsewhere: on the edges of the playfield, such as in a menu the player consults during a pause.

In accretions games, any response to losing one's fragile "self" in a heteropathic identification is framed by the promise of restoration. So, the world of an accretions game seems to serve an idiopathic identification as well, at least in the sense that it exists for player consumption. The *Mega Man* games of the late 1980s and 1990s exemplify this idea, as Mega Man even somewhat resembles the foes he has destroyed and absorbed, as if identified with them while using their powers. Rarely in any accretion game is care taken to provide motivation in plot for the player's ability to ransack and plunder any space, public or private, or to take any power and make it their own without remorse. The metaphor of destroying by consuming that Silverman evokes for thinking of idiopathic identification (characteristic of Freud's oral phase of psychosexual development) is apt since the accretion is like a last stop on the road to oblivion. As Julian Stallabrass notes of many games, "Objects when captured or destroyed may become, at the moment of their extinction, a floating number."[87] The number—this ghostly after-image of the videogame object—reflects destruction through consumption. In the assumed ethos of most accretions games, the "good" we claim as our own is closely stitched to the "bad," which must be destroyed to progress. It is standard that fallen foes surrender a chunk of experience at the moment of their extinction (a floating number) and even that their corpses can subsequently be looted for rare gear and valuable items (the stronger the enemy, the better the loot). *Divinity: Original Sin II* (2017) takes this process one step further in that players can additionally choose to *consume* the "source" (aka spiritual essence or soul) of a fallen adversary. The result is an especially severe illustration of how moving through an accretions quest often means sifting the world into the *accreted* and the *excreted*: players gain a source point (for casting powerful spells) and leave behind a pile of bones and viscera on the ground.

Perhaps deciding how accretions games position their players requires thinking about the structure of collecting itself.[88] There is significance in how an object becomes "reframed as collectible"—meaning, as Brenda Danet and Tamar Katrial put it, how an object is made "a potential member of a category of objects" that can become part of a collection.[89] Framing is not necessarily the same thing as *reframing*, the latter of which for Danet and Katrial emphasizes the special value of objects that collectors organize into a new, more selective context (e.g., collections of rare postal stamps). When it comes to collection quests in digital games, the player's stake is established early on by how the game *itself* reframes— and so isolates and elevates as collectable—certain parts of its wider storehouse of objects. Collection quests can be initiated, their collectable objects specified, by a number of devices, including cinematic cutscenes, action commands that suddenly appear on-screen such as "investigate" or "pick up," a telltale twinkle (e.g., the diamond-in-the-rough effect of *Dark Souls*), or merely by convention.

Jill Rettberg notes the quest "syntax" of *World of Warcraft* includes "quest-giver, background story, objectives, rewards."[90] Within such a syntax—common to many RPGs—one can discern both *collectable* (reward) and *framing* devices (quest-giver, background, and objective),[91] though the latter devices rarely frame the collectable in quite the same manner as the accretion system itself (the whole of which each accretion is a part). The accrued item can either pass into the player's possession with no notice at all, or else may be marked by the game with much fanfare. Either way, as Danet and Katrial point out, collecting is a "future-oriented activity," an "agenda for future action" that one plans "for oneself."[92] Collecting is fundamentally optimistic—one has a future in it. Collecting speaks explicitly and directly to the player's agency, to what is within reach. Ultimately, reframing something as collectible speaks to the collector at the heart of every collection.

Any accretion in a digital game may be viewed as a special part of a larger collection of objects or abilities. Many games encourage this by giving accretions unique names (e.g., the Varia Suit in *Metroid Dread* [2021]), tying them to specific, in-game objects, effects, and special affordances, and hiding each in a specific place (often right after a memorable boss fight). Some games even offer bonus stats for wearing each item in a set at once (a set bonus).[93] In these cases, each accrued item forms part of a whole (a set) but resists being reduced to that whole.

The alternative case—where a numerical amalgam absorbs and dissolves each individual accretion into a running total—can be found in the leveling systems of most RPGs. Level-ups often simply elevate some of the player's core stats, which accumulate over time as a stable quantity. What matters is not the level itself (each is soon replaced by the next) but the difference *between* levels. This difference represents a numerically defined experience of growth. Numbers are part of a closed, rational system of signification predicated on difference (like language or mathematics), what Freud calls a *secondary system*. Normally such systems are understood to offer us control but also to "dampen down the affective and sensory appeal" of the world.[94] But this is not always the case. We can, at times, invest a secondary term—a number, a key stat, for instance—"with all the affective and sensory intensity" of a beloved object in the world.[95] Someone who has not played a game with stratified progression may think of level designations as arbitrary or artificial (purely symbolic). But players come to understand these differences viscerally. Key scores and metrics can carry the full force of our involvement in a game if such numbers specify a crucial aspect of the situation of play (with the precision and finality that numerical distinctions offer). We learn to both fear and avoid the level 15 foe that our level 12 party cannot yet defeat in an open-world RPG.

Becoming invested in the process of accrual in an implicit, embodied manner involves what might be termed *numerical specularization*, an identification with numbers—the scores, metrics, levels, and so on—that define one's situation in play. These are not necessarily the numbers that underlie and codify a digital game's rules or systems but rather the numbers presented at the level of enunciation, in the game's very images and as an explicit part of play: health meters, ability levels, mana costs, damage indicators, cooldown timers, power bars, and so on. Such numbers often appear on the heads-up display or in menus and so tend to work against any cinematic illusion of depth employed by a game. The accretions quest represents a special kind of numerical specularization, an identification with the numbers that represent and encapsulate growth.

In psychoanalytic theory, specularization very roughly means an identification with one's mirror image.[96] In numerical specularization, we identify with a modified projection that is significantly abstracted from our flesh-and-blood bodies. This projection is especially enticing because its growth is undeniable, expressed as part of a unified, closed system—something external, stable, and incontrovertible. Accretions benefit from the specificity offered by numeric systems—as Stallabrass observes of games: "Measured by number, self-improvement is always unambiguous."[97] Or, as Roger Caillois puts it, rule-bounded games "are played *for real. As if* is not necessary."[98] This distinction is helpful when thinking about projection as a way of expressing a difficult truth about ourselves by attaching that truth to something *external* that we encounter in the world. Doing so enables an active and constructive response. Numbers in an accretions game may form part of an abstract, symbolic system. But the relations between their terms are real and capable of being put into play as the place where we store what we have won, measure what we hope to become, and slowly cover over that single mortal place. The notion of projection reminds us that our subjective boundaries extend beyond our literal bodies and can include certain people and objects from the world, even when those things do not belong to our consciously acknowledged self. Though accretions play focuses on covering over feelings of vulnerability, we do occasionally catch necessary glimpses of our mortal and finite self reflected in the game—in the consumable resource we deplete, in the door we cannot open, or even in the *smallness* of the individual accretion, that tiny change that makes our ears perk up. New accretions always occasion another glance in this mirror. We are like Oscar Wilde's Dorian Gray, apparently untouched by forces external or internal (immune even to time itself), when really our vulnerable and finite self is registered elsewhere, the object at the heart of our collection.

Conclusion

● ●

Surface Narratives and the
Contrivance of Fantasy

When I began thinking about games as assemblages of distinct but interrelated fantasy processes, such as tethers and accretions, the best examples seemed to be role-playing games where players venture into the field, face adversity, and retreat to a safe space (campsite or village) to take stock of what their efforts have won: gold, experience points, new equipment, and so on. By drawing accretions in, the hero's tether (their ability to venture into dangerous spaces from a point of safety) is modified and capable of stretching farther. The burgeoning stats and crowded inventory screens in these games help illustrate how tethers become gilded by accretions; in turn, the requirement to leave safety and face new enemies in unfamiliar places demonstrates how the pursuit of stability of an accretions quest is repeatedly disrupted by a tether's extension.

One might view such patterns as the stuff of games and as distinct from the stuff of stories. But of course these fantasies appear in stories as well. And even in their most gamic moments, it is possible to think of these patterns or loops as telling their own slow and repetitive stories about stretching out, encountering threats, and recovering to safety—and about gradually gaining confidence in the self. Henry Jenkins and Mary Fuller suggest that most videogames are made up of two distinct narratives. For instance, in 1990s-era side-scrolling *Mario* games, there is of course the stated motive for adventure: "a quest to free the Mushroom Princess from the evil Koopa" (as the instruction booklet for *Super Mario Bros.* puts it). But there is also an underlying narrative—the endlessly extendable spatial story that play itself tells about pushing toward the edge of the screen as if it were the frontier of exciting new worlds. Jenkins and Fuller hint at a kind of ludonarrative dissonance (a tension between story and gameplay), but as an incongruity between the two story layers within a single game.

Jenkins and Fuller implicitly hierarchize their narrative layers—one is apparent at a glance, the other *underlies* the first and is available only to those who play. The first is shallow, problematic, and quickly forgotten during play—the other becomes a key motivating factor throughout (apparently, we never tire of it). In truth, the meanings games contain are located somewhere in the relationship between the two story layers—a relationship that varies from game to game. And there is not necessarily always discord there. The surface and underlying narratives can also resonate with one another, such as when tethers stretch across both (e.g., *Gone Home* [2013], *Subnautica* [2018], or *Dying Light* [2015]). The relationship between apparent and underlying (aka fantasy) narratives is a site of active experimentation.

One tendency that does seem to emerge from the interplay of these layers is *contrivance*. Contrivance can refer to an ingenious act of invention or scheming as well as to an adaptation of means to some end, such as in a design or mechanical device. When the design is too transparent, too mechanical, perhaps, then contrivance can be meant contemptuously (e.g., as a literary device that seems artificial).[1] Of course, fantasy itself can be a contrivance in this sense—it is scheming, ends-oriented, and fairly transparent (if it is indeed wish fulfilling). And contrivance (as design or mechanical device) is also a good term for a videogame's relationship with its fantasy systems, those counterfeit coins that *just happen* to "make the machine work when dropped into the slot."[2] And so contrivance might apply best in moments when an underlying narrative *protrudes* through a surface narrative, breaking its cohesiveness and signaling the presence of an alternative motivational rationale. There are, for instance, fantasy conventions in RPGs that would stretch the coherence of any framing narrative: the fact that the world is so agonistic, that townspeople go about daily life despite monsters freely roaming the fields, that death is impermanent, that combat unfolds in discrete temporal chunks (turns), that fighting makes the player's character stronger (rather than weaker), that players end up controlling the central figure who alone accrues strength, and so on. These conventions protrude from even the most carefully planned surface narrative in games such as *The Elder Scrolls V: Skyrim* (2011) or *Divinity: Original Sin* (2014), which seek to fold many RPG conventions into a plausible diegesis. In these games, players can still loot a nonplayer character's private dwelling, but they must do so furtively if they do not want to be attacked or branded a thief.[3]

If surface narratives in games often reference real-world spaces and observe certain social conventions (such as rules protecting private property), a game's underlying fantasy systems instead tend to reflect that game's theory of mind for its player. In this sense, fantasy conventions tend to work against fourth-wall boundaries and diegetic immersion: they represent the player's structural position *within* the game itself. Simulation genres excepted, videogames do not faithfully simulate the real world represented in image and setting. As Kurt Squire puts it, "Games differ from simulations in that they give roles, goals, and agency" to players.[4] As a result, Squire says, the realism attached to a game's diegetic roles must sometimes be sacrificed in favor of interesting goals. Fantasy makes goals interesting. There seems to be at least some unavoidable heterogeneity in a game that frames fantasy-driven play with diegesis, at least if fantasy's interests are not merely mimetic—that is, if the fantasy is not about making believe we are a direct participant in story events.

From the point of view of story, most fantasy mechanisms are pure contrivance. We laugh at their absurdity when we isolate them from the context that renders them legible as fantasy (i.e., a videogame's core loops) and introduce them into a new context, such as with films poking fun at videogame conventions like temporal mutability or numerical specularization—for instance, *Scott Pilgrim vs. The World* (2010) or *Jumanji: Welcome to the Jungle* (2017). The contrivance of an empowering fantasy welcomes critique, even when videogames are not directly involved. In James Cameron's *Avatar* (2009), for instance, the villain—Colonel Quaritch—is not simply the antagonist; he is the very *sign* of villainy, the embodiment of everything evil in the world. He has been shaped by and now leads the violent, racist, and unfeeling military-industrial machine destroying the planet Pandora and brutally displacing its native population. It is a contrivance that Quaritch must also be the one who thwarts the heroes' plans (again and again), who shoots and kills Dr. Grace Augustine, who kills Neytiri's bonded mount, the giant cat (thanator), who happens upon Jake Sully's trailer hidden in the woods during the final confrontation, and who then disrupts Jake's link with his avatar. Quaritch is a device, a contrivance, a container for the film's accumulated injustices so they might combine into a single force of maximal amplitude (and clarity) at the dramatic moment when Neytiri, the native woman whom Quaritch dehumanizes and underestimates, buries an arrow in his chest.

As spectators, we may chuckle at fantasy's contrivance when it is presented as a misfit to our experiential world; as dreamers of a future with *Hamlet* on the holodeck, we may assail its diegetic heterogeneity; as artists, we may celebrate it for its power to defamiliarize assumed narrative or social tendencies; as public intellectuals, we can advocate for transplanting such contrivances into business models as a way to revivify a workforce. I suggest viewing contrivances as beginnings, as points of entry for thinking about how fantasy unfolds in a shadowy, second narrative beneath the surface.

The following section considers a specific game's fantasy systems with an eye toward contrivance. The game, *Deep Rock Galactic* (2020), represents its own unique combination of each of this book's empowerment fantasies—body transcendence, tether, and accretions.

"Danger. Darkness. Dwarves."

Deep Rock Galactic frames its play with the premise that "the richest mine ever discovered just happens to be on the deadliest planet in the galaxy. It's also where you work." Players control mercenary dwarves sent to plunder precious materials from planet Hoxxes IV, eradicating any indigenous species that get in the way. *Deep Rock Galactic* not only exemplifies the three fantasy traditions in this book, but as the game's subtitle ("Danger. Darkness. Dwarves.") intimates, it does so with a touch of self-awareness. The one-to-four-player cooperative, first-person POV game is broken into missions where dwarves explore destructible, procedurally generated tunnels and caverns deep underground. The Tolkienesque miners must drill down, light up the darkness, and defend themselves against the occasional swarm of giant insect creatures, all while they mine minerals and fuel sources, recover lost equipment, or destroy an enemy target on behalf of the corporation that employs them. The dwarven miners are frequently reminded that the ores they gather and launch into space are far more valuable than their lives. And at the end of each mission, an extraction ship for the crew is sent only *after* the haul is safely away. Even then, the extraction vessel drops in an absurdly random place and only waits several minutes before leaving—no exceptions. As if aware of this fact, Hoxxes IV's vengeful giant insects pour out of every crevice in ceaseless pursuit at the conclusion of each mission.

The need to rush to the extraction point, the arbitrary countdown, the sudden emergence of monsters—contrivance upon contrivance only partially justified as a tongue-in-cheek joke about the expendability of the workaday laborer for corporate capitalism on a galactic scale. Of course, from the point of view of tether play, these contrivances are the game's entire raison d'être. Tethers pervade play at every turn. The team lands in a dark, unexplored cave and gradually lights the way in search of their objective, deeper and deeper, all the while leaving behind a trail of breadcrumbs (a traversable path with ziplines or tunnels) in case they must return this way for extraction. Players are tethered to one another by a cooperative structure where fallen dwarves can be revived by teammates, and where each class (engineer, gunner, driller, scout) uniquely complements the others.

When not under attack, players may split up. The highly mobile scout, as the name implies, may search ahead, grappling to new areas and lighting the way. The driller may opt to follow the scout, steadily cutting a sloping path others can follow. The engineer may lag behind with their platform gun, as collecting unreachable resources from a lofty cave wall takes time. The gunner may opt to stay near and protect the engineer, or else may venture bravely in a new direction, confident in the safety provided by their heavy firepower. In this way, the crew may be split up, divided across a complex three-dimensional map at the moment when the insect swarm attacks. Then, the tether tightens and all must band together, mounting a joint defense for their own sake, or else converging on some fragile objective they must protect.

Each mission type comes with its own quirky complications meant to ensure the experience of a tether: ores conveniently located at the farthest reaches of the cave, oil pipes that spring leaks every time an attack happens and must be repaired under duress, and so on. Most illustrative is the "Escort Duty" mission where players protect and travel with a "drilldozer" vehicle that cuts a large horizontal tunnel toward the objective, the Ommoran Core. While in motion (and ostensibly because of the noise it generates), the drill draws enemy attention continuously and must be defended as it moves. Here, the interplanetary corporation's immense cheapness provides a surface narrative that winks as it pretends to motivate the game's tether play: the drilldozer comes with enough fuel for only *part* of the journey. Put differently, at the behest of a tether fantasy, players will run out of fuel in special caverns full of oil shale. They must heft fuel canisters from the back of the drilldozer and split apart to search for shale. While collecting, the drilldozer is still a target for the insect swarm, which can (and always does) attack during the refueling process. Players must drop what they are doing and respond. One task is interrupted at its midpoint (drilldozer on its path to the Ommoran Core), in order for a second task (collecting oil shale in the cavern) to also be interrupted by an emergent threat: tension upon tension. But then blissful diminution: when the bugs are gone, players can return to the discarded canisters, finish refueling, and then set the drilldozer off again. Of course, smaller tensions may crop up on top of the two major interruptions built into the mission—someone may, for instance, opt to stay behind in an opened cavern and mine material for an upgrade or a secondary mission objective. As their teammates ride the departing drilldozer, the isolated dwarf is at greater risk of losing their way or being swarmed by bugs. And the entire party is vulnerable when split apart, since the mission's finale (when the drill penetrates the core) requires active defense from all sides.

In general, however, dwarves must collect resources whenever they can. Accrual is essential for mission success. And it extends the tether's reach. Every weapon's ammunition is finite; the bugs infinite. As a contrivance for both tether and accretions play, dwarves must pay their corporate overlords for ammo resupply pods, which cost eighty units of "Nitra," a red mineral found along the way. The result of the game's interlocking fantasy systems is a sometimes complex interplay between venturing forth, exploring, collecting, fighting, and retreating—tasks pile on and are interrupted; some can be completed by one dwarf, others require teamwork.

One more contrivance along these lines: each dwarf can carry only a limited amount of any resource (e.g., forty Nitra), so all pickups are tallied at the bottom of the screen. As a result, collecting often involves stopping midtask to transfer what one has gathered into a mobile reservoir (the Mining Utility Lift Engine or MULE). There is only one MULE, so players must sometimes wait after calling it with full pockets (and likely some surplus resources scattered on the ground). Once something is stored there, the MULE acts as a team

Stalled drilldozer with empty fuel canister nearby in *Deep Rock Galactic* (2020).

inventory that can be accessed immediately. The resource limits in the MULE system may seem arbitrary, but this system ensures that players remain aware of the burden of minerals and ores they carry (in ways they likely would not if inventory space were unlimited). The system also introduces a rhythm into the game's accretions play, an oscillation between feeling empty and oriented toward gathering, and feeling full and oriented toward a return. While chipping at a Nitra deposit, players are in an accretions mode, automatically collecting each mined bit. Suddenly, the Nitra tally reaches its limit and one or two mined chunks fall into the darkness below. In place of accrual, the resource limit has substituted tether play: we must turn attention toward the MULE, which may be nearby or far off (with others). Players may also try to remember the location of surplus resources left on a cave wall or floor, at least if they plan to return later (a mental tether). At any moment, an insect swarm can introduce an additional and much more significant interruption than the resource limit.

Player characters do grow stronger in the breaks between missions at home base, when they review newly available upgrades and perks (e.g., extra ammunition, faster sprinting, armor-piercing bullets, etc.). However, no amount of accrual will alter the tether dynamics built into each mission—collecting will always be interrupted by a tether, and that tether will be interrupted as well. There is certainly an eagerness to test new upgrades in the next outing. And even modest changes in gear can make the difference between completing or failing a mission. But the game's accretions project seems even more closely related to its fantasy of body transcendence, its joy of being a cause. Players experience this each time they chip their way into a brittle patch of Nitra, bore through a cave wall, grapple to the top of a large cavern, or witness the light from their weapon illuminate the darkness.

Accretions ultimately emphasize and frame—often in dazzling and kinetic ways—each dwarf's contribution to the mission, the unique manner in which they move or project force through space. Accretions serve a kind of specialism that is defined in relation to one's role in a group. In yet another contrivance, each dwarf is "special" only in ways that happen to complement the others. For instance, the gunner dwarf can summon a bubble-like shield of light to force all enemies away. This shield lasts just long enough to revive a fallen teammate or restock ammunition and health at a supply pod. With a long cooldown period and a limited number of uses, the shield will never behave like a permanent armoring of the body; it will never consume the game's tethers. But upgrading it makes it a bit more useful and so helps cement the gunner's role as a kind of anchor for the others, someone with a Gatling gun to duck behind who can revive a teammate in even the direst circumstances. Progress in *Deep Rock Galactic* is guaranteed not by accretions but rather by a combination of accrued powers and experience (skill). However, skilled play and the structurally useful ability become blurred during a fight. We assume both when we make a game's kinetics our own and mark our own body memory with the bursts and explosions that register our intervention into game space.

As Katherine Isbister argues, cooperative multiplayer games often divide roles in such a way that personal preference and playstyle must be weighed against the functions that are most needed in the group.[5] When first playing *Deep Rock Galactic* with friends, I had predicted at the outset that one friend in particular would gravitate toward the scout class. He initially bristled at the possibility of being so predictable. But after testing each class in turn, he made me blush and admitted I was right. In the games we have played together over the past six years, I have noted this friend's preference for the tether stretched to its limit. In *Minecraft* (2011), while I preferred breaking ground and designing a home base within a natural environment (e.g., on the side of a cliff, in the middle of a lake, etc.), and another friend preferred refining and optimizing systems (farming, inventory management), this friend had always sought new caves or built portals to other worlds. In *Valheim* (2021), the same friend had specialized in a melee build with a shield for parries. I would send arrows from a safe distance, while he consistently dove into the fray. There were times in the game *Dying Light* (2015) when this friend departed a safe zone at night and slipped into the darkness while I stood on the edge of the lit rooftop and decided I could not follow. I would rather stop playing than risk another encounter with a "volatile" zombie type, a nocturnal monster that cannot be outrun.

Of course, we each tend to gravitate toward different fantasy arrangements, different optimal orbits around a secure base. I can play a dungeon crawler endlessly, taking pleasure in the slow but assured pursuit of constancy. But the friend who prefers to organize home base is bored by these games. The same friend ultimately called off my own group's engagement with *Deep Rock Galactic* as well; our time together is finite and best spent with shared enthusiasm. Rather than framing such differences in terms of personal preference, Laplanche and Pontalis might point to fantasy's "structural link"—that element of any person's daydream that resists categorization, that runs deeper than the fantasy's "typical and repetitive scenarios."[6] More than preference, the structural link is *part* of the fantasy scenario—and perhaps it is related to the point of entry we choose (i.e., the role we tend to adopt in a shared fantasy framework). The path in and out of the fantasy represents a crucial juncture between games and other media—but also between players.

Though my initial playthrough of *Deep Rock Galactic* concluded prematurely, I have continued to reflect upon the game, even while seeking new cooperative experiences with friends. In a way, one does not ever stop playing a game one has enjoyed. Thinking about games (as well as playing them) is my own *dark playground*, the place where I consume leisure activities instead of doing what my superego thinks I should.[7] And *Deep Rock Galactic* reflects this dark playground for me—it is an endless rabbit hole. Its metaphor of depth rings true: here, there is danger and darkness indeed.

Acknowledgments

I should begin by acknowledging the University of Iowa for its support of this book. Special thanks are due to Teresa Mangum and the University of Iowa's interdisciplinary Obermann Center for Advanced Studies, which has supported this project with a generous Book Ends: Obermann/OVPR Book Completion Workshop award. Warmest thanks to Sheila Murphy, Patrick Jagoda, Corey Creekmur, and Rosemarie Scullion for their participation in this workshop, and for their indispensable feedback on an initial draft of the full manuscript. Thanks once more to the Obermann Center for underwriting the Film Theory and Comparative Literature Working Group, which provided feedback on an early chapter draft. And thanks to Corey Creekmur, Kathleen Newman, Eric Gidal, and Elke Heckner for their frank and constructive discussion of this draft. Particular thanks to Kathleen Newman for providing detailed feedback on my book proposal. And I must also thank Rutgers University Press and my editor there, Nicole Solano, for her unwavering belief in this project's potential, even as its completion was delayed by a pandemic. Thanks as well to John Donohue and Joseph Dahm of Westchester Publishing Services for their scrupulous review and copyediting of the finalized manuscript. Special thanks to Alex Trotter for compiling this book's index, and to the College of Liberal Arts and Sciences and Department of Cinematic Arts at the University of Iowa for the generous book subvention grant that supported this task.

This research was supported in its earliest days by amazing advisors at UC Berkeley, Kristen Whissel, Linda Williams, and Abigail De Kosnik. Kristen Whissel in particular must be thanked not only for her superhuman patience, but ultimately for seeing promise in my project when it was at its most nebulous. Special thanks also to Kaja Silverman for instilling a lifelong passion for psychoanalytic inquiry, and to Karen Gilmore and Salman Akhtar for their guidance in the world of clinical psychoanalysis.

I must acknowledge the moral support of friends and colleagues: Damon Young, Josef Nguyen, Bo Ruberg, Kristopher Fallon, Margaret Rhee, Jen Schradie, Doug Cunningham, Nicholaus Gutierrez, Renée Pastel, Andrew Cheng, Andy Owens, Alenda Chang, Irene Chien, Fareed Ben-Youssef, Norman Gendelman, and Brooke Belisle. Along these lines, I must also thank my colleagues and students in the Department of Cinematic Arts at the University of Iowa—especially the crucial guidance of Paula Amad, Steven Ungar, and Michael Cowan. My family (Jaclyn Goetz, Darryl Goetz, Catherine Edgerly, and Chris Edgerly) must also be thanked for understanding how much of me this work has demanded these past several years. Special thanks to Ianto Xi for both moral support and technical assistance. And thanks to every friend and peer who joined me for games or reading on the sunny Memorial Glade at the heart of UC Berkeley's campus, where this project began in spirit.

This book is dedicated to my uncle, Larry Goetz, and my grandmother, Eldrus Ann Goetz. I will forever miss the tradition of card and board games with them in the Michigan countryside. Though my uncle frequently offered to finish writing this book himself (in jest), neither he nor my grandmother lived to see its completion. I know they would have been proud.

Notes

Introduction

1 As of July 2021, this video was still accessible at https://www.facebook.com/watch/?v=1688168281324047.

2 Examples of this meme can be found at knowyourmeme.com: https://knowyourmeme.com/memes/video-games-appeal-to-the-male-fantasy, last accessed January 2022.

3 Mulvey, 843. Mulvey famously argues that cinema's optical powers align with the perspective and desires of male characters and men in the audience as both groups fix women in the position of fetishistic spectacle.

4 Anita Sarkeesian's commentary on gaming's "princess rescue plot" and its gendered subject/object dichotomy (where men act and women are acted upon) renders a widespread pattern in the industry and culture visible (and problematic). Recent game studies scholarship has cemented the necessity of attending to the representational content of videogames (e.g., Adrienne Shaw, Jennifer Malkowski, TreaAndrea Russworm, or Bonnie Ruberg).

5 To be clear, I do not endorse the caricature of Restrepo depicted in the meme, which understands her remarks about *Grand Theft Auto V* as a brazen extrapolation: all of gaming from one moment. The strip club in that game more likely reflects for Restrepo a wider truth about the industry: that, whatever their content, games are designed, distributed, and played within a culture largely structured by this gender binary. Often (but of course not *always*), games reflect this context in especially clear and problematic ways.

6 Consider Irene Chien's use of the term "empowerment fantasy" in a thoughtful passage about how dying in military-themed games threatens their essential "fantasy of control": "The loss of control inherent to the military video game's empowerment fantasy is an unexamined crack in the wargame's seemingly impervious body armor, the place where it registers killing and being killed as trauma" ("Playing against the Grain," 250). For Chien and others, empowerment—especially when joined in the context of commercial videogames with its partner in crime, fantasy—evokes the nexus between military masculinity, hyperviolence, industrial capitalism, and an ideology of control and domination. For another notable example, see Daniel Dooghan's discussion of an "economic fantasy" (which validates

an expansionist, neoliberal worldview) operating broadly across commercial gaming, especially in sandbox games such as *Minecraft*. Such fantasies "habituate players to myths of empire and capital that rationalize political and economic inequality" (67–68).

7 In anticipation of backlash for her unfavorable review of *Grand Theft Auto V*, game critic Leigh Alexander writes, "What, you want to leave me death threats? Go for it! Games are about feeling powerful, and about you getting your way" (Schroeder). Alexander ties feeling powerful to feeling entitled, and links empowerment in commercial games to antifeminist backlash and misogyny in gaming culture.

8 This list of examples is drawn from action, adventure, survival, idle clicker, farming, and match-three puzzle games.

9 For instance, see Linda Williams ("Film Bodies"), Carol Clover, and Valerie Walkerdine.

10 Laplanche and Pontalis, "Fantasy," 128. Laplanche and Pontalis draw on a Freudian fantasy scenario, "A father seduces a daughter," in which nothing "shows whether the subject will be immediately located as daughter; it can as well be fixed as father, or even in the term *seduces*" (128). Their notion of fantasy as a "scenario with multiple entries" has been taken up by film scholars in order to reconsider rigid subject-object dichotomies popularized by Laura Mulvey's "Visual Pleasure" essay. In fantasy, one might identify across gender lines, may locate oneself in the position of the object, as either the hero or the monster, or even in the position of the verb—to slash, etc.—in the cinematic examples of the slasher film and other "body genres" that Clover and Williams consider.

11 Laplanche and Pontalis, 128.

12 Freud, "Creative Writer," 26.

13 Freud, 28. A wish expresses a want but also its prohibition: some want has gone unfulfilled due to life circumstances, such as when a parent (or some internalized voice) prohibits sweets before bed. A wish emerges as a response to the prohibited want as an imagined scenario where the want is presented as satisfied. Freud sees wish fulfilment as the motivating force behind all mental activity, including not just dreams and fantasies but even rational thought. Further, Freud understands wants as representations of some bodily impulse or "drive." Sometimes, we can openly acknowledge these impulses. Sometimes, however, he theorizes that they conflict with our waking sense of self, our ego—for instance, Oedipal impulses. Wants of this nature become repressed, and their corresponding wish can be expressed only in a disguised form.

14 Freud, 26.

15 Freud, 27.

16 Freud, 28.

17 Laplanche and Pontalis, "Fantasy," 118. This is how Laplanche and Pontalis phrase Lacan's notion of a fundamental fantasy, itself based on Freud's notion of a primal or unconscious fantasy, which plays an organizing role on the subject's psychological and sexual development.

18 Sandler and Sandler, "Phantasy," 83.

19 Freud's notion of conscious fantasy does not permit this final binary pair since conscious fantasy for Freud is weighted by the ego. The lack of subjectivization is a quality of *unconscious* fantasy that I suggest should nevertheless be extended to games. Games involve us in a variety of tasks leading away from the moors of waking identity. The wishes considered in this book tend to stick closer to Freud's model of the daydream—i.e., wishes that can be directly expressed without serious distortion by an internal censor.

20 Not all wishes are repressed, barred from consciousness, and heavily revised. Some are only hidden from others or slightly modified to satisfy what Sandler and Sandler term a *second censorship*. As opposed to the "first" kind of censorship (at work on unconscious wishes), the second censorship's "*fundamental orientation is towards the avoidance of shame, embarrassment and humiliation*" ("'Second Censorship,'" 421). Based largely in Freud's daydream essay, the second censor originates "early in life, when the child can experience such emotions and begins to substitute conscious fantasying for play that meets with social disapproval" (421).

The fantasies discussed in this book are framed as conscious (i.e., engaged with a second censor) because their manifest forms and structures are—like play—immediately and viscerally legible. However, it must be kept in mind that conscious fantasies are not completely "reducible to an intentional aim on the part of the desiring subject," as Laplanche and Pontalis put it (*Language of Psychoanalysis*, 318). Instead, fantasy almost always expresses *more* than we intend, *more* than we might even understand about ourselves. Fantasy can readily be "the locus of defensive operations: it facilitates the most primitive defense processes, such as turning round upon the subject's own self, reversal into the opposite, negation and projection" (318). There will be moments in the chapters ahead when the structure of a fantasy (its aim) seems to undergo a reversal.

21 The "Ars Poetica" (The Art of Poetry) is an ancient, self-reflexive poem by a Roman poet known as Horace (Quintus Horatius Flaccus) full of maxims on writing poetry. Freud's reference here signals his approach to questions of art and craft that might not be suitably discussed in his avowedly scientific framework. Of course, Freud nevertheless advances two hypotheses about the creative writer's secret art: first, "the writer tones down the character of the egoistic daydream by modifying and disguising it"; second, the writer "bribes us with the purely formal— that is aesthetic—bonus of pleasure that he offers us in the way he presents his fantasies" ("Creative Writer," 33). In short, Freud argues that aesthetic appreciation in art is a displacement away from the creative work's egoistic daydream, which itself features a displacement from the ego to the hero of the story (two relatively transparent revisions in the name of avoiding shame over openly enjoying one's fantasy).

22 Freud, "Creative Writer," 33.

23 Daniel Reynolds, 3.

24 Daniel Reynolds, 3.

25 Daniel Reynolds, 79.

26 So argue Stephanie Boluk and Patrick LeMieux in their book *Metagaming*.

27 Gombrich, 4.

28 Gombrich, 4.

29 The term "self-involving" comes from Robson and Meskin.

30 Žižek, *Looking Awry*, 5.

31 Žižek, 6.

32 Žižek, *Plague of Fantasies*, 12, 18.

33 Mulvey, 840.

34 Williams, *Hard Core*, 204.

35 Stillar, 211.

36 Along with numerical representation, automation, and cultural transcoding, modularity and variability constitute Lev Manovich's five principles of new media. Manovich poses the possibility that the loop may be a "new narrative form appropriate for the computer age"—a potential he helpfully situates within a wider

historical tradition of media making use of loops, including not only games but also cinema, internet pornography, and computer programming itself (317).

37 Of a game's many looping structures, the audio loop seems to have received the most serious scholarly attention. Karen Collins's careful taxonomy of game audio introduces helpful terms for thinking of loops in distinct scalar categories across a game's fractal structure: "microloops," "mesoloops," and "macroloops" (212). For further discussion of musical loops, see Middleton, Brown, or Stillar.

38 Guardiola, 3.

39 Bogost, ix.

40 Wardrip-Fruin, 13. Both Wardrip-Fruin and Bogost discuss algorithmic processes in somewhat affectively muted terms. However, neither goes quite as far as Alexander Galloway's contention that as a "software system," a digital game "has more in common with the finance software *Quicken* than it does with traditional games like chess, roulette, or billiards"—and that, further, we should refer to those who play games as operators, not players (6).

41 Theories of affect and fantasy seem to offer similar benefits for the study of media. Both Jagoda and Anable emphasize affect's ability to "[move] through lived bodies and everyday experience" (Jagoda, 27). As an "experience of intensity that is nonconscious and relational," affect is also helpful for discussing a game's nonrepresentational dimensions (27). This, for instance, is how Anable suggests approaching an imagined space *between* a game's "representational qualities" and its "mechanical properties" (xvi). Fantasy shares much in common with affect: it is situated (especially in Lacanian models) between bodily drives and the external world, can be both conscious and nonconscious, and is inherently relational. However, this book's emphasis on consciously experienced fantasy highlights a similarity with emotion, or the *closure and capture* of affect. Naming and describing specific fantasy traditions and their role within wider systems of meaning making implicitly aligns fantasy with the "formed, qualified, situated perceptions and cognitions" that Brian Massumi suggests truncate and contract the fuller experience of affect (35). It is helpful to keep in mind that fantasy can be oriented both toward the body and its affective energies as well as toward specific textual notions of emotion, meaning, story, and context.

42 Mechanic, 641.

43 This is not to say that there are only three fantasies to consider—far from it. In developer commentary, Riot Games talks about its online game, *League of Legends* (2009–present), as if every one of their 160 playable characters (or champions) provided a unique fantasy experience for players: e.g., the fantasies of becoming invisible, of stalking prey, of healing and protecting teammates, and so on. Each champion's abilities constitute a distinctly empowering set of possibilities that the developer apparently organizes and assembles (renders internally coherent) under separate fantasy headings. And whether players gravitate toward one champion or another might reflect a predisposition that is itself related to the diverse and personal fantasies we all invent, inherit, and entertain throughout our daily lives. This book's focus on three broad fantasy traditions seeks fantasies that seem to repeat within and across games, game genres, and even apparently disparate media—fantasies that have become part of a broader cultural preoccupation.

44 Žižek, *Plague of Fantasies*, 7.

45 Purse, "Digital Heroes," 8.

46 Though Žižek's notion of fantasy as a schema is based on a Lacanian argument, it shares an affinity with Laplanche and Pontalis's famous description of fantasy as the

"mise-en-scène of desire" (*Language of Psychoanalysis*, 318). This description is meant to evoke the defensive function of fantasy, as "a mise-en-scène in which what is prohibited (l'interdit) is always present in the actual formation of the wish" (318). Put differently, a wish is not simply something realized in fantasy, but accounts for fantasy's very structure.

47 Freud, *Beyond the Pleasure Principle*, 8.

48 Consider, for example, Sheila Murphy's characterization of contemporary media convergence: "In the past few decades, once seemingly discrete media technologies such as film, television, and computers have increasingly coalesced through the industrial convergence of production and delivery methods and the narrative crossovers and linkages now commonly found between co-positioned media objects such as film franchises, television programs, or the adaptation of one medium's content into another format" (4).

49 Silverman, *Subject of Semiotics*, 67–68.

50 Silverman, 67.

51 Laplanche and Pontalis, "Fantasy," 128.

52 Murphy, 9.

53 Jenkins, *Convergence Culture*, 14. Here, Jenkins distills Lisa Gitelman's more extended and nuanced discussion of media technologies and protocol.

54 Jenkins, 14.

55 Ludology—or the study of games qua games—was originally intended to establish an interpretive method uniquely designed to address videogames as games, not in the terms of an already established discipline (such as film studies). This mission was first expressed in a series of contentious essays challenging the notion that video-games were a platform for storytelling.

56 These are Dan Fleming's words for discussing videogame identification. He employs the compounded terms "spectator" and "player" to describe an oscillation between a game's narrative moments and their "subject-fixing processes" (e.g., seeing Mario as a white, heterosexual male), and the game's "underlying geometry of playability" that presents expanded possibilities for identity through play (178, 192).

57 Klinger, 139.

58 Klinger's discussion of "the ritual of return" is meant to apply to repeat movie viewing in the home. And Thomas Apperley's work extends this line of thought to the question of how games intersect with the rhythms of daily life. But it is Valerie Walkerdine's essay that first attests to the role fantasy plays in the complex intersections of public and private, media text and family, within the home. In her ethnographic study of home viewing practices, Walkerdine insists on looking beyond the boundaries of the text and, as Candida Yates puts it, she "thus makes a key intervention into the study of film and its reception by drawing our attention to the identifications and fantasies that take place within and among the viewers, the text and the lived experience of family; she disrupts the conceptual duality that hitherto has located the processes of fantasy in opposition to the experience of 'real life'" (405–406).

59 Jenkins, "Complete Freedom of Movement," 346.

60 Chief among these reasons are Freud's own sexist, racist, and colonialist mind-sets—which are built into his theoretical models. Not for nothing does Laura Mulvey reflect on what it means to address patriarchy through one of its key institutions (psychoanalysis). On top of this, Freud is also criticized for lacking empirical methodologies that would allow his theories to be tested.

61 Rose, 5.

62 Rose, 3.

63 Bainbridge, 64.

64 Jagoda, 193.

65 Many, but not all, experimental games target empowerment. Some embrace it, others take aim obliquely, without completely dismantling it. Jason Rohrer's experimental online game *The Castle Doctrine* provides a relevant example. Its play seems predicated on a tether fantasy: players build defensive structures (mazes, traps, guard dogs, etc.) to protect their in-game resources. However, the game is also harshly punitive and pervaded by anxiety: death is permanent and players risk life and limb to invade one another's vaults; all they have gathered can be stolen away by other players. The game freezes its tether in a tense state of exposure, and nothing gained can be banked upon. Unlike with commercial games, the point is not to capture the player in an empowering loop for profit. Instead, Rohrer hopes the player will reflect on the anxiety they feel toward the boundaries of their home and belongings. In Rohrer's words, "I wanted to make a game that makes you feel violated and makes you want to protect stuff that's yours, and puts you in the process of securing what's yours"—adding that "there is this temptation to discount the suffering of others and elevate your own suffering" (Meer). Rohrer sees his game as an experimental means of exploring this dynamic.

66 Rose, 4.

67 The queer game studies movement provides a number of relevant examples (e.g., Bonnie Ruberg's *Video Games Have Always Been Queer* and Ruberg and Shaw's *Queer Game Studies*).

Chapter 1   The Fantasy of Bodily Transcendence

1 The term "transcendence" carries at least two common associations: first, with the theological principle situating God beyond material reality; second, with the nineteenth-century American philosophical movement Transcendentalism. Though this book's use of the term exceeds religious frameworks, it does not exclude them. In fact, the narratives discussed in relation to this fantasy sometimes reference religious mythology, such as with Neo's evocation of Christ in *The Matrix*. The fantasy of bodily transcendence resonates with Transcendentalism's emphasis on the individual standing in opposition to the corruptive forces of institutions and constraints from the past. The belief in one's specialness, much like the anticipation of a future moment of recognition (or the revelation of latent powers), is a central narrative trope in the texts I connect with this fantasy.

2 Ward, 123–124.

3 Magrì, 28.

4 Magrì, 38.

5 Sutton-Smith, 21.

6 Sutton-Smith, 21.

7 Purse, "Digital Heroes," 8.

8 "The Tetris effect" is a term for the general experience of having played any game long enough to see its play continued when one closes one's eyes or before bed, as a side effect of prolonged (embodied) engagement with the game, its images, and its systems. It is named for the commonly reported afterimage experience following long play sessions of Pajitnov's famous game.

9 Understanding the body as a "project" that is undertaken on both individual and cultural levels is a relatively recent (late modern) notion. Archaeologists of the body

link it specifically to commercial media, recent constructs of individuality, as well as representations of beauty, youth, fitness, sex, class, and race in the developed world (Hamilakis, Pluciennik, and Tarlow, 2).

10 Fuchs, "Collective Body Memories," 333.

11 How such videos are habitually watched and circulated online seems to exemplify Wendy Hui Kyong Chun's notion of "habitual new media." Chun's framework adopts a macro view focusing more on networked interactions than granular techniques such as wave dashing. However, especially apt for a discussion of wave dashing videos is Chun's reading of Natalie Bookchin's *Mass Ornament and Testament*, a video installation depicting a "mass dance" from hundreds of found-footage YouTube clips. Chun emphasizes the neoliberal condition in the video—the paradox of individuality undercut by repetition, "unconscious community," and, more optimistically, "found collectivity" (173).

12 Spectators are participants in spite of not holding a controller, even if only through the activation of *mirror neurons* (the neurobiological basis of mimesis). As Giacomo Rizzolatti puts it, "Mirror neurons are a particular type of neurons that discharge when an individual performs an action, as well as when he/she observes a similar action done by another" (419). Scientists hypothesize mirror neurons play an important role in the acquisition of language as well as "action understanding, imitation, intention understanding, and empathy" (419).

13 In addition to parodic references such as *Deuce Bigalow: Male Gigolo* (1999) and more flattering repetitions in action films such as *Swordfish* (2001), bullet time has also been the focus of academic conversations about digitally mediated action cinema, such as Bob Rehak's "The Migration of Forms."

14 In Loftus and Loftus's example, "the letter string MGAE is perceived as four separate letters—four chunks. But the same letters presented as GAME are perceived as one word—one chunk" (79). In general, "the fewer the chunks you have to process in order to accomplish some task, the more efficiently the task can be done" (79)—a fact that has clear application to developing skills related to game play. The authors use the example of chess:

> Various studies have linked the acquisition of expertise in game playing to the fusing of many small chunks into fewer large ones. Consider chess. In one experiment, various board positions were shown either to chess experts or to chess novices. The board positions were either random configurations of the chess pieces or they derived from actual games. Later the subjects had to reproduce the board positions they had seen. Neither the novices nor the experts could reproduce the random board configurations very well. The novices couldn't reproduce the actual game configurations very well either, but the experts could.
> The boards involved perhaps twenty pieces. Apparently, however, the experts saw the game configuration boards as a small number of chunks, because any configuration resulting from an actual game was bound to be very similar to some configuration that the experts had seen many times before. This wasn't true for the novices; hence for them twenty pieces constituted about twenty separate chunks. The random board configurations were unfamiliar to everyone and were thus perceived by all as many chunks. (79)

15 Fuchs, "Body Memory," 91.

16 Fuchs, 92.

17 Fuchs, "Collective Body Memories," 336.

18 For a detailed discussion of how the earliest flowerings of fantasy are propped upon but also deviate from the vital function of nourishment, see Jean Laplanche (15–24).

19 Abraham and Torok, 30.
20 Abraham and Torok, 24.
21 Abraham and Torok, 30.
22 Abraham and Torok, 25.
23 Of course, in analysis, the interrupted moment is twofold: the fantasy intrudes upon both the dinner party and the ongoing discussion between patient and analyst.
24 Schusterman, 100.
25 Tannahill, Tissington, and Senior, 2.
26 Tannahill, Tissington, and Senior, 2.
27 Stickgold et al., 350.
28 Stickgold and colleagues have found that "amnesic patients with extensive bilateral medial temporal lobe damage produced similar hypnagogic reports [aka the Tetris effect] despite being unable to recall playing the game, suggesting that such imagery may arise without important contribution from the declarative memory system" (350).
29 Shanton and Goldman; Jerome Singer, 16.
30 Diedrichsen and Kornysheva define motor skill learning as "neuronal changes that allow an organism to accomplish a motor task better, faster, or more accurately than before," adding that beyond this very broad definition "there is little agreement in the literature about a more precise, scientific definition" (227).
31 Cathy Caruth refers to trauma as "unclaimed experience" because traumatic events cannot be integrated into our normal manner of perceiving or remembering (11). The American Psychological Association's term for behavioral therapies effective in the treatment of trauma (or, rather, posttraumatic stress disorder) is *cognitive processing therapy*. When the experience cannot be processed, it remains at an implicit or bodily level, as a memory that is prevented from becoming a cohesive element of consciousness: "Because of trauma's intense shock and pain, the victim cannot properly integrate it into a clear, conscious, meaningful memory, since the experience overwhelms one's normal sense of self, rupturing the narrative continuity that gives meaning and stability to experience, including remembered experience. Instead, as the explicit narrative memory of trauma is significantly blurred or even lost in many of its details, so the traumatic memory thrives in implicit behavioral form in terms of somatic complaints such as flashbacks (that repeatedly relive the trauma)" (Shusterman, 100).
32 Žižek, *Plague of Fantasies*, 6.
33 In Lacanian theory, it is not quite correct to say that fantasy conceals the Real. As Claudia Lapping puts it, "In traditional conceptions of fantasy, what is repressed is a truth about reality; in Lacanian conceptions, what is repressed is the illusory nature of the relation between language/signifier and reality/signified" (720).
34 Žižek, *Plague of Fantasies*, 6.
35 The ambiguity Žižek acknowledges in fantasy's screening function—how fantasy "creates what it purports to conceal, its 'repressed' point of reference"—attests to our fascination with narratives of disaster ("are not the images of the ultimate horrible Thing, from the gigantic deep-sea squid to the ravaging twister, phantasmic creations *par excellence*?"; *Plague of Fantasies*, 6). Disaster narratives in entertainment media exemplify fantasy's function in mediating encounters with potentially traumatizing realities.
36 In his study of the national reaction to the terror attack, Kevin Rozario relays the sentiment widely shared among witnesses and reporters that the attacks and

subsequent destruction were like a movie. In the words of a *New Yorker* film critic, in reference to the looped news footage of the collapsing Twin Towers, "people saw—literally saw, and are continuing to see, as it airs in unforgiving repeats—that day as a movie" (Rozario, 177). Relaying an account of one reporter, who kept expecting Bruce Willis to land on the roof and fly people to safety, Rozario points out that this news footage was reminiscent of "images of mass destruction" that had been "the film industry's bread and butter for decades" (177). The national trauma of the terror attack—while preceded by widely shared images of destruction in cinema, games, and other popular media—exemplifies the detachment from lived experience of trauma more generally (a separation of body and mind). As concerns our collective processing of the terror attacks of 9/11, see Smith for a discussion of how fantasy helps screen such a traumatizing reality and King for a discussion of how the attacks were remediated by cinematic convention in news coverage.

37 Jerome Singer, 16; Classen, Koopman, and Spiegel, 178.
38 Such a view is even broached in Marshall McLuhan's theory of media, specifically his designation of games as "artificial situations that rival the irritations and stresses of real life under controlled conditions of sport and play" (42). In this passage, games join with other media as "counter-irritants" or homeostatic formations meant to counteract some "cause of irritation" in the world (42).
39 Groos, 315.
40 Groos, 325; emphasis added.
41 Groos, 88–89.
42 Children's play exemplifies *paidia* for Caillois, who interprets this play in direct reference to Groos as a "primitive joy in destruction" or a "moral vertigo" projected outward—"an impulse to touch, grasp, taste, smell, and then drop any accessible object," such as with the monkey's game of pulling the dog's tail, or "the pleasure of endlessly cutting up paper with a pair of scissors, pulling cloth into thread"—in short, the feeling of being "the *cause*" (*Man, Play and Games*, 28).
43 Fleming, 190.
44 James Newman, "The Myth of the Ergodic Videogame."
45 Jenkins, "Games," 36. David Myers reinforces both Newman's and Jenkins's ideas about movement in games, arguing that "object play" and the more visible "social play," which videogame commentators tend to prioritize, are both predicated on "locomotor play" ("running, jumping, and using our bodies"; 46–49).
46 Freud, "Creative Writer," 26.
47 These words are Iris Marion Young's (35). They refer to her discussion of Merleau-Ponty's notion of transcendence in the lived body, which is the root of intentionality.
48 Freud, "Creative Writer," 28.
49 Niedzviecki's major concern does not lie with teachers' or parents' generic messages to children that they are special and unique. Rather, Niedzviecki fears what he claims is a tendency within recent media for the equation of specialness with celebrity, an unrealistic goal for so many who nevertheless feel compelled to pursue it in order to experience self-worth.
50 Dyer, 8.
51 Dyer, 8.
52 Dyer argues that the 1994 action film *Speed*, aside from being a "celebration of sensational movement," serves as an excuse to fantasize the destruction of the "great frustration of modern urban living—getting about" (8).
53 Dyer, 8.

54 Dyer, 8. Though straight white male protagonists are still very well represented in action cinema and television series, there are reassuring signs of a shift toward better parity. Action heroes who are women have become much more common since the publication of Dyer's article. Examples include Captain Kathryn Janeway in *Star Trek: Voyager* (1995–2001); Wai Lin in *Tomorrow Never Dies* (1997); Buffy Summers in *Buffy the Vampire Slayer* (1997–2003); Trinity in *The Matrix* (1999); Storm, Mystique, Jean Grey, and Rogue in *X-Men* (2000); Yu Shu Lien and Jen in *Crouching Tiger, Hidden Dragon* (2000); Lara Croft in *Lara Croft: Tomb Raider* (2001); Patience Phillips in *Catwoman* (2004); Landlady in *Kung Fu Hustle* (2004); Elastigirl and Violet Parr in *The Incredibles* (2004); Susan Storm in *The Fantastic Four* (2005, 2015); River Tam in *Serenity* (2005); Toph Beifong and Katara in *Avatar: The Last Airbender* (2005–2008); Hit-Girl in *Kick-Ass* (2010); Arya Stark in *Game of Thrones* (2011–2019); Hermione Granger of the *Harry Potter* books and films; Black Widow in *The Avengers* (2012); Avatar Korra in *The Legend of Korra* (2012–2014); Elsa and Anna of Arendelle in *Frozen* (2013); Susan Cooper (Melissa McCarthy) in *Spy* (2015); Rey in *Star Wars: Episode VII—The Force Awakens* (2015); Jessica Jones in *Jessica Jones* (2015–2019); Angel Dust and Negasonic Teenage Warhead in *Deadpool* (2016); Abby Yates, Erin Gilbert, Jillian Holtzmann, and Patty Tolan in *Ghostbusters* (2016); Diana Prince in *Wonder Woman* (2017); Michael Burnham and Philippa Georgiou in *Star Trek Discovery* (2017–present); Okoye in *Black Panther* (2018); Wanda Maximoff in *Avengers: Infinity War* (2018) and *WandaVision* (2021); Carol Danvers in *Captain Marvel* (2019); Allison and Vanya Hargreeves in *The Umbrella Academy* (2019–present); Sersi, Thena, Ajak, and Sprite in *Eternals* (2021); Kamala Khan in *Ms. Marvel* (2022–present); Evelyn Quan Wang in *Everything Everywhere All at Once* (2022); and many others.

55 Dyer, 8.

56 The situation Dyer describes is established in both sociological accounts of boys' culture (e.g., Anthony Rotundo) as well as in fantasies of erotic domination where men "negate" and women are negated (e.g., Jessica Benjamin). Henry Jenkins highlights this same disparity when arguing that videogames offer boys virtual substitutes for spaces outside the home where they might test the body's limits ("Complete Freedom of Movement").

57 Dyer, 8.

58 Carlson, 6–7.

59 Carlson, 7–8.

60 Iris Marion Young, 36.

61 Iris Marion Young, 36.

62 James Newman, *Videogames*, 14.

63 Altice, 175. A game engine is a software infrastructure containing built-in systems and graphical-mechanical assets that streamline the game development process. Of the *Mario* engine, Altice highlights "metatile elements like pipes, blocks, and pits," which developers could place in the game, "in various lengths and widths atop a looping backdrop of repeated scenery," lending visual consistency to game spaces without ever asking them to "cohere into a holistic world" (175).

64 As Barthes puts it, with pachinko, "everything is determined in the initial dispatch" (*Empire of Signs*, 27).

65 Fleming, 192.

66 Parkour began as a kind of military obstacle course training and developed into its own sport or pseudo martial art (without combat). It involves using the body (freed of assistive technologies and equipment) to move over complicated spaces quickly

and efficiently, including scaling walls, vaulting over obstacles, rolling through landings, jumping over gaps, etc.

67 Dyer, 8.

68 Frisch, 178.

69 In other words, Cole might embody the same wish David Nye identifies with the figure of the cyborg: "to escape the 'meat body' into the matrix of electronic communications, literally to become disembodied" (205). Cyberspace discourse has certainly grappled with notions of disembodiment of the sort that Nye refers to here (for instance, the virtual worlds in *Neuromancer* or *The Matrix*). But Nye's characterization of the cyborg raises questions. Donna Haraway's account of cyborg bodies (in her well-known "Cyborg Manifesto") advocates for an affinity politics that *critiques* mind-body dualisms in Western thinking. Further, consider Claudia Springer's argument about the sheer corporeality of cyborgs. Springer argues that popular cultural texts rather than "effacing the human body" actually "intensify corporeality in their representation of cyborgs. A mostly technological system is represented as its opposite: a muscular human body with robotic parts that heighten physicality and sexuality" (303). In this respect, the figure of the cyborg can actually help ground VR and cyberspace fantasies about leaving the body behind and existing as pure information or energy in a machine or simulation.

70 Frisch, 178.

71 Richard Reynolds, 14.

72 Merleau-Ponty, 115.

73 Merleau-Ponty, 115.

74 Whissel, *Spectacular Digital Effects*, 21, 22.

75 Whissel, 22.

76 Whissel, 21.

77 Richmond, 121.

78 Richmond, 121, 123.

79 Iris Marion Young, 37–38.

80 Iris Marion Young, 38.

81 Jesper Juul describes two "extreme ways of creating challenge for players" in game design: "*emergence* (rules combining to provide variation) and *progression* (challenges presented serially by way of special-case rules)" (*Half-Real*, 56). Emergence games establish a sandbox of rules and allow play to unfold in unpredictable ways, and progression games are a series of (often narratively inflected) challenges carefully designed for players to encounter in sequence.

82 Fleming, 192.

83 In a 2017 interview with ESPN Esports, Ken Hoang estimates that the move combination became named after him in 2005. Hoang explains, "I was the one who invented most of the Marth meta-game at the time. Not a lot of people knew what Marth could really do, so when they saw me do a Forward-Air to Down-Air, they decided to call it the 'Ken Combo.' I think it has a nice ring to it" (Sam Stewart).

84 Psychologists use the term "interference" to describe situations where one's ability to learn something new is inhibited by past memories that conflict with the new material. Interference requires that long-term memory be pulled back into working memory, which runs against the independence of cognitive and motor functions. With Hoy Quarlow's rotating attack, players have to go back to thinking about dodging instead of performing it reflexively. Series reboot *Punch-Out!!* (2009) builds an entire opponent around this concept. Aran Ryan (who first appears in the SNES title) inverts the typical dodge/counterattack pattern; players who dodge any

of Ryan's moves will be unable to land a follow-up. Instead, players must strike before his attack lands. And this requires unlearning the game's well-established rhythms.

85 Ngai says, of "animatedness," that "the affect manages to fuse signs of the body's subjection to power with signs of its ostensive freedom—by encompassing not only bodily activity confined to fixed forms and rigid, specialized routines (Fordist or Taylorist animation), but also a dynamic principle of physical metamorphosis by which the body, according to Eisenstein, seems to 'triumph over the fetters of form' (what we might call 'animistic' animation)" (100–101). A recent high-profile videogame, *Cuphead: "Don't Deal with the Devil"* (2017), emulates the style of early Disney animation to which Eisenstein and, subsequently, Ngai refer in their theorizing of the form. But games in general seem to exemplify the sentiment behind animatedness—in both their rigid routines and looped repetitions, and in the dynamic metamorphosis by which their animated figures seem to *triumph* over these fetters of form. It is interesting that *Cuphead* is a run-and-gun shooter, since this genre of game is among the most visually dynamic.

86 Mike Rugnetta's PBS Idea Channel, which explores connections between pop culture, technology, and art, devotes a YouTube video to the notion that bullet hell games are meditative and that their complex action forces players into a passive state where they act "without intention." The video even compares bullet hell to watching crowds of people in the city: "Maybe you focus on one thing here, one thing there. You focus on yourself. Or you go on a kind of autopilot. This autopilot in the face of complexity." Rugnetta links bullet hell games to an interesting array of visually complex cultural objects, from *Where's Waldo?* books to films such as *Kill Bill: Vol. 1* (2003) and *The Matrix*.

87 Goto-Jones evokes the Zen arts (including martial arts) in a discussion of how players develop mastery in action videogames: "The key is a form of habituation through repetition, in which complex, nuanced movements are broken down into simple constituent parts that are then repeated and repeated until their performance no longer requires conscious thought" (48–49). He concedes that there are many "everyday" examples of "habituated and sublimated movements" other than Zen art ("tying our shoelaces, driving a car, etc."; 49).

88 *Undertale* is a kind of an action role-playing game where enemies attack with bullet hell dakka. The game's characters express their own personalities in text interactions as well as in the dakka itself. In one mini-boss encounter, for example, players must subdue a sad ghost whose tears fall into the bullet hell arena. Players are free to attack the enemies in the game but may also seek other means of resolving fights, such as attempting to cheer up the ghost with a joke.

89 Cheng, 11.

90 Bukatman, "Why I Hate Superhero Movies," 120.

91 Caillois, "Mimicry and Legendary Psychasthenia," 98.

92 Caillois, 99.

Chapter 2   The Fantasy of Bodily Transcendence in Narrative Media

1 Groos, 315.

2 As of March 2022, Box Office Mojo shows that four of the ten top grossing films of all time feature comic book superheroes: *Avengers: Endgame* (2019), *Avengers: Infinity War* (2018), *Spider-Man: No Way Home* (2021), and *The Avengers* (2012). Five of the top ten lack an explicit superhero theme but are still like comic heroes in

their use of action-melodrama (stories structured by the melodramatic mode's dialectic of pathos and action): *Avatar* (2009), *Titanic* (1997), *The Lion King* (2019), *Furious 7* (2015), and *Star Wars: Episode VII—The Force Awakens* (2015). Such a trend continues well beyond the top ten. Also worth notice is the recentness of most top earners—one must go back more than thirty spots to find a film made before 2000 (with the single exception of James Cameron's *Titanic*).

3 Of course, comic books are often the literal source material for characters and storylines of post-1990s superhero cinema—and many of the narrative conventions discussed in this chapter would apply to comics written decades earlier: stark contrasts between good and evil, the pursuit of moral legibility, and bodies caught in spectacular, kinetic action.

4 Bolter and Grusin, *Remediation*.

5 Gaming's incorporation of the formal qualities of cinema has been documented by scholars such as Will Brooker, Jessica Aldred, Jonathan Mack, Geoff King, and Tanya Krzywinska. King and Krzywinska's edited volume *ScreenPlay: Cinema/Videogames/Interfaces* considers this topic at length.

6 Jenkins identifies a generation of consumers "educated on nonlinear media like video games" who came to prefer a fragmented cinema in order to "make the connections on their own time and in their own ways" (*Convergence Culture*, 119). Jenkins's examples include *Fight Club* (1999), *Being John Malkovich* (1999), *The Sixth Sense* (1999), *The Matrix* (1999), and *Memento* (2000).

7 Fuchs, "Collective Body Memories," 336.

8 Galloway, 62.

9 Caillois, *Man, Play and Games*, 7–8.

10 For work on the connections between spectator sports and popular videogames, see the edited volume on sports videogames by Mia Consalvo, Konstantin Mitgutsch, and Abe Stein.

11 Ben Singer, 41.

12 Ben Singer, 41.

13 This is an allusion to Peter Brooks's early writing on the melodramatic mode, discussed further below.

14 Pribram, 243.

15 Clint Hocking is a game designer known in game studies circles for coining the term "ludonarrative dissonance," meaning conflict between a game's story and its interactive gameplay elements. The references to Hocking in this paragraph are paraphrased from his address at the 2013 Interactive Storytelling Symposium at UC Santa Cruz (titled "Inventing the Future of Games").

16 Fleming, 171. Fleming reworks Marsha Kinder's analogy between videogame play and a child's sleep-bargaining ritual (the request for one more story before bed). Along these lines, Kinder points to videogames as spiritual successors to metanarratives such as *One Thousand and One Nights*.

17 Moretti, 160.

18 Williams, "Mega-Melodrama!," 523; emphasis added.

19 Brooks, *Melodramatic Imagination*, 15; Williams, *Playing the Race Card*.

20 Williams, *Playing the Race Card*; Williams, "Mega-Melodrama!"; Williams, "'Tales of Sound and Fury.'"

21 Linda Williams argues that excess was the rule rather than the exception to classical cinema's supposed subordination of style to plot ("'Tales of Sound and Fury'"). In fact, she suggests we avoid referring to Hollywood cinema between the 1920s and 1950s as "classical" at all.

22 Williams, *Playing the Race Card*, 12. This phrase references Henry James's description of Harriet Beecher Stowe's book *Uncle Tom's Cabin* (1852).

23 Williams, "World and Time," 172.

24 Williams, 172.

25 Superhero narratives in comic books have long drawn on the melodramatic mode to structure their narratives. Jason Bainbridge notes a stronger correspondence between melodrama and Marvel comics than DC, since DC exemplifies a kind of premodern, mythological hero archetype ("Superman, Batman, and Wonder Woman could just as easily be Hercules, Orpheus, and Athena"; 66). Bainbridge suggests that Marvel not only exemplifies but also "deepens" the melodramatic mode by using its long-running serial format both to introduce "shades of grey" (morally ambiguous characters) and to reorder traditional roles (e.g., a villain such as Spider-Man's Norman Osborn, who is also the father figure).

26 Williams, *Playing the Race Card*, 41.

27 Building on Peter Brooks's historical account of melodrama, Mellor and Shilling argue that "the decline of the religious frameworks which constructed and sustained existential and ontological certainties residing outside the individual" in tandem with "the massive rise of the body in consumer culture as a bearer of symbolic value" has led to "a tendency for people to place more importance on the body as constitutive of the self" (413).

28 Niedzviecki claims that "each and every manifestation of pop culture purports to be telling the story of how the individual transcends obstacles and the masses to earn recognition, success, happiness" (68). Specialism is discussed at greater length in chapter 1.

29 Williams, "Film Bodies."

30 Purse, "Digital Heroes," 7.

31 Purse, 22–23.

32 Brooks, *Melodramatic Imagination*, 35.

33 Brooks, 36.

34 Where competitive games are concerned, a player's definition of the situation must include a theory of mind for their opponent, or at least for their opponent's own definition of situation. In the academic study of situational awareness, understanding the nature of the situation is as important as understanding the nature of awareness itself, thus the ecological question "what is the head inside of?" rather than the more conventional "what is inside the head?" (Flach, Mulder, and van Paassen, 42–43).

35 Bordwell, 146.

36 Bordwell, 141, 154.

37 Bordwell, 154.

38 Note that Henry Jenkins applies Bordwell's notion of expressive amplification to videogames when he describes them as an "art of expressive movement" ("Games," 36).

39 Caillois, *Man, Play and Games*, 7–8.

40 The metagame is what matters: every act of play comes with its own framing rules or what Bernard Suits famously terms a game's *"prelusory* goal" (37). Playing in order to deliberately lose (or at least to lose one's bearings) is a perfectly valid use of game software. For one thing, Caillois identifies "ilinx" or vertigo as a fundamental category of games based on efforts "to momentarily destroy the stability of perception and inflict a kind of voluptuous panic upon an otherwise lucid mind" (*Man, Play and Games*, 23). Bonnie Ruberg's discussion of a queer art of failure in

games—losing on purpose—explores this pleasure in the context of queer responses to competitive gamer culture.

41 Bordwell, 133.

42 Brooks, *Body Work*, 1, 3.

43 Niedzviecki, 69, 71.

44 Henry Jenkins uses the term "additive comprehension" to describe films in which plot revelations alter the meaning of previous events, occasioning a review of the plot from the beginning (*Convergence Culture*, 123).

45 "Iconic imagination" is Richard Allen's term for the imagination's power to release pleasure from imagined satisfaction, which Allen analogizes with an audience's fantasmatic play with cinematic images (122). Imagining what will happen next in an unfolding action sequence may seem like a "problem-solving use of the imagination," which Allen contrasts with "wish-fulfilling fantasy" in terms of the effect of pleasure it produces (123). However, this use of imagination is likely much closer to wish fulfillment when it involves the need to grasp the full kinetic significance of a moment of peripety, a new situation, and especially new powers of the body.

46 Whissel, *Spectacular Digital Effects*, 6. Whissel distinguishes a traditional "emblem" with her term, the "effects emblem": "At its most basic level, an 'emblem' is defined as a pictorial image that represents or epitomizes a concept, expresses a moral or lesson, or serves as a 'representation of an abstract quality, an action, state of things, class of persons, etc.' In contemporary cinema, spectacular visual effects often function as 'effects emblems.' I define the 'effects emblem' as a cinematic visual effect that operates as a site of intense signification and gives stunning (and sometimes) allegorical expression to a film's key themes, anxieties, and conceptual obsessions—even as it provokes feelings of astonishment and wonder" (6).

47 For this total, I am counting the revelation of experts or masters hiding in workaday settings. But I am also counting the inverted form of the fantasy that emphasizes weakness, failure, and humiliation—such as when Jiang, one of the residents of the Alley, believes he may be special but is immediately shut down by Landlady or when Sing, as a child, is unable to save Fong from bullies stealing her lollipop. Fong's character—a mute girl whose candy is stolen—seems to exist only to connote virtue, reflecting the more general sexist tendency within the melodramatic tradition to view women (and apparently more, women who do not speak) as sources of virtue.

48 Dyer, 8.

49 "Though Truth and Falsehood bee Neare twins, yet Truth a little elder is": so says John Donne's epigraph in Daniel Gilbert's essay about belief. Gilbert is persuasive in arguing Spinoza's philosophy of belief, in which comprehension entails some degree of acceptance, and where *incredulity* is a separate process that requires additional effort. Thus, there is no such thing as suspending disbelief (as if we were skeptics at base). Like the innocent child, we are inclined to believe until we learn otherwise. Even when we hear a patently false piece of information, this temporal ordering is repeated—we first comprehend (and believe) and then assess (and either certify or reject) new information. Crucially, this two-part process can be disrupted in the middle. One strategy for propagandists, for instance, is to flood the airwaves with so much misinformation that fact-checking efforts are overwhelmed and something false eventually slips through as a truth. Our information-processing resources are finite, thus our capacity to exercise doubt is limited as well.

50 Williams, "World and Time."

51 Brooks, *Body Work*, 2.

52 Of course, deferral itself is at least one goal, given that the anime are often close adaptations of manga. In addition to writing new, tangential plotlines (aka "filler"), drawing out and forestalling a climactic encounter by inserting flashback material is one strategy to avoid "catching up" to or "running out" of canonical source material.

53 Note the risk of porting structures directly between narrative media and video-games: the same strategies anime often use to support and maintain definitions of the situation of play (the temporal manipulations and protractions) would have the opposite effect if used in most games. In action-oriented games, at least, the definition of play is fluid and constantly changing. Temporal interruptions would destabilize the player's ability to make these definitions and respond in intended ways.

54 To be precise, the fight featured in this episode takes place during a preliminary round of eliminations before the final phase. However, the rules and stakes are effectively the same.

55 Bordwell, 140.

56 Whissel, *Spectacular Digital Effects*, 14.

57 Brooks, *Body Work*, 2.

58 Though the fight is short-lived and motivated by the random selection process of the Chūnin exam (i.e., Lee knows nothing of Gaara's victims and does not act during the fight on behalf of the virtuous or suffering), each fighter is so strongly con-trasted along moral lines that it is as if Lee fights on behalf of virtue; moreover, as viewers, we know that Lee (who was rescuing a woodland creature while Gaara was murdering fellow shinobi in cold blood) risks being made an innocent victim himself in the course of the fight. The moral contrast is made even clearer as the fight unfolds by interposed narrative flashbacks that reveal the circumstances shaping Lee's ability to compete (i.e., the bodily training, sources of moral support, and reasons for fighting). The moral contrast comes sharply into focus once more at the fight's conclusion as Lee and Guy's paternal bond stands symbolically above Gaara, who stands alone—nobody has (ever) needed to come to Gaara's aid.

59 Efforts to define the narrative qualities of digital media are a remnant of new media studies' interest in hypertext narrative in the 1990s. Though videogames are understood as distinct from hypertext today, there is still much interest in mapping their unique narrative structure. For a general introduction to narrative-based theories of convergence, see Marie-Laure Ryan's edited volume *Narrative across Media*. The question "What is narrative?" expands in both scope and obscurity over the course of this volume, which broadly considers narrative's philosophical and cultural functions, including its role as an instrument of human thought, alongside more practical concerns, such as what sort of a narrative is shared across distinct media (e.g., cinema and digital games). Efforts to describe this shared narrative thread inevitably return capacious or open-ended definitions.

60 Ryan, 337.

61 Ryan, 337.

62 Grodal, 130–131.

63 In the context of game studies, there are meaningful political stakes to the question of whether games can be considered narrative media. From a certain perspective, even questioning whether something is a story reflects privilege—the privilege (i.e., callousness) to doubt the legitimacy of another person's emotional investment in a media object (especially when that person is already from a marginalized group within the gaming community). Accommodative definitions of narrative can counteract an exclusionary formalist approach to game criticism and are valid for this reason if no other.

64 Freud's *The Interpretation of Dreams* provides the remarkable account of a dream experienced at the moment of being awakened by a wooden object that falls upon a man's neck. In the instant between the external stimulus and his waking, the man supposedly experiences a lengthy, elaborate dream about the French Revolution that culminates in his being beheaded by guillotine. Freud suggests that the dream's temporal compression can be explained if the falling object is understood to have triggered "a phantasy which had been stored up ready-made in his memory for many years" (500). Freud further suggests that ready-made fantasies are frequently incorporated into dreams with relatively little modification and that they serve the purposes of secondary revision (a kind of dream censorship where the mind works to fill in gaps and render dream contents more intelligible). Throughout his career, Freud frequently returned to the idea of ready-made fantasies that can be activated in an instant and then orient us in certain ways with respect to both internal and external reality.

65 For instance, Kristen Whissel has identified bullet time as one of the key "calling cards of a new generation of films featuring computer-generated (CG) images" ("Digital Multitude," 90). Lisa Purse has described bullet time as a flaunting of "the verisimilitude of the image," all the while calling attention to itself as a spectacle, as an effect ("New Spatial Dynamics," 158). Purse thus positions the effect within a wider historical framework harking back to the cinema of attractions. Bob Rehak has described the effect as a "microgenre"—an uncanny effect that has traveled or made "guest appearances" in a range of movies from different genres, but that originates in experimental artwork from decades prior (artwork that itself recalls Muybridge's precinematic experiments with photography and motion).

66 Manovich, 242.
67 Manovich, 251.
68 Spectacular action sequences occurring prior to narrative exposition may inevitably seem (for a moment) to exceed in their form the demands of transparent narration, or what Bordwell, Staiger, and Thompson deem "classical" Hollywood's "self-effacing craftsmanship": the notion that Hollywood style presents narration invisibly, as if viewers are directly observing the unmediated events themselves (3).
69 Rehak, 26.
70 Galloway, 66.
71 Galloway, 65.
72 Bordwell, 144.
73 Juul, *Half-Real*, 179.

Chapter 3   The Tether Fantasy

1 Barthes, "Nautilus," 65.
2 Kaika, 265.
3 Freud, *Civilization*, 40.
4 Referring to the protagonist of Freud's anecdote as the "bedclothed bourgeoisie" marks the historical significance of notions of comfort and domesticity contemporary to Freud. Along with comfort, the idea of a private space called home is tied to the rise of the bourgeois class in the Middle Ages (Rybczynski, 24). Though such concepts long predate Freud, their meaning has continued to shift. Freud did not enjoy many of the contemporary luxuries my own readers might take for granted, such as central heating. The winter air for Freud's bedclothed bourgeoisie would have likely been quite cold. But imagining a cozy space of retreat from such

cold is partly what marks Freud's protagonist bourgeois in spirit. In fact, John Lukacs describes the "bourgeois spirit" as both "Free" but "also secure": "Not for nothing did the satirical draftsmen and writers depict the bourgeois wearing a nightcap, tucking himself under a large comforter on a rainy or wintry night. When we think of a bourgeois scene, we seldom think of nature outdoors; we usually think of something that is human, comfortable, cozy. We seldom think of a bright glittering morning; we think of an afternoon or evening" (622).

5 Freud, *Civilization*, 40.

6 This passage of Freud's has been referenced in an essay by Tom Gunning that historicizes cinema's own role in mediating anxieties about new communications technologies entering home spaces in the early 1900s. The short film Gunning discusses (*The Lonely Villa*, 1909)—about a home invasion that takes place after Father leaves for town—seems to confirm Freud's argument that technology is not our savior. In the film, the distance from home generated by an automobile (which quickly breaks down) is bridged by a desperate plea for help made via phone. The scenario is Freud's "cheap enjoyment" all over again. Although Gunning omits mention of the game played under Freud's bedclothes, the film structurally reenacts this game, albeit in an inverted form where the sanctity of a home base is threatened from without while someone far away rushes back to help.

7 Spufford, 47.

8 Turner.

9 Burn and Carr, 23.

10 Tolkien's Middle-earth fantasy setting is generally considered the inspiration for medieval themes in table-top role-playing games, especially *Dungeons & Dragons* (1974), a game which, in turn, is understood as perhaps the single biggest influence for the RPG videogame genre—one of the core genres in commercial gaming since the late 1980s. However, Burn and Carr go beyond *Baldur's Gate*'s fictional setting and address its game mechanics by arguing that the oscillation between the game's action and its pause menu instantiates the pattern scary/safe.

11 Freud, *Beyond the Pleasure Principle*, 8–9.

12 Through fort-da, Freud describes the mind's fledgling ability to tone down the intensity of lived experience in order to coolly encounter the world and preserve one's place in it. Fort-da stands for the creation of what Freud terms the precon- scious mind and is connected for many readers to Freud's eventual discovery of the death drive. For Jacques Lacan—and thus many psychoanalytically inclined scholars in the humanities—Freud's discussion of fort-da also speaks to the creation of the unconscious.

13 Lacan's discussion of fort-da shifts emphasis away from the child's active agency and toward the space that is produced by the parent's departure—a space that becomes "a ditch" or an "ever-open gap" into which Freud's grandson lets loose a piece of himself attached to a thread reel and there enacts his "centrifugal tracing" of the world (*Four Fundamental Concepts*, 62).

14 Note within these examples the emphasis on the centripetal action of retractions inward that, in their compulsive and daily repetition, seem to express the wish to return to a prior state.

15 Akhtar, *Comprehensive Dictionary of Psychoanalysis*, 284.

16 Akhtar, *Damaged Core*, 75.

17 Akhtar, 76–77.

18 "Rapprochement" is a reference to one of the subphases of separation-individuation originally identified by Margaret Mahler. Rapprochement is said to occur between

months fifteen and twenty-five and involves a return to the parent after the explorations of the surrounding world via crawling that characterize the "practicing" subphase (when the child is ten to fifteen months old; Mahler, 407).

19 Akhtar, *Inner Torment*, 257.

20 Of course, Turkle does engage digital games in several of her studies, including *Alone Together*. However, none of her claims about tethers in that book are extended to games. Most likely, this opportunity is missed because emphasis in psychoanalytic studies of digital games tends to fall on the game's presumed status as an idealized substitute, a second reality for a second self. Such a dualistic mind-set about games seems influenced by popular representations of the medium, such as the matrix in Gibson's *Neuromancer* (1984) or the OASIS in *Ready Player One* (2011). While some videogames do explicitly present themselves as fully coherent virtual spaces meant to simulate and supplant the real world—such as *Second Life* (2003–present)—most do not.

21 Ainsworth et al., 20.

22 Behavioral psychology and psychoanalytic theory cannot be easily reconciled with one another in a general sense; there is, however, quite a bit of similarity in the theories employed for understanding this particular set of developmental phenomena (see, for instance, Lyons-Ruth or Holmes).

23 Lyons-Ruth, 4.

24 Holmes, 29.

25 Holmes, 8.

26 Holmes, 9, 29.

27 Holmes, 29.

28 Holmes, 7.

29 Frost, 91–92.

30 Bachelard, 39, 40.

31 Quoted in Bachelard, 30–31.

32 Bachelard, 30.

33 "Turn Your Home into a Fortress."

34 May, 102.

35 Klinger, 9.

36 Klinger, 51.

37 Klinger, 10.

38 Klinger, 10.

39 The untranslatable word *koselig* (pronounced "Koohshlee") is often described as a pleasure taken in practices that make one feel cozy during winter. But it has been better understood as "a sort of shared, safe togetherness" by a Scandinavian language expert: "It can describe a house, a situation, a meal, a conversation, or a person," as long as the reference somehow is related to a "feeling of safe, warm, and good" (quoted in Ware). Koselig is often evoked in relation to winter and seasonal affective disorder, which people in the northernmost parts of Norway seem to avoid by embracing winter's enforced inwardness: by staying indoors, enjoying cozy rituals (fireplaces, warm drinks, quiet mornings), making connections with others, and embracing nature.

40 These are terms Klinger pulls from a 2003 *New York Times* story on stay-at-home film buffs (25).

41 APN News.

42 Barr and Copeland-Stewart, 129.

43 Klinger, 9.

44 Turner.

45 Many attachment researchers subscribe to a universality hypothesis that the theory applies to all cultures, all people—and even many animals. Infant research consistently shows no statistically significant variance between sexes. However, some researchers disagree, suggesting at the very least that there are meaningful differences in how attachment outcomes are expressed in different cultures. Wang and Mallinckrodt offer a review of the debate, which they suggest may never be resolved. The authors cover a relatively limited set of empirical cross-cultural adult attachment studies, call for more research, and devote the remainder of their article to laying some of the conceptual groundwork for how the core term in the theory— the secure attachment—is defined differently in various cultural contexts. They are especially persuasive in one regard: the widely used tests that measure attachment styles, such as the Experiences in Close Relationships Scale (ECRS), express a bias toward Western cultural ideals. Using such measures outside of an American or European context could potentially skew results (193).

46 Porteous, 387–388.

47 Wolff, 37.

48 Massey, 7.

49 Jessica Benjamin, 148.

50 Bachelard, 6.

51 Bachelard, 41.

52 Jacobson, Silverstein, and Winslow, 208.

53 Jacobson, Silverstein, and Winslow, 231.

54 Tether imagery likely speaks to wellness even when we fantasize about the tether being stretched beyond its limit, such as in fantasies about our home's defenses failing. Spufford identifies "a sublime of defeat," "a dreamed-of conquest *by* raging elements" in disaster narratives about cataclysmic floods, epic snowstorms, or, in our post-9/11 context, a zombie apocalypse (26). Even in these cases, we are imagining a scenario that ultimately speaks to our security, that centers its protagonists in the universe as witnesses to the end, as perhaps the last people on earth (so much more reason to claim what love remains). More than a simple pleasure taken in pain, John Kucich suggests that masochism can be understood as a kind of empowerment that is achieved by evoking "a powerful or punitive other": "If parental figures have become identified with the pain they cause, then aggravating such pain can magically evoke their presence and overcome separation anxiety" (84). As one patient puts it, "When I'm feeling good, I feel alone; when I'm feeling bad, I'm with my mother."

55 The film resonated at least with the voting members of the Academy of Motion Picture Arts and Sciences: *Parasite* won Best Picture, Best Director, Best Original Screenplay, and Best Foreign Language Film at the 92nd Academy Awards.

56 Salman Akhtar's research on tether fantasies focuses on pathological cases of unresolved separation-individuation. So too is attachment theory employed to address problems that arise in the attachment patterns a child forms early in life. A child with a "secure" attachment pattern "is confident that his parent (or parent figure) will be available, responsive, and helpful should he encounter adverse or frightening situations. With this assurance, he feels bold in his explorations of the world" (Bowlby, 123). Unfortunately, many children experience trauma at a young age from physical or sexual abuse, neglect, abandonment, or other causes. Problems a child faces with early attachment figures can influence relationship patterns throughout life. Further, it is a tenet of the theory that attachment patterns tend to

reproduce themselves generationally, as a central factor influencing a parent's caretaking style is the attachment habits formed in childhood based on their own parenting.

57 Fog-Olwig, 226.

58 Morley, 56.

59 Fraser, 37.

60 hooks, 33.

61 hooks, 34.

62 Jenkins, "Complete Freedom of Movement," 335.

63 Flanagan, 53.

64 Flanagan, 53.

65 Flanagan, 52–53.

66 Flanagan, 52.

67 Holmes, 29.

68 Holmes, 9.

69 The possibility of an irretrievable "game over" invests every action with seriousness. There is no respite, no recovery, like a tether stuck forever in the extended position until it snaps, once and for all. This is an anxious tether. One of the genre's pleasures lies in its requirement to tread lightly, to respect every threat, and to act with care and deliberateness. Rob Parker makes sense of permadeath genres such as roguelikes in terms of terror management theory and the strategies it identifies for avoiding conflict between life-preservative instincts and the realization that death awaits us all.

70 In speed running, there are scant moments of rest until the run is complete. Their metagame is about setting records. If they have time to experience a tether, one might expect it to take the form of an ever-expanding anxiety since the better one does and the longer one plays, the more the pressure mounts. However, for many runs, the tensest moments differ from what typical players would think of as a game's challenge points. Speed runs are made or broken by difficult tricks or exploits to which most players remain oblivious.

71 *Ori and the Blind Forest*'s unique save mechanic reflects an awareness of this player latitude. Rather than attempting to guess where players will feel comfortable saving their progress, the game allows players to situate a check point nearly anywhere they like by consuming a limited but renewable resource. The game's player-determined checkpoints are anchoring positions from which play may progress with confidence, instantiating the attachment theory tenet that exploratory behavior (and therefore progress) extends outward into the unknown from a point of security.

72 Akhtar, *Damaged Core*, 78.

73 In dungeon crawlers and MOBAs, the directionality of protective relationships is typically fixed in one's character class or build. In other games, these roles are reversible and depend on spatial position. *Fire Emblem: Awakening* (2013) employs a support mechanic offering stat bonuses to characters attacking or defending while occupying spaces adjacent to one another. Characters earn a relationship grade that reflects their general compatibility in battle. In Microsoft's *Gears of War* games (2006, 2008, 2011, 2013), players can revive one another on the battlefield for a short period of time after falling. These games incentivize keeping teammates nearby and so sharing in the experience of play. However, lifeline tether play may emerge in nearly any fluidly cooperative game if one reflects on the added security a nearby ally provides.

74 While it is true that many RPGs have prominent narrative elements, such as the lavish cinematics for which the *Final Fantasy* series is known, there are also RPGs

with scant storylines (or with cutscenes that players can easily skip or ignore). Dungeon crawlers, puzzle RPGs, and other interesting, hybrid formats sometimes minimize narrative in favor of a sustained focus on play's mechanics. The iOS game *Sword & Poker* (2010), which stages its combat on a grid of playing cards, eschews not only narrative but navigation as well. Admittedly, *Sword & Poker* does not contain much of a tether fantasy. Often, the strength of a tether and the prominence of fictional settings are correlated.

75 See note 54 above.

76 Queer theorists such as Jack Halberstam and Kathryn Bond Stockton have embraced failure as a subversive act. Along similar lines, Bonnie Ruberg argues that we might queer commercial games by embracing our failure to complete their challenges or by rejecting a game's given goals and playing in ways not intended by developers ("playing the wrong way"; 156).

77 It is worth noting that this archetype is widespread not only among role-playing and adventure games but also in works of fantasy fiction that influence and inspire these games, such as in Tolkien's tendency to anchor his adventure stories in the idyllic domestic space of the Shire, which is left behind only reluctantly. Home is able to maintain an air of innocence, perhaps only by being left behind early in plot.

78 Some games combine siege narratives with progression gameplay that incorporates a home space throughout play, such as Ubisoft's *Beyond Good & Evil* (2003). Such games express a clear hope that players will develop a narrative attachment to home and its occupants and will feel compelled by the story to protect such a place in fantasy as well.

79 One notable exception is *Dwarf Fortress* (2006) and the games it has inspired, such as *RimWorld* (2018), *Stonehearth* (2018), *Oxygen Not Included* (2019), and perhaps even *Factorio* (2016). The home base tethers in these games take a backseat to simulation and players will probably spend more time in menus delegating tasks and customizing characters than reflecting on the borders of home base. Nevertheless, despite the very steep learning curve, the abstract visuals, the focus on automation, and the general absence of player-controlled characters, there is some home base tether play in each example that is worth acknowledging.

80 *Minecraft* is perhaps more interesting for its departures from what inspired it (e.g., *Dwarf Fortress*) than the similarities. *Minecraft* has become one of the most successful and influential games of the past decade, often credited with inspiring a new videogame genre (called crafting or survival), with dozens of copycat games in the subsequent decade. As Mojang (the developer's company) playfully points out, if every one of the 200 million people who purchased the game were to form a nation, it would be the eighth most populous nation in the world. Despite being developed a decade ago, *Minecraft* still boasted 126 million monthly players as of 2021 (Warren). Much of the game's success is attributed to the unique manner in which it assembles its world, which allows the game to serve as the ultimate sandbox where players can build three-dimensional models of nearly anything they imagine.

It is difficult to measure the full extent of *Minecraft*'s influence on games designed in the 2010s. As a popular and cultural phenomenon almost without parallel in the videogame industry, and as an independently designed game kept alive by a vibrant modding and streaming community, *Minecraft* disrupted conventional understandings of production, distribution, and reception. Sometimes, a detectable influence on commercial production is subtle, such as with the settlement system (a small part of a much larger game) where players construct bases through resource management, such as in Bethesda's *Fallout 4* (2015). However, there is a striking number of games directly influenced not only by *Minecraft*'s design (its combination of survival, crafting, and exploration built around home base and lifeline tether fantasies) but also in many cases by its independent production model: *Junk Jack* (2011), *Starmade* (2012), *7 Days to Die* (2013), *Don't Starve* (2013), *King Arthur's Gold* (2013), *Rust* (2013), *DayZ* (2013), *Block Fortress* (2014), *The Castle Doctrine* (2014), *Craft the World* (2014), *The Long Dark* (2014), *Dying Light* (2015), *Terasology* (2015), *Trove* (2015), *Kerbal Space Program* (2015), *Starbound* (2016), *Dragon Quest Builders* (2016), *No Man's Sky* (2016), *Planet Centauri* (2016), *Space Engineers* (2016), *Stardew Valley* (2016), *Factorio* (2016), *Ark: Survival Evolved* (2017), *Colony Survival* (2017), *Castle Story* (2017), *Robocraft* (2017), *Lego Worlds* (2017), *The Flame in the Flood* (2017), *The Forest* (2018), *Subnautica* (2018), *Dragon Quest Builders 2* (2018), *Eco* (2018), *Conan Exiles* (2018), *Cube World* (2019), *Astroneer* (2019), *Necesse* (2019), *Volcanoids* (2019), and *Valheim* (2021). Many of these games were developed with grassroots Kickstarter campaigns, and many were independently designed and depended on player interest during early access.

81 In addition to the game's unique visual style, its voxel design has played a large part in its longevity. The voxel is inseparable from *Minecraft*'s flexibility as a platform for showcasing and playing with user-generated content (it is often compared to other block-based toys such as Lego). The game's endless modifiability (along with Mojang's decision to actively support player mods) has broadened the game's appeal to Twitch.tv streamers and YouTube personalities who have, in turn, ensured the game's continued popularity.

82 *Minecraft*'s basic Survival Mode tasks players with staying alive and progressing through a series of open-ended challenges in a sandbox-style, modifiable play space. Monsters will attack (they roam at night or in dark places underground), players can take damage from a variety of sources and die, and resources are limited to what they collect while playing the game.

83 Although there are randomly positioned villages of indigenous people in *Minecraft*, and although players will sometimes happen upon a long-abandoned mine shaft, *Minecraft*'s world is generally untouched when players begin; it is procedurally ripe for the taking. When viewed ecologically, *Minecraft* seems to impart a narrative of colonialist expansion and domination. Daniel Dooghan provides a thorough discussion of what he terms *Minecraft*'s neoliberal apologetics, its perpetuation of myths of empire that justify economic inequality. Moreover, *Minecraft* joins a long list of games that Alenda Chang argues mythologize nature as a fount of unlimited and untouched resources intended for our consumption—in short, the myth of wilderness. What the notion of a tether brings to this conversation is an emphasis on how the game's exploitative consumption of natural resources is *galvanized* by the urgency of security-seeking.

In attachment theory, when security-seeking takes over, it disables other, *nonessential* behavior systems. So there is considerable metaphoric power in aligning a theme of natural resource exploitation with the dynamics of meeting basic survival needs. Contemporary U.S. politics have illustrated the potency of such an alignment in emboldening binary, us-versus-them thinking. For many survivalists and conspiracy theorists, the apocalypse expresses the imaginary social, spatial, and ecological relations that loom powerfully over our present moment. Their daily lives are framed and enclosed by backyard bomb shelters, surveillance equipment, gas-powered generators, and stockpiles of weapons, food, water, and munitions. The survivalist's world verges on an imagined future when urban industrialism has collapsed, global populations succumb to starvation, and families can survive only by tightly closing ranks and defending what is theirs. In this future, feelings don't matter, environmental conservation is moot, and identity politics are frozen in place (or even rolled back).

84 Of course, there are unavoidable discontinuities to play at the start and end of any play session or when players collectively sleep through the night in beds. There are also portals players travel through within Survival Mode—these are rare and fictionally motivated discontinuities to play. Perhaps more significantly, *Minecraft*'s aesthetic of continuity is predicated on a pervasive discontinuity. Even without considering the discrete, binary logic of digital code, it is worth considering that *Minecraft*'s voxel system itself is an illusion; what we think of as one continuous world that dynamically changes as we interact with it is actually many different completely static worlds. Every time we move a block, the game presents us with a new world image that reflects that single change.

85 Klapp, 12. Klapp sees patterns of opening and closing as "a feature of human collectives," and, far beyond that, even "as part of a natural tide or rhythm throughout the living world":

> The sea anemone in a tide pool outstretches and retracts its green tentacles. The turtle and snail withdraw into shells when openness gets to be too much. Hibernation is a seasonal closure. The Old Testament says: "to everything there is a season . . . a time to get and a time to lose; a time to keep and a time to cast away . . . a time to keep silence, and a time to speak" (Ecclesiastes 3:1–7). The sabbath is a traditional closure to worldliness once a week. The pupil dilates when light is dim and contracts when it is bright. Youth is a time of risk, whereas old age is one of saving and stocktaking. The child crawls, reaches, tastes, then curls up to rest. From such things, we see that what we call aliveness—resilience, adaptability—is not continual intake, nor any constant policy, but sensitive alternation of openness and closure. The mind listens alertly, then turns off to signals. The natural pattern is alternation, and the more alive a system is, the more alertly it opens and closes. In such a view, closing is not, as some suppose, merely a setback to growth and progress, but evidence that the mechanisms of life are working, that the society has resiliency. More alarming than swings to closure would be a lack of public response. A perpetually open society would suffer the same fate of a perpetually open clam. (14–15)

The range of examples in Klapp's writing is breathtaking and seems to follow an intuitive path through imagination (like fantasy). However, his interweaving of examples from social, psychological, informatic, homeostatic, and developmental levels threatens at times to cast nuanced social issues in simple, binary terms. This is a problem that threatens to naturalize closed-mindedness and resistance to social change by analogy with nonconscious physiological responses to stimulus, such as a pupil contracting in bright light.

86 Klapp, 15.

87 For most of the game, players explore a dark underground world by carrying torches, lamps, and glowsticks into that darkness to light a path. The narrow pathway cut by play's activity typically represents only a small portion of the screen's total area, which dwarf's the tiny player character, helping to restrict vision and knowledge of all surrounding blocks and materials to the player character's rough visual field.

88 In a "Blood Moon," more powerful monsters emerge and zombies are able to open doors. But the Blood Moon pales in comparison to the invasion of the goblin or

pirate armies, when hordes lay siege to home base, picking locks and attacking both players and important nonplayer characters.

89 One particularly illustrative example is the Sol Duc River cabin, a one-of-a-kind, private steelhead fly fishing cabin that rests on ten-foot stilts to protect it from seasonal flooding, given its location near the shore of Washington State's Sol Duc River. The client who commissioned a Seattle-based architect (Olson Kundig) to design the cabin describes it as "a comfortable, small rural refuge from city life, a fishing base in an area where wildlife abounds—a place to escape to read, take in the landscape and its surroundings and recharge" (Trumpp). The vacation home employs a large sliding steel panel that completely encloses its windows to the outside world when not in use (to protect the home from the elements as well as "intruders"). When the panel is open, it affords a two-story, floor-to-ceiling view of the grove of alder trees beyond the river. Though remote in its location, and capable of closing up in a tight cube, the cabin boasts a full range of amenities, including electricity, plumbing, internet access, ventilation, natural light, and a covered and elevated outdoor deck.

When I first encountered a post about the Sol Duc River cabin on a fly fishing blog, during the summer of 2020, at the height of the global COVID-19 pandemic and amid nightly protests of police brutality in Philadelphia, where I was staying, I imagined climbing its stairs during a flood—riverboat docked below—and finding temporary haven from the world.

90 Rank, 100.

91 "Perpetual Motion."

92 The Rankian comparison between this sensation of motion and a uterine state has already been popularly observed in a range of fields (from sleep science to developmental psychology). Personally, I need *white noise* to sleep at night—so, when traveling and deprived of my bedroom, I instead play a ten-hour YouTube video that purports to be the room tone aboard the Starship *Enterprise*, the sound of its always-humming engines. I once lived in an apartment above a restaurant and became accustomed to the rhythmic vibrations of its grill fans during the day. I would feel suddenly deflated or even lonely when the fans were powered down each evening—it's a sensation similar to when a moving vehicle comes to rest suddenly and prematurely. The restaurant's large grill fans put my home *in motion*.

93 Edwards, 320.

94 Edwards, 8.

95 Edwards describes a series of exhibits at the 1964 World's Fair in New York City that reveal "a remarkable range of images representing closed, artificial systems in hostile environments": "space capsules, undersea communities inhabiting pressurized domes, underground houses, and space stations. Many of the images . . . depict smiling, prosperous white nuclear families going about their ordinary daily activities inside the walls of these bubble-like shells. . . . [On] a symbolic level all of these amount to fallout shelters: tiny artificial containers in which the white nuclear family would avoid the perils of nuclear holocaust" (425). Perpetuum mobile tethers are common in Edwards's discussion of closed-world aesthetics in popular media, which focuses largely on science fiction set in outer space. However, it would be misleading to tie perpetuum mobile tethers exclusively to this historical period, given their indebtedness to narratives of maritime exploration, articulated at least a century prior in Jules Verne's 1870 novel *Twenty Thousand Leagues under the Sea*, which was itself apparently inspired by Verne's encounter with the French submarine, the *Plongeur* (built in the early 1860s).

96 Edwards, 13.

97 Diana Wynne Jones's 1986 novel of the same name is just as strongly a perpetuum mobile narrative—perhaps even more so given its tighter emphasis on the mechanics of the castle itself as well as the castle's role in protecting its inhabitants from the Witch of the Waste. However, Miyazaki's film better exemplifies Edwards's category of green-world aesthetics by reframing the narrative more explicitly against the backdrop of a world war, the ultimate limit to the enlightenment's embrace of "rationality, authority, convention, and technology" (Edwards, 13).

98 The dramatic conclusion to *The Matrix* is a perpetuum mobile fantasy. The film's protagonists evade their machine overlords by hiding in an abandoned underworld in a perpetuum mobile vessel, the *Nebuchadnezzar*. From this ship, the heroes hack into the virtual reality system (the Matrix) that enslaves humanity. Their telepresence within an abstracted virtual space is anchored in this mobile vessel (which houses their vulnerable flesh-and-blood bodies). And if their connection to the Matrix is severed before they can safely withdraw, they die. In the conclusion, with Neo still trapped inside the Matrix and Sentinels clawing their way through the *Nebuchadnezzar*'s hull, Morpheus is much like Bill Adama, hand above the throttle (in this case, an electromagnetic pulse that would stop the Sentinels but also immediately sever Neo's neural connection), waiting until the last possible moment so Neo might return aboard.

99 For instance, the space opera *Skylark* novels from the 1920s and 1930s were an influence for the fictional setting of Steve Russell's *Spacewar!* (1962), an early and influential game designed and played on PDP-1 computers on college campuses in the 1960s. In turn, *Spacewar!* was a direct inspiration for some of the earliest coin-operated commercial videogames the following decade, such as *Galaxy Game* (1971) and *Computer Space* (1971). Though *Spacewar!* features no real tether mechanics in its two-dimensional, dogfight gameplay, the game's very impetus is explicitly tied to the wish to carry *Skylark*'s perpetuum mobile story forward in a new medium (purportedly out of frustration for a lack of compelling cinematic adaptations of the source material). Fantasy also bridges the divide between what one does while playing and what one imagines doing.

100 Moore's law is not a law in a legalistic or scientific sense. It roughly states that the speed and efficiency of computers increase every several years.

101 The design of the Nintendo DS was more directly inspired by Nintendo's own handheld *Game & Watch* games from the early 1980s such as *Oil Panic* (1982), which feature both multiscreen play and a clasping clamshell design.

102 Susan Stewart, 61.

103 Klinger, 10.

104 *Astroneer* is unique because of its oxygen tether system. As players explore, they must craft literal tethers or lines supplying oxygen and power from a central source, home base. These lines eventually crisscross the planet's surface in areas that have undergone exploration.

105 Freud, *Civilization*, 40.

106 This analogy appears in Freud's *Introductory Lectures on Psycho-Analysis* (Lecture XXVI), "On Narcissism" and "A Difficulty in the Path of Psychoanalysis."

Chapter 4   The Fantasy of Accretions

1 Bettelheim, 44.

2 Bettelheim, 44.

3 Cramer, 70.

4 Note that the series' English subtitled version is the source for this translated text.

5 *Naruto* and *Naruto: Shippûden* frequently juxtapose the bodily harm and self-sacrifice of their titular protagonist against villains who have already built some power or ability that prevents bodily injury: a foe with armored skin who can be damaged only with a self-dealt blow; a foe who is more prosthesis than body, whose only point of vulnerability (a small lump of flesh) is encased and nested within deadly and invincible puppets he controls; a foe surrounded by sentient sand, which reflexively forms a defensive barrier; or a foe who can selectively slip through objects or allow them to pass through without incidence (a body that isn't really there). The fantasies of invulnerability proliferate. None of these opponents need lift a finger in self-defense. The contrast with Naruto's vulnerability frames Naruto's gradual acquisition of new powers and competencies throughout the series.

6 Game designer Shigeru Miyamoto (creator of Mario, Zelda, Donkey Kong, Star Fox, and others) is likely being sardonic when describing RPGs this way in a 1994 interview for the Japanese magazine *Famicom Tsushin*. In Chris Kohler's translation of the interview, Miyamoto emphasizes how, in RPGs, players begin "completely bound hand and foot and can't move"—no amount of skill can change this situation (quoted in Kohler 88). It is "only gradually, as your character gains powers, [that] you become able to move your hands, your feet . . . you come untied slowly. And in the end, you feel powerful" (88). In an echo of Freud's "cheap enjoyment" (discussed in chapter 3), Miyamoto questions whether genuine happiness can result from arbitrarily denying basic freedoms before gradually restoring them.

7 The trope of premature encounters with difficult bosses in games has many variations, including fights that cannot be won, fights that are nearly impossible to win, and fights that are lost entirely in narrative cinematics. For instance, at the start to *Paper Mario* (2000), Mario faces his rival, Bowser, during the game's prologue. This fight is interactive, but only one outcome is possible. Because he cannot be harmed while in possession of the "Star Rod," Bowser defeats Mario and initiates the game's accretions project. In addition to accruing gear, coins, and experience points, Mario must also rescue and absorb the powers of seven "Star Spirits" imprisoned throughout the Mushroom Kingdom. These spirits strip Bowser of his invulnerability at the start of the game's final boss fight. The trope of the premature boss (or difficult enemy) encounter cuts across game genres and includes many prominent examples, such as *Mega Man X* (1993), *Chrono Trigger* (1995), *Super Mario RPG: The Legend of the Seven Stars* (1996), *The Legend of Zelda: The Ocarina of Time* (1998), *Resident Evil 2* (1998), *Dino Crisis* (1999), *The Legend of Zelda: Majora's Mask* (2000), *Silent Hill 2* (2001), *Metroid Fusion* (2002), *Fatal Frame II: Crimson Butterfly* (2003), *Metal Gear Solid 3: Snake Eater* (2004), *God of War II* (2007), *Demon's Souls* (2009), *Amnesia: The Dark Descent* (2010), *Dark Souls* (2011), *Metal Gear Rising: Revengeance* (2013), *Alien: Isolation* (2014), *Star Wars Jedi: Fallen Order* (2019), *Devil May Cry 5* (2020), *Sekiro: Shadows Die Twice* (2020), and *Metroid Dread* (2021).

8 This is to borrow Hal Foster's Freudian phrasing for describing a fascist fixation on body armor (or the body as armor) as a way of shoring up a shattered ego (73).

9 See, for instance, Ling et al. for a discussion of goal setting theory's contention that specific and immediate goals are more effective motivators than abstract and long-term goals. See Locke et al. for a general introduction to the theory.

10 In *Final Fantasy Tactics A2: Grimoire of the Rift* (2008), for instance, players build teams and send them to complete quests for gold and loot. While in combat,

teammates gain experience, gradually mastering abilities that their equipment allows them to perform—once mastered, they can perform these abilities without the equipped gear, which allows them to equip different gear and master new abilities. Defeated enemies drop loot, which can be brought to a trader to unlock new items that can be purchased with gold and equipped to train new abilities. Each quest entails specific demands and requirements (bring certain items, defeat certain enemies, protect certain friendly nonplayer characters, etc.) and introduces its own tactical complications on the battlefield. But the skill mastery, experience, and loot system underlies all else as a cascading set of small goals and tasks that build gradually over a complex accretions project. Every new loot drop, like every encounter with enemies, prompts a review of accretion menus: players will need to regularly review their party members' progress in mastering skills, just as they will need to regularly check the trader's inventory options. Decisions must be made about allocating scarce loot resources or possibly swapping gear among party members so each has a turn learning useful abilities. These decisions relate meaningfully to every other aspect of play, including which quests to accept, where to travel, and which party members to include in a mission.

11 Each time I play *Super Mario RPG* (*SMRPG*), I anticipate one particular end-game accretion: the Lazy Shell, a piece of armor that makes whoever equips it extremely "tanky" (high defense) but at the cost of reduced attack damage and speed. It has always seemed like a dominant strategy to equip Princess Toadstool with the Lazy Shell armor since she has few damage-based offensive abilities. With the Lazy Shell, she generally survives most attacks and can heal and revive teammates, making it unlikely you will see the "Game Over" screen (lose your entire party during combat). Though there are other options for equipping gear in *SMRPG*, I've completed the game's roughly seventeen-hour narrative adventure at least a half dozen times, and I've never strayed from this upgrade path or excluded Toadstool from my party.

12 The term "rogue-lite" is meant to strike a comparison with (while maintaining some difference from) the genre of "rogue-like" or "roguelike" games, an RPG subgenre featuring tile- or grid-based movement, turn-based gameplay, procedurally generated terrain, and permanent death. All terms reference an ASCII game from 1980 titled simply *Rogue*. Rogue-lite games diverge formally from roguelikes in a number of ways, blending key aspects (such as procedurally generated encounters and permanent death) with other popular genres, like side-scrollers or action RPGs. Often, rogue-lites are relatively short games that reset on avatar death. All upgrades or accretions gained during any one "run" are lost, though there are certain accretions that persist. For example, *Hades* (2020) features different kinds of currency: Charon's Obol, or gold coins, can be spent on valuable upgrades during any run, but the currency is lost (along with all accrued upgrades) upon death. However, on each run, players can also collect gems or "darkness," currencies that are kept after death and can be spent to unlock permanent upgrades that will assist all future runs (e.g., an extra life, an extra dash, a higher chance of encountering rare upgrades, etc.).

13 These stats are drawn from the NeoSeeker FAQ for *Aria of Sorrow* and have not been independently verified. As of June 2021, the game FAQ can be found here: https://www.neoseeker.com/castlevania-aria/faqs/1053296-castlevania-aos-enemy -list.html.

14 Juul, "Zero-Player Games." Alharthi et al. provide a helpful taxonomy of idle-clicker games. Their review reveals a surprising variation of game mechanics and degrees of player involvement. *Cookie Clicker* is currently running in the background of my

laptop, and each time I proof this paragraph, I am reminded to check on my cookie totals and rate of accrual.

15 In multiplayer games where accretions play a large role, such as with *League of Legends*, the positive feedback loops are two-sided. They help whichever team builds an early lead gain momentum and potentially "snowball" a win (and whichever team falls behind early is likely to fall further behind as the game progresses, barring an upset). Conversely, negative feedback loops work to restore a state of balance or offer the players who are behind (in gold or in the race) a chance to catch up. Nintendo's *Mario Kart* series (1992, 1996, 2001, 2003, 2005, 2008, 2011, 2014, 2017, 2020) is built around a negative feedback loop where racers who are farther behind receive more powerful items than those in the lead. But even *League of Legends* installs a negative feedback loop into its play with a "bounty" system that rewards the losing team with extra gold for managing to take down objectives or opponents.

16 As Siang and Rao argue, while extrinsic game rewards such as coins from a slot machine are immediately intelligible to players, rewards that are intrinsically motivating rely on some degree of prior familiarity with a game's rules and the wider stakes of play. Understanding an accretion's marginal shift in the balance of power from the game world to the player requires a basic awareness of how power is distributed in the first place, such as is communicated with particular clarity in some games by a premature encounter with a much stronger foe. But even in the absence of this trope, games offer numerous ways to clarify the situation of play in terms that are relevant to the accretions process. For instance, most accretions games convert action into numerical expression. *League of Legends* displays the damage dealt by each attack as a number that crops up and quickly fades near the attack's target. As players upgrade skills and accrue items, these numbers grow in size and frequency. They are even color coded to clarify between different kinds of damage: physical, magical, or "true" damage that ignores resistances.

17 Peterson, 341. Though Gary Gygax's influential tabletop role-playing game *Dungeons & Dragons* (1974) is often thought of as single-handedly introducing and popularizing stratified progression, Jon Peterson's history of tabletop wargames demonstrates that versions of this system were in place in earlier games as well, such as the medieval-themed *Chainmail* (1971), on which Gygax himself worked. And Gygax took inspiration from even older war-themed games. To illustrate that stratification "has existed in some form since the very beginning of wargaming," Peterson notes a 1780 edition of chess featuring a "leaping queen" that combined the move sets of rooks, bishops, and knights (342).

18 Peterson, 342.

19 Peterson, 343.

20 Peterson, 343.

21 In their book on the German philosopher, Robert Solomon and Kathleen Higgins track a number of distinct and even contradictory ways that Nietzsche has characterized strength and weakness. One especially prevalent metaphor Nietzsche evokes for strength is as a "response to ill-health," and Solomon and Higgins note that "Nietzsche's own response to his debilitating infirmities was a muscular and aggressive prose, full of vitality, displaying a strength that only the strongest souls can fully comprehend" (122).

22 In other words, Peterson adopts a perspective akin to Ian Bogost's notion of procedural rhetoric, the idea that games make arguments about the world through their interactive systems.

23 Peterson, 345.

24 Chang, 73.

25 Fine, 76–77.

26 Žižek, *Plague of Fantasies*, 11.

27 For a comprehensive overview and discussion of games and questions of motivation told from the point of view of "gamification," see Richter, Raban, and Rafaeli. Additionally, consider Patrick Jagoda's book, *Experimental Games*, which persuasively positions gamification as a counterpart to neoliberalism.

28 King, Delfabbro, and Griffiths note gaming's general "kitchen sink" tendency to overlay different methods of motivating play (99). Theirs follows Nick Yee's oft-cited essay on reasons for playing MMORPGs such as *World of Warcraft* (*WOW*) ("Motivation for Play"). Yee organizes his discovery of multiple, overlapping motivations into broad categories, such as "achievement," "social," and "immersion." His identification of different motivations produces a psychological taxonomy of *WOW* players. Bateman and Nacke, as well as Nacke, Bateman, and Mandryk, have since updated and extended Yee's approach. Of course, researchers have been interested in gaming's motivational powers for much longer than this. See, for instance, Turkle's chapter in *The Second Self* on "Computer Holding Power" or Malone's 1981 essay on intrinsic motivation.

29 Self-determination theory posits that any task will be more deeply and internally motivated when it meets one or more of three basic psychological needs: competence, autonomy, and relatedness. Nir Eyal has applied these general categories to digital and social media, breaking down their means of "hooking" users into three broad sorts of rewards—rewards of the hunt, of the self, and of the tribe. Though Eyal situates digital games mainly in the category of rewards of the self (i.e., experiences that are intrinsically motivating and make us feel competent when we complete them), it is also clear that games help us feel connected, accepted, and important to others (rewards of the tribe) and that games provide some outlet for "the need to acquire physical objects, such as food and other supplies that aid our survival" (rewards of the hunt) (77).

30 Consider Abraham Maslow's hypothesis in his hierarchy of needs that physiological needs (like food and shelter) and foundational psychological needs (like a sense of safety and security) underlie more complex social and psychological needs, such as belongingness, self-esteem, and self-actualization (the full realization of life goals and ambitions). Scholarship applying Maslow's hierarchy of needs to games might take many forms. For instance, gamification scholars such as Richter, Raban, and Rafaeli are interested in the foundational elements of a game's system that must be in place to foster more complex kinds of motivation. Richter et al. draw on theories of learning (e.g., Siang and Rao) and situate "rules need" at the base of a modified Maslow pyramid, suggesting that the most foundational need for anyone to become motivated to play a game is to understand the rules (2).

31 See, for instance, King, Delfabbro, and Griffiths for a discussion of variable ratios in games (100). As Bateman succinctly puts it, neurochemical research has shown that "even if we fail at an activity, the decision center will release dopamine *if it assesses that we nearly won.* In other words, when we come close to triumph, the limbic system spurs us into another attempt" (*Imaginary Games*, 34). Variable reward ratios, where players are genuinely unsure whether the next attempt will be met with success, produce this dopamine release with every pull of the lever.

32 Bateman, "Grind Mystery." As Bateman points out on his blog, videogames seem to follow the same pattern employed by animal trainers of gradually reducing the

percentage of instances when a desired behavior is rewarded until the response is firmly established, after which time it is rewarded on a random basis ("Grind Mystery"). For instance, players earn experience points from defeating enemies and will level up relatively frequently early in the game *Castlevania: Symphony of the Night* (1997). But the level ups will occur less frequently later in the game, when the emphasis of accretions play will likely instead fall on the search for special weapons such as the Crissaegrim or the Heaven's Sword, which specific enemies in Dracula's castle drop a tiny percentage of the times they are defeated.

33 Bateman, *Imaginary Games*, 33.

34 Hopson.

35 Madigan, 100. As Madigan points out, while the Zeigarnik effect seems to speak to the game design strategy of motivating play with multiple, overlapping tasks or quests—denying closure—it also speaks to more granular game dynamics, such as a gap in accumulated blocks in a round of *Tetris*.

36 Bateman, *Imaginary Games*.

37 Goggins; Yee, "Labor of Fun." Trebor Scholz's edited volume *Digital Labor: The Internet as Playground and Factory* is an invaluable resource on this topic.

38 Scott Rettberg, 24. For further reading on this topic, Dyer-Witheford and de Peuter's *Games of Empire* illuminates the various ways gaming exemplifies modern notions of global, immaterial capital.

39 It should be noted, however, that the absence of embodied labor does not necessarily pose as much of a challenge to Dyer-Witheford and de Peuter's argument about games and immaterial labor. In fact, games with delay mechanics or that function ambiently in the background may continue to exert a presence on the fringe of consciousness (through, for instance, the Zeigarnik effect) so that even while not actively playing them, they still occupy thoughts and intrude in time that might be spent doing other things.

40 This comment comes from the October 16, 2014, episode of IGN's *Nintendo Voice Chat* podcast. It refers to the process of grinding to win rare item drops. In *Aria of Sorrow*, enemies regenerate or "respawn" whenever players enter a room. In order to optimize this process, which might need to be repeated hundreds of times, players will often target a specific instance of the enemy that spawns near the entrance to a particular room. Note that the brain's reward center is not quite at the *back* of the head (it is centralized because it is evolutionarily old, present across the animal kingdom).

41 This is a reference to Mihaly Csikszentmihalyi's theory of *flow*, which he describes as "joy, creativity, [and] the process of total involvement with life" (xi). Flow describes a state of happiness related to moments of optimal experience when we "feel in control of our actions, masters of our own fate" (3). Such moments are shaped by activities that challenge us but that ultimately offer some balance between anxiety (or tasks that are difficult) and boredom (tasks that are too easy). We enter a flow state when we feel that our "skills are adequate to cope with the challenges at hand, in a goal-directed, rule-bounded action system that provides clear clues as to how well one is performing" (71). Games clearly serve as key examples of activities that allow us to "*join all experience into a meaningful pattern*" (7).

42 See, for instance, Lisa Nakamura's essay "Don't Hate the Player" on gold farming in *World of Warcraft*.

43 Neurotransmitters cannot speak to the specificity of the meanings rewards acquire within a game's wider systems, nor to what makes one sort of reward more or less important (in the game's terms) than another. Neurobiology may not even differentiate

between videogames and slot machines, two vastly different cultural objects that share little in common besides the use of variable reward ratios (which all slot machines employ, but which many videogames do not).

44 Jill Rettberg references endless "to-do lists" in RPGs that are also quests "for personal betterment" (176). Rettberg discusses the quest structure in these games in terms of deferral and repetition. Taking *World of Warcraft* (2004–present) as the exemplar, Rettberg suggests "we humans have finally succeeded in creating something that we can desire endlessly, have entirely, and never consume. This game has no end; it is an endless deferral of an end" (176). This book's framework speaks to gaming's tendency to combine deferral and repetition by conceiving of this process as the intersection of distinct fantasy processes that reinforce one another.

45 Laplanche and Pontalis, *Language of Psychoanalysis*, 272.

46 Laplanche and Pontalis, 341.

47 Laplanche and Pontalis, 341–342.

48 This language comes from Freud's discussion in *Beyond the Pleasure Principle* of "fort-da," which Freud interprets as an effort of the child to "master" or "bind" the "unpleasure" of his mother's departure (24). Kaja Silverman discusses this game in terms of Freud's account of language's power to strip memories of their affective intensity (*Subject of Semiotics*, 70–71). In a sense akin (at least in effect) to what Silverman says of language, accretions games provide a formal system or structure that shifts the player's relationship with painful or threatening impressions.

49 Malabou, 78.

50 Freud, *Beyond the Pleasure Principle*, 32.

51 Freud, 32.

52 Freud, 20, 21.

53 Freud, 21.

54 Freud, 32.

55 Freud, "Economic Problem of Masochism," 160.

56 Freud, *Beyond the Pleasure Principle*, 33.

57 Žižek, "Cogito," 76.

58 This is a reference to Aristophanes's myth in Plato's *Symposium* where humans once had four legs and arms (and hands, eyes, ears, etc.), two faces, and so on—but were split in half by Zeus when they attempted to dethrone the gods of Olympus. Each split piece would instead spend the rest of time seeking out its missing half, its perfect counterpart, to restore a lost condition of completeness. *Metroid Prime* games situate accretions play in a similar vein, as the search for a sense of fulness lost at the outset of play.

59 Rank, 107.

60 Rank, v.

61 The epigraph is from Nietzsche's *The Birth of Tragedy* and is normally associated with Nietzschean nihilism. Of course, Rank's characterization of birth as a traumatic separation differs from the emphasis in Nietzsche's account of "the terrors and horrors of existence" into which one is born (3).

62 Martin, 141.

63 Bauman, 206.

64 Bauman, 206. Sarah Tarlow references these words in a discussion of funerary practices that "emphasize the beauty of the dead body," suggesting death is "a suspension in the relationship" rather than "its closure or failure" (92). Along these lines, the pursuit of an inorganic state in accretions play might be made sense of as a wish to freeze or eternally suspend an advantageous relationship with the world.

65 Foster, 66.

66 Foster, 67.

67 Theweleit, 164.

68 Theweleit, 164. Derek Burrill's book on masculinity in videogames is a helpful resource for further pursuing a connection between the masculine ego and the experience of pain. Burrill argues that displays of violence in games and other media constitute one of masculinity's key formations and that this includes not simply the domination of an external object or other but also violence to one's own body.

69 Foster, 71.

70 This phrasing (the "dreamt-of metalization of the human body") is explicitly mentioned in the epilogue of Walter Benjamin's essay "Work of Art in the Age of Mechanical Reproduction" as one of several ways fascists tend to render war aesthetic, hoping war might "supply the artistic gratification of a sense perception that has been changed by technology" (241). Benjamin's thesis that urban modernity has transformed how we perceive the world could certainly be discussed in relation to contemporary computer technology and digital games that render war beautiful—as well as in relation to our era of superhero cinema (with its own dreams of metalized bodies). In fact, Scott Bukatman has connected contemporary superhero comics to Theweleit's argument about the armored body (specifically, German soldiers' "careful deployment of disciplinary and military apparatuses that turn the body into a part of a machine, delibidinalized through the imposition of boundaries drawn from outside the subject"; *Matters of Gravity*, 55). Bukatman connects this idea to masculine figures in comics with literal and figurative armoring, defending their bodies and projecting vulnerability outward onto the feminized others they destroy without mercy ("The armored body enforces categories of being by buttressing self against nonself"; 68).

71 Theweleit's original observation was based on a culture that emphasized "the punishments of parents, teachers, masters, the punishment hierarchies of young boys and of the military," confronting soldier males with "the existence of their periphery (showing them their boundaries), until they 'grow' a functioning and controlling body armor, a body capable of seamless fusion into larger formations with armorlike peripheries" (164). In other words, overlapping cultural institutions disciplined the male body and helped create these soldier males with ruined egos. Before applying this idea to games, it would be necessary to further consider the extent to which anything similar has taken place in the contemporary context of masculinized gaming communities in America (and globally, since these communities transcend national borders).

72 Foster, 83.

73 Caillois, "Myth of Secret Treasures," 257.

74 Caillois, 258–259.

75 Caillois, 261, 255.

76 Caillois, 261.

77 Caillois, 255, 260.

78 Cramer, 74–75. Cramer suggests that in the milder forms of projection exemplified by a child's engagement with folktales (or, we might add, with digital games), projection "does not seriously distort reality, and may even serve a positive function" related to empathy (92).

79 This is a reference to the Jungian concept of collective images and structures appearing across different times and geographic localities, the shared but unconscious origins of mythology.

80 Stockton, 4.
81 Negative capability is poet John Keats's term for the capacity of remaining "in
   uncertainties, mysteries, doubts, without any irritable reaching after fact and
   reason"), the ability of a line of thinking to endure and grow in complexity
   (Stockton would say grow sideways, to thicken in suspension) by resisting as long as
   possible the urge to conclude (Keats, 277).
82 Stockton, 13.
83 McGonigal, 87. McGonigal cites Edward Castronova's claim that "there is zero
   unemployment in *World of Warcraft*," meaning that it is perhaps in games where we
   are at our most productive, our most useful (Castronova, 124). Of course, *World of
   Warcraft*'s world is less the simulation of a real-world economy than a means by
   which its producers sell a subscription service to players. Its developers could
   instantly spawn any needed commodity with no cost. Its only real economic
   interest, what it *sells* to players, is the feeling of being eternally useful, being able to
   endlessly progress and grow through effort.
84 Laplanche and Pontalis, "Fantasy," 128.
85 Shaw, 56. Shaw suggests that we cannot derive knowledge about how a text positions
   its audience by consulting textual identifiers alone. Identification is ultimately an
   empirical question more suited to ethnographic studies such as the one her book
   undertakes. As Valerie Walkerdine's observational work has demonstrated, fantasy
   is a useful theoretical tool for studying the multiple, contradictory ways actual
   people engage with entertainment media.
86 Silverman, *Male Subjectivity*, 264. Note that the quoted phrase here as well as its
   key terms ("idiopathic" and "heteropathic") come from Max Scheler's *The Nature
   of Sympathy* (1922), which Silverman quotes and expands through a discussion of
   Freudian models of identification (and sadism and masochism).
87 Stallabrass, 90. Though his observations are helpful, Stallabrass ultimately defaults
   to a Marxian reading of gaming's interest in numbers, suggesting that software
   operates under a "tyranny of number" in its enactment of alienating, machinelike
   labor ("reaction, regulation and economy in discrete, repetitive acts"; 90).
88 Burn and Carr note that RPGs such as *Baldur's Gate* (1998) emphasize "collect-
   ables" in a way that "recalls hobby-gaming miniatures, and cult or subcultural
   practices in general, as well as fantasy's generic tendency to revel in detail" (24).
   They add that aside from weapons and armor, players "accumulate gems, necklaces,
   gloves, gauntlets, girdles, magic boots, cloaks and tunics."
89 Danet and Katrial, 225.
90 Jill Rettberg, 168.
91 Jill Rettberg suggests that narrative elements might even be stripped away, leaving
   only the "bare essentials," or simply objective and reward (coordinates and amounts:
   numbers; 174).
92 Danet and Katrial, 224.
93 The Captain Armor Set in the downloadable content of *Divinity: Original Sin II*
   (2017), for instance, includes a set bonus that automatically charms opponents who
   move too close (provided they have no magical armor to block the charm status).
94 Silverman, *Subject of Semiotics*, 83.
95 Silverman, 84. These are "moments of fixation" when desire erupts "into the relational logic of the secondary process" and a particular term exceeds the logic of that
   closed system (83).
96 For a thoughtful and extended theoretical application of the notion of specularization, see Judith Butler.

97 Stallabrass, 89–90.
98 Caillois, *Man, Play and Games*, 8.

Conclusion

1 These common meanings can be found in the *Oxford English Dictionary* entry for "contrivance."

2 Gombrich, 4.

3 Note that restrictions on looting in games such as *Skyrim* and *Divinity: Original Sin* do not undermine a fantasy of accretions by rendering accrual inconvenient. Rather, the demand for diegetic coherence actually *reinforces* the fantasy. In part, this is because such accrual is presented as a special opportunity (when nobody is watching) and so becomes a game within a game. The narrative prohibition against theft actually expands the possibilities of accrual in play by generating new patterns for an accretions fantasy in noncombat skills and upgrade paths related to thievery itself (e.g., lockpicking, persuasion, or sneaking). The option to specialize in such mechanics meets the games' complex social systems halfway, demonstrating the fecundity of efforts to put a game's two narrative layers more fully into dialog with one another.

   Other games cleverly shape a surface narrative around an already established fantasy pattern. For instance, Soma Cruz is empowered by the monsters he slays in *Castlevania: Aria of Sorrow* (2003) because he is apparently the reincarnation of Dracula and possesses the legendary vampire's control over creatures of the night (in this case, the ability to absorb the souls of those he has defeated, ultimately making their power his own). The spiritual mythos surrounding Dracula works to motivate the game's extended accretions quest.

4 Squire, 29.

5 Isbister, 56.

6 Laplanche and Pontalis, "Fantasy," 128.

7 Ferrari and Tice's study of procrastination demonstrates that chronic procrastinators are more "concerned and protective of their self-presentational image" than those who do not procrastinate and therefore do not attempt "to avoid situations that may show an adverse negative image": "For [chronic procrastinators] it is better to do nothing than risk failure and look foolish," and, further, the subsequent avoidance of the necessary task is a form of "self-handicapping" that may well lead to failure, but this is a kind of failure that "may be attributed to the handicap or obstacle and not to a personal lack of ability" (74). When procrastination involves playing a game, there is a clear distinction between actual empowerment—the confidence to begin and complete tasks—and a fantasy of empowerment.

Works Cited

Abraham, Nicolas, and Maria Torok. *The Shell and the Kernel: Renewals of Psycho-analysis*. Edited and translated by Nicholas Rand. University of Chicago Press, 1994.

Ahmed, Sara. *Queer Phenomenology: Orientations, Objects, Others*. Duke University Press, 2006.

Ainsworth, Mary, Mary Blehar, Everett Waters, and Sally Wall. *Patterns of Attachment: A Psychological Study of the Strange Situation*. Lawrence Erlbaum Associates, 1978.

Akhtar, Salman. *Comprehensive Dictionary of Psychoanalysis*. Karnac Books, 2009.

———. *The Damaged Core: Origins, Dynamics, Manifestations, and Treatment*. Aronson, 2009.

———. *Inner Torment: Living between Conflict and Fragmentation*. Aronson, 1999.

Aldred, Jessica. "All Aboard *The Polar Express*: A 'Playful' Change of Address in the Computer-Generated Blockbuster." *Animation: An Interdisciplinary Journal*, vol. 1, no. 2, 2006, pp. 153–172.

Alharthi, Sultan, Olaa Alsaedi, Zachary Troups, Theresa Tanenbaum, and Jessica Hammer. "Playing to Wait: A Taxonomy of Idle Games." *Proceedings of the 2018 CHI Conference on Human Factors in Computing Systems*. ACM, 2018, pp. 1–15.

Allen, Richard. *Projecting Illusion: Film Spectatorship and the Impression of Reality*. Cambridge University Press, 1995.

Altice, Nathan. *I Am Error: The Nintendo Family Computer / Entertainment System Platform*. MIT Press, 2015.

Anable, Aubrey. *Playing with Feelings: Video Games and Affect*. University of Minnesota Press, 2018.

APN News. "Activision CEO Bobby Kotick Discusses the Pandemic's Effects on the Gaming Industry." May 25, 2022. https://www.apnnews.com/activision-ceo-bobby -kotick-discusses-the-pandemics-effects-on-the-gaming-industry/.

Apperley, Thomas. *Gaming Rhythms: Play and Counterplay from the Situated to the Global*. Institute of Network Cultures, 2010.

Bachelard, Gaston. *The Poetics of Space*. Beacon Press, 1958 [1994].

Bainbridge, Jason. "'Worlds within Worlds': The Role of Superheroes in the Marvel and DC Universes." *The Contemporary Comic Book Superhero*, edited by Angela Ndalianis. Routledge, 2009, pp. 64–85.

Barr, Matthew, and Alicia Copeland-Stewart. "Playing Video Games during the COVID-19 Pandemic and Effects on Players' Well-Being." *Games and Culture*, vol. 17, no. 1, 2022, pp. 122–139.

Barthes, Roland. *Empire of Signs*. Macmillan, 1983.

———. "The *Nautilus* and the Drunken Boat." *Mythologies*, selected and translated from the French by Annette Lavers. Noonday Press, 1957 [1991], pp. 65–68.

———. "The Third Meaning." *Image-Music-Text*, translated by Stephen Heath. Macmillan, 1978, pp. 52–68.

Bateman, Chris. "The Grind Mystery: Escalating Reward Schedules." *International Hobo*, January 19, 2011. https://blog.ihobo.com/2011/01/the-grind-mystery-esca lating-reward-schedules.html.

———. *Imaginary Games*. Zero Books, 2011.

Bateman, Chris, and Lennart Nacke. "The Neurobiology of Play." *Proceedings of the International Academic Conference on the Future of Game Design and Technology*. ACM, 2010, pp. 1–8.

Bauman, Zygmunt. *Mortality, Immortality and Other Life Strategies*. Stanford University Press, 1992.

Bazin, André. "The Ontology of the Photographic Image." *What Is Cinema?*, vol. 1, translated by Hugh Gray. University of California Press, 1967 [2004], pp. 9–16.

Benjamin, Jessica. "The Bonds of Love: Rational Violence and Erotic Domination." *Feminist Studies*, vol. 6, no. 1, 1980, pp. 144–174.

Benjamin, Walter. "The Work of Art in the Age of Mechanical Reproduction." *Illuminations*, edited by Hannah Arendt and translated by Harry Zohn. Schocken Books, 1968 [2007], pp. 217–251.

Bettelheim, Bruno. *The Uses of Enchantment: The Meaning and Importance of Fairy Tales*. Vintage Books, 1975 [2010].

Bizzochi, Jim. "*Run, Lola, Run*—Film as Narrative Database." *Fourth Media in Transition Conference*, 2005.

Bogost, Ian. *Persuasive Games: The Expressive Power of Videogames*. MIT Press, 2007.

Bolter, Jay David, and Richard Grusin. *Remediation: Understanding New Media*. MIT Press, 1999.

Boluk, Stephanie, and Patrick Lemieux. *Metagaming: Playing, Completing, Spectating, Cheating, Trading, Making, and Breaking Videogames*. University of Minnesota Press, 2017.

Bordwell, David. *Planet Hong Kong: Popular Cinema and the Art of Entertainment*. Harvard University Press, 2000.

Bordwell, David, Janet Staiger, and Kristin Thompson. *The Classical Hollywood Cinema: Film Style and the Mode of Production to 1960*. Columbia University Press, 1985.

Bowlby, John. *A Secure Base: Parent-Child Attachment and Healthy Human Development*. Basic Books, 1988.

Brooker, Will. "Camera-Eye, CG-Eye: Videogames and the 'Cinematic.'" *Cinema Journal*, vol. 48, no. 3, 2009, pp. 122–128.

Brooks, Peter. *Body Work: Objects of Desire in Modern Narrative*. Harvard University Press, 1993.

———. *The Melodramatic Imagination*. Yale University Press, 1976.

Brown, Lee. "Phonography, Repetition and Spontaneity." *Philosophy and Literature*, vol. 24, no. 1, 2000, pp. 111–125.

Bukatman, Scott. *Matters of Gravity: Special Effects and Superman in the 20th Century*. Duke University Press, 2003.

———. "Why I Hate Superhero Movies." *Cinema Journal*, vol. 50, no. 3, 2011, pp. 118–122.

Burn, Andrew, and Diane Carr. "Defining Game Genres." *Computer Games: Text, Narrative, and Play*, edited by Diane Carr, David Buckingham, Andrew Burn, and Gareth Schott. Polity, 2006, pp. 14–29.

Burrill, Derek. *Die Tryin': Videogames, Masculinity, Culture*. Peter Lang, 2008.

Butler, Judith. *Bodies That Matter: On the Discursive Limits of "Sex."* Routledge, 1993.

Caillois, Roger. *Man, Play and Games*. University of Illinois Press, 1958.

———. "Mimicry and Legendary Psychasthenia." *The Edge of Surrealism: A Roger Caillois Reader*, edited by Claudine Frank, translated by Claudine Frank and Camille Naish. Duke University Press, 1935 [2003], pp. 89–103.

———. "The Myth of Secret Treasures in Childhood." *The Edge of Surrealism: A Roger Caillois Reader*, edited by Claudine Frank, translated by Claudine Frank and Camille Naish. Duke University Press, 1942 [2003], pp. 252–261.

Carlson, Jody. *George C. Wallace and the Politics of Powerlessness: The Wallace Campaigns for the Presidency, 1964–1976*. Transaction Publishers, 1981.

Caruth, Cathy. *Unclaimed Experience: Trauma, Narrative, and History*. Johns Hopkins University Press, 1996.

Castronova, Edward. *Exodus to the Virtual World: How Online Fun Is Changing Reality*. Palgrave Macmillan, 2007.

Chang, Alenda. *Playing Nature: Ecology in Video Games*. University of Minnesota Press, 2019.

Cheng, William. *Sound Play: Video Games and the Musical Imagination*. Oxford University Press, 2014.

Chien, Irene. "Playing against the Grain: Machinima and Military Gaming." *Joystick Soldiers: The Politics of Play in Military Video Games*, edited by Nina B. Huntemann and Matthew Thomas Payne. Routledge, 2009, pp. 239–251.

———. "This Is Not a Dance." *Film Quarterly*, vol. 59, no. 3, 2006, pp. 22–34.

Chun, Wendy Hui Kyong. *Updating to Remain the Same: Habitual New Media*. MIT Press, 2016.

Classen, Catherine, Cheryl Koopman, and David Spiegel. "Trauma and Dissociation." *Bulletin of the Menninger Clinic*, vol. 57, no. 2, 1993, pp. 178–194.

Cline, Ernest. *Ready Player One*. Dark All Day, 2011.

Clover, Carol. *Men, Women, and Chain Saws: Gender in the Modern Horror Film*. Princeton University Press, 1992.

Collins, Karen. "In the Loop: Creativity and Constraint in 8-Bit Video Game Audio." *Twentieth-Century Music*, vol. 4, no. 2, 2008, pp. 209–227.

Condis, Megan. *Gaming Masculinity: Trolls, Fakes, Geeks, and the Gendered Battle for Online Culture*. University of Iowa Press, 2018.

Consalvo, Mia, Konstantin Mitgutsch, and Abe Stein. *Sports Videogames*. Routledge, 2013.

Cramer, Phebe. *Protecting the Self: Defense Mechanisms in Action*. Guilford Press, 2006.

Csikszentmihalyi, Mihaly. *Flow: The Psychology of Optimal Experience*. Harper Perennial, 1990.

Danet, Brenda, and Tamar Katrial. "No Two Alike: Play Aesthetics in Collecting." *Interpreting Objects and Collections*, edited by Susan M. Pearce. Routledge, 1994 [2003], pp. 220–239.

Diedrichsen, Jörn, and Katja Kornysheva. "Motor Skill Learning between Selection and Execution." *Trends in Cognitive Science*, vol. 19, no. 4, 2015, pp. 227–233.

Dooghan, Daniel. "Digital Conquerors: *Minecraft* and the Apologetics of Neoliberalism." *Games and Culture*, vol. 14, no. 1, 2019, pp. 67–86.

Dyer, Richard. "Action!" *Sight and Sound*, vol. 4, no. 10, 1994, pp. 6–10.

Dyer-Witheford, Nick, and Greig de Peuter. *Games of Empire: Global Capitalism and Video Games*. University of Minnesota Press, 2009.

Edelman, Lee. *No Future: Queer Theory and the Death Drive*. Duke University Press, 2004.

Edwards, Paul. *The Closed World: Computers and the Politics of Discourse in Cold War America*. MIT Press, 1996.

Entertainment Software Association. "2020 Essential Facts about the Video Game Industry." August 3, 2020. https://www.theesa.com/resource/2020-essential-facts/.

Eyal, Nir. *Hooked: How to Build Habit-Forming Products*. Portfolio, 2014.

Ferrari, Joseph, and Dianne Tice. "Procrastination as Self-Handicap for Men and Women: A Task-Avoidance Strategy in a Laboratory Setting." *Journal of Research in Personality*, vol. 34, 1999, pp. 73–83.

Fine, Gary Alan. *Shared Fantasy: Role-Playing Games as Social Worlds*. University of Chicago Press, 1983.

Flach, John, Max Mulder, and Marinus M. van Paassen. "The Concept of the Situation in Psychology." *A Cognitive Approach to Situation Awareness: Theory and Application*, edited by Sébastien Tremblay and Simon Banbury. Ashgate, 2004, pp. 42–60.

Flanagan, Mary. *Critical Play: Radical Game Design*. MIT Press, 2009.

Fleming, Dan. *Powerplay: Toys as Popular Culture*. Manchester University Press, 1996.

Fog-Olwig, Karen. "Contested Homes: Home-Making and the Making of Anthropology." *Migrants of Identity: Perceptions of Home in a World of Movement*, edited by Nigel Rapport and Andrew Dawson. Berg, 1998, pp. 225–236.

Foster, Hal. "Armor Fou." *October*, vol. 56, 1991, pp. 65–97.

Fraser, Nancy. "What's Critical about Critical Theory? The Case of Habermas and Gender." *Feminism as Critique: On the Politics of Gender*, edited by Seyla Benhabib and Drucilla Cornell. University of Minnesota Press, 1987, pp. 31–56.

Freud, Sigmund. *Beyond the Pleasure Principle. Standard Edition of the Complete Psychological Works of Sigmund Freud*, vol. 18, translated by James Strachey. W. W. Norton, 1920 [1961], pp. 1–64.

———. *Civilization and Its Discontents. Standard Edition of the Complete Psychological Works of Sigmund Freud*, vol. 21, translated by James Strachey. W. W. Norton, 1930 [1961], pp. 5–119.

———. "The Creative Writer and Daydreaming." *The Uncanny*, translated by David McLintock. Penguin Books, 1908 [2003], pp. 23–34.

———. "A Difficulty in the Path of Psychoanalysis." *Standard Edition of the Complete Psychological Works of Sigmund Freud*, vol. 17, translated by James Strachey. Hogarth, 1917 [1953–1974], pp. 135–144.

———. "The Economic Problem of Masochism." *Standard Edition of the Complete Psychological Works of Sigmund Freud*, vol. 19, translated by James Strachey. W. W. Norton, 1924 [1961], pp. 157–170.

———. "Formulations on the Two Principles of Mental Functioning." *The Freud Reader*, edited by Peter Gay. W. W. Norton, 1911 [1989, 1995], pp. 301–306.

———. *The Interpretation of Dreams*. Translated by James Strachey. Basic Books, 1899 [2010].

———. "On Narcissism: An Introduction." *Standard Edition of the Complete Psychological Works of Sigmund Freud*, vol. 14, translated by James Strachey. Hogarth, 1914 [1953–1974], pp. 69–102.

Frisch, Max. *Homo Faber*. Harcourt Brace, 1987.

Frost, Robert. "Stopping by Woods on a Snowy Evening." *New Hampshire*. Henry Holt, 1923, pp. 91–92.

Fuchs, Thomas. "Body Memory and the Unconscious." *Founding Psychoanalysis Phenomenologically: Phenomenological Theory of Subjectivity and the Psychoanalytic Experience*, edited by Dieter Lohmar and Jagna Brudzinska. Springer, 2011, pp. 86–103.

———. "Collective Body Memories." *Embodiment, Enaction, and Culture: Investigating the Constitution of the Shared World*, edited by Christoph Durt, Thomas Fuchs, and Christian Tewes. MIT Press, 2017, pp. 333–352.

Fuller, Mary, and Henry Jenkins. "Nintendo and New World Travel Writing: A Dialogue." *Cybersociety: Computer-Mediated Communication and Community*, edited by Steven Jones. Sage Publications, 1994, pp. 57–72.

Galloway, Alexander. *Gaming: Essays on Algorithmic Culture*. University of Minnesota Press, 2006.

Gibson, William. *Neuromancer*. Gollancz, 1984.

Gilbert, Daniel. "How Mental Systems Believe." *American Psychologist*, vol. 46, no. 2, 1991, pp. 107–119.

Gitelman, Lisa. *Always Already New: Media, History, and the Data of Culture*. MIT Press, 2006.

Gledhill, Christine. "Signs of Melodrama." *Stardom: Industry of Desire*, edited by Christine Gledhill. Routledge, 1991, pp. 207–229.

Goggins, Joyce. "Playbour, Farming, and Labour." *Ephemera: Theory and Politics in Organization*, vol. 11, no. 4, 2011, pp. 357–368.

Gombrich, Ernst. *Meditations on a Hobby Horse*. Phaidon, 1963 [1978].

Goto-Jones, Chris. "Playing with Being in Digital Asia: Gamic Orientalism and the Virtual Dōjō." *Asiascape: Digital Asia*, vol. 2, 2015, pp. 20–56.

Grodal, Torben. "Stories for Eye, Ear, and Muscles: Video Games, Media, and Embodied Experiences." *The Video Game Theory Reader*, edited by Mark J. P. Wolf and Bernard Perron. Routledge, 2003, pp. 129–155.

Groos, Karl. *The Play of Animals*. Translated by Elizabeth Baldwin. D. Appleton and Company, 1898.

Guardiola, Emmanuel. "The Gameplay Loop: A Player Activity Model for Game Design and Analysis." *ACE 2016: Proceedings of the 13th International Conference on Advances in Computer Entertainment*. ACM, 2016, pp. 1–7.

Guins, Raiford. "'Intruder Alert! Intruder Alert!' Video Games in Space." *Journal of Visual Culture*, vol. 3, no. 2, 2004, pp. 195–211.

Gunning, Tom. "Heard over the Phone: *The Lonely Villa* and the de Lorde Tradition of the Terrors of Technology." *Screen*, vol. 32, no. 2, 1991, pp. 184–196.

Halberstam, Jack. *The Queer Art of Failure*. Duke University Press, 2011.

Hamilakis, Yannis, Mark Pluciennik, and Sarah Tarlow. "Introduction: Thinking through the Body." *Thinking through the Body: Archaeologies of Corporeality*, edited by Yannis Hamilakis, Mark Pluciennik, and Sarah Tarlow. Kluwer Academic Publishers / Plenum Publishers, 2002, pp. 1–21.

Haraway, Donna. "A Cyborg Manifesto: Science, Technology, and Socialist-Feminism in the Late Twentieth Century." *Simians, Cyborgs and Women: The Reinvention of Nature*. Routledge, 1991, pp. 149–181.

Hocking, Clint. "Ludonarrative Dissonance in Bioshock." *Click Nothing: Design from a Long Time Ago*, October 7, 2007. https://clicknothing.typepad.com/click_nothing/2007/10/ludonarrative-d.html.

Holmes, Jeremy. *The Search for the Secure Base: Attachment Theory and Psychotherapy*. Brunner-Routledge, 2001.

hooks, bell. "Homeplace: A Site of Resistance." *Undoing Place? A Geographical Reader,* edited by Linda McDowell. Arnold Press, 1991 [1997], pp. 33–38.

Hopson, John. "Behavioral Game Design." *Gamasutra: The Art & Business of Making Games,* April 27, 2001. https://www.gamasutra.com/view/feature/131494/behavioral _game_design.php.

Isbister, Katherine. *How Games Move Us: Emotion by Design.* MIT Press, 2016.

Jacobs, Lea. "The Woman's Picture and the Poetics of Melodrama." *Camera Obscura,* vol. 31, 1993, 121–147.

Jacobson, Max, Murray Silverstein, and Barbara Winslow. *Patterns of Home: The Ten Essentials of Enduring Design.* Taunton Press, 2005.

Jagoda, Patrick. *Experimental Games: Critique, Play, and Design in the Age of Gamification.* University of Chicago Press, 2020.

Jenkins, Henry. "Complete Freedom of Movement: Video Games as Gendered Play Spaces." *The Game Design Reader: A Rules of Play Anthology,* edited by Katie Salen and Eric Zimmerman. MIT Press, 1998 [2006], pp. 330–363.

———. *Convergence Culture: Where Old and New Media Collide.* New York University Press, 2006.

———. "Games, the New Lively Art." *The Wow Climax: Tracing the Emotional Impact of Popular Culture.* New York University Press, 2007, pp. 19–40.

Johnson, Mark. *The Body in the Mind: The Bodily Basis of Meaning, Imagination, and Reason.* University of Chicago Press, 1987 [2013].

Jones, Diana Wynne. *Howl's Moving Castle.* HarperCollins, 1986.

Jones, Gerard. *Killing Monsters: Why Children Need Fantasy, Super-Heroes and Make-Believe Violence.* Basic Books, 2002.

Julius, Anthony. *Transgressions: The Offences of Art.* University of Chicago Press, 2002.

Juul, Jesper. *The Art of Failure: An Essay on the Pain of Playing Video Games.* MIT Press, 2013.

———. *A Casual Revolution: Reinventing Video Games and Their Players.* MIT Press, 2010.

———. *Half-Real: Video Games between Real Rules and Fictional Worlds.* MIT Press, 2005.

———. "Zero-Player Games: Or, What We Talk about When We Talk about Players." Presented at the Philosophy of Computer Games Conference, Madrid, 2012.

Kaika, Maria. "Interrogating the Geographies of the Familiar: Domesticating Nature and Constructing the Autonomy of the Modern Home." *International Journal of Urban and Regional Research,* vol. 28, no. 2, 2004, pp. 265–286.

Keats, John. *The Complete Poetical Works and Letters of John Keats.* Cambridge ed. Houghton Mifflin, 1899 [2010].

Kinder, Marsha. *Playing with Power in Movies, Television, and Video Games: From Muppet Babies to Teenage Mutant Ninja Turtles.* University of California Press, 1991.

King, Daniel, Paul Delfabbro, and Mark Griffiths. "Video Game Structural Characteristics: A New Psychological Taxonomy." *International Journal of Mental Health and Addiction,* vol. 8, no. 1, 2010, pp. 90–106.

King, Geoff. "'Just Like a Movie?' 9/11 and Hollywood Spectacle." *The Spectacle of the Real: From Hollywood to "Reality" TV and Beyond,* edited by Geoff King. Intellect Books, 2005, pp. 47–57.

King, Geoff, and Tanya Krzywinska. "Introduction: Cinema/Videogames/Interfaces." *ScreenPlay: Cinema/Videogames/Interfaces,* edited by Geoff King and Tanya Krzywinska. Wallflower Press, 2000, pp. 1–32.

Klapp, Orrin. *Opening and Closing: Strategies of Information Adaptation in Society.* Cambridge University Press, 1978.

Klinger, Barbara. *Beyond the Multiplex: Cinema, New Technologies, and the Home.* University of California Press, 2006.

Kocurek, Carly. *Coin-Operated Americans: Rebooting Boyhood at the Video Game Arcade.* University of Minnesota Press, 2015.

Kohler, Chris. *Power-Up: How Japanese Video Games Gave the World an Extra Life.* BradyGames, 2004.

Kucich, John. "Olive Schreiner, Masochism, and Omnipotence: Strategies of a Preoedipal Politics." *Novel: A Forum on Fiction*, vol. 36, no. 1, 2002, pp. 79–109.

Lacan, Jacques. *The Four Fundamental Concepts of Psychoanalysis.* Edited by Jacques-Alain Miller. Translated by Alan Sheridan. W. W. Norton, 1973 [1998].

———. "The Mirror Stage as Formative of the *I* Function as Revealed in Psychoanalytic Experience." *Écrits: The First Complete Edition in English*, translated by Bruce Fink. W. W. Norton, 1949 [2006], pp. 75–81.

Laplanche, Jean. *Life and Death in Psychoanalysis.* Translated by Jeffrey Mehlman. Johns Hopkins University Press, 1970 [1976].

Laplanche, Jean, and Jean-Bertrand Pontalis. "Fantasy and the Origins of Sexuality." *Unconscious Phantasy*, edited by Riccardo Steiner. Karnac Books, 1968 [2003], pp. 107–143.

———. *The Language of Psychoanalysis.* Translated by Donald Nicholson-Smith. Hogarth Press, 1973 [1988].

Lapping, Claudia. "Reflexivity and Fantasy: Surprising Encounters from Interpretation to Interruption." *Qualitative Inquiry*, vol. 22, no. 9, 2016, pp. 718–724.

Ling, Kimberly, Gerard Beenen, Pamela Ludford, Xiaoqing Wang, Klarissa Chang, Xin Li, et al. "Using Social Psychology to Motivate Contributions to Online Communities." *Proceedings of the 2004 ACM Conference on Computer Supported Cooperative Work.* ACM, 2005, pp. 212–221.

Locke, Edwin, Karyll Shaw, Lise Saari, and Gary Latham. "Goal Setting and Task Performance: 1969–1980." *Psychological Bulletin*, vol. 90, no. 1, 1981, pp. 125–152.

Loftus, Geoffrey R., and Elizabeth F. Loftus. *Mind at Play: The Psychology of Video Games.* Basic Books, 1983.

Lukacs, John. "The Bourgeois Interior: Why the Most Maligned Characteristic of the Modern Age May Yet Be Seen as Its Most Precious Asset." *The American Scholar*, vol. 39, no. 4, 1970, pp. 616–630.

Lyons-Ruth, Karlen. "Rapprochement or Approchement: Mahler's Theory Reconsidered from the Vantage Point of Recent Research on Early Attachment Relationships." *Psychoanalytic Psychology*, vol. 8, no. 1, 1991, pp. 1–23.

Mack, Jonathan. "Evoking Interactivity: Film and Videogame Intermediality since the 1980s." *Adaptation*, vol. 9, no. 1, 2016, pp. 98–112.

Madigan, Jamie. *Getting Gamers: The Psychology of Video Games and Their Impact on the People Who Play Them.* Rowman & Littlefield, 2016.

Magrì, Elisa. "The Problem of Habitual Body and Memory in Hegel and Merleau-Ponty." *Hegel Bulletin*, vol. 38, no. 1, 2017, pp. 24–44.

Mahler, Margaret. "A Study of the Separation-Individuation Process and Its Possible Application to Borderline Phenomena in the Psychoanalytic Situation." *The Psychoanalytic Study of the Child*, vol. 26, no. 1, 1971, pp. 403–424.

Malabou, Catherine. "Plasticity and Elasticity in Freud's 'Beyond the Pleasure Principle.'" *Diacritics*, vol. 37, no. 4, 2007, pp. 78–85.

Malkowski, Jennifer, and Treaandrea Russworm, eds. *Gaming Representation: Race, Gender, and Sexuality in Video Games.* Indiana University Press, 2017.

Malone, Thomas W. "Toward a Theory of Intrinsically Motivating Instruction." *Cognitive Science*, vol. 5, no. 4, 1981, pp. 333–369.

Manovich, Lev. *The Language of New Media*. MIT Press, 2001.

Martin, George R. R. *A Clash of Kings*. Bantam Books, 1999.

Massey, Doreen. *Space, Place, and Gender*. University of Minnesota Press, 1994.

Massumi, Brian. *Parables for the Virtual: Movement, Affect, Sensation*. Duke University Press, 2002.

Mauss, Marcel. "Les techniques du corps." *Journal für Psychologiei*, vol. 32, 1935, pp. 271–293.

May, Elaine Tyler. *Homeward Bound: American Families in the Cold War Era*. Rev. ed. Basic Books, 1988 [2008].

McGonigal, Jane. *Reality Is Broken: Why Games Make Us Better and How They Can Change the World*. Penguin Books, 2011.

McLuhan, Marshall. *Understanding Media: The Extensions of Man*. MIT Press, 1964 [1994].

Mechanic, David. "Adolescents at Risk: New Directions." *Journal of Adolescent Health*, vol. 12, no. 8, 1991, pp. 638–643.

Meer, Alec. "Rohrer on the Castle Doctrine, Guns & Chain World, Pt 2." *Rock Paper Shotgun*, February 1, 2013. https://www.rockpapershotgun.com/rohrer-on-the-castle -doctrine-guns-chain-world-pt-2.

Mellor, Philip, and Chris Shilling. "Modernity, Self-Identity and the Sequestration of Death." *Sociology*, vol. 27, no. 3, 1993, pp. 411–431.

Merleau-Ponty, Maurice. *Phenomenology of Perception*. Translated by Colin Smith. Routledge, 1945 [2005].

Middleton, Richard. "'Play It Again Sam': Some Notes on the Productivity of Repetition in Popular Music." *Popular Music*, vol. 3, 1983, pp. 235–270.

Moretti, Franco. *Signs Taken for Wonders*. Translated by Susan Fischer, David Forgacs, and David Miller. Verso, 1983 [2005].

Morley, David. *Home Territories: Media, Mobility, and Identity*. Routledge, 2000.

Mulvey, Laura. "Visual Pleasure and Narrative Cinema." *Film Theory and Criticism: Introductory Readings*, edited by Leo Braudy and Marshall Cohen. Oxford University Press, 1975 [1999], pp. 833–844.

Murphy, Sheila. *How Television Invented New Media*. Rutgers University Press, 2011.

Murray, Janet. *Hamlet on the Holodeck: The Future of Narrative in Cyberspace*. MIT Press, 1999.

Myers, David. "The Video Game Aesthetic: Play as Form." *The Video Game Theory Reader 2*, edited by Bernard Perron and Mark J. P. Wolf. Routledge, 2009, pp. 45–63.

Nacke, Lennart, Chris Bateman, and Regan Mandryk. "BrainHex: A Neurobiological Gamer Typology Survey." *Entertainment Computing*, vol. 5, no. 1, 2014, pp. 55–62.

Nakamura, Lisa. "Don't Hate the Player, Hate the Game: The Racialization of Labor in *World of Warcraft*." *Digital Labor: The Internet as Playground and Factory*, edited by Trebor Scholz. Routledge, 2013, pp. 187–204.

Newman, James. "The Myth of the Ergodic Videogame." *Game Studies*, vol. 2, no. 1, 2002.

———. *Videogames*. Routledge, 2004.

Newman, Michael. *Atari Age: The Emergence of Video Games in America*. MIT Press, 2017.

Ngai, Sianne. *Ugly Feelings*. Harvard University Press, 2005.

Niedzviecki, Hal. *Hello, I'm Special: How Individuality Became the New Conformity*. City Lights Books, 2006.

Nietzsche, Friedrich. *The Birth of Tragedy*. Edited by Raymond Guess and Ronald Speirs. Translated by Ronald Speirs. Cambridge University Press, 1999.

NPD Group. "Fourth Quarter 2020 U.S. Consumer Spending on Video Game Products Increased 26% while Annual Spend Gained 27% Compared to 2019." February 1, 2021. https://live-npd-group.pantheonsite.io/news/press-releases/2021/the-npd-group-fourth-quarter-2020-u-s-consumer-spending-on-video-game-products-increased-26-while-annual-spend-gained-27-compared-to-2019/.

Nye, David. *Technology Matters: Questions to Live With*. MIT Press, 2006.

Parker, Rob. "The Culture of Permadeath: Roguelikes and Terror Management Theory." *Journal of Gaming & Virtual Worlds*, vol. 9, no. 2, 2017, pp. 123–141.

"Perpetual Motion." *Oxford English Dictionary*. Accessed July 15, 2018. https://oed.com.

Peterson, Jon. *Playing at the World: A History of Simulating Wars, People, and Fantastic Adventures, from Chess to Role-Playing Games*. Unreason Press, 2012.

Porteous, J. Douglas. "Home: The Territorial Core." *Geographical Review*, vol. 66, no. 4, 1976, pp. 383–390.

Pribram, E. Deidre. "Melodrama and the Aesthetics of Emotion." *Melodrama Unbound: Across History, Media, and National Cultures*, edited by Christine Gledhill and Linda Williams. Columbia University Press, 2018, pp. 237–251.

Purse, Lisa. "Digital Heroes in Contemporary Hollywood: Exertion, Identification, and the Virtual Action Body." *Film Criticism*, vol. 32, no. 1, 2007, pp. 5–26.

———. "The New Spatial Dynamics of the Bullet-Time Effect." *The Spectacle of the Real: From Hollywood to "Reality" TV and Beyond*, edited by Geoff King. Intellect Books, 2005, pp. 151–160.

Rank, Otto. *The Trauma of Birth*. Robert Brunner, 1929 [1952].

Rehak, Bob. "The Migration of Forms: Bullet Time as Microgenre." *Film Criticism*, vol. 32, no. 1, 2007, pp. 26–49.

Rettberg, Jill. "Quests in *World of Warcraft*: Deferral and Repetition." *Digital Culture, Play and Identity: A World of Warcraft Reader*, edited by Hilde G. Corneliussen and Jill Walker Rettberg. MIT Press, 2008, pp. 167–184.

Rettberg, Scott. "Corporate Ideology in World of Warcraft." *Digital Culture, Play and Identity: A World of Warcraft Reader*, edited by Hilde G. Corneliussen and Jill Walker Rettberg. MIT Press, 2008, pp. 19–38.

Reynolds, Daniel. *Media in Mind*. Oxford University Press, 2019.

Reynolds, Richard. *Super Heroes: A Modern Mythology*. University Press of Mississippi, 1992.

Richmond, Scott. *Cinema's Bodily Illusions: Flying, Floating, and Hallucinating*. University of Minnesota Press, 2016.

Richter, Ganit, Daphne R. Raban, and Sheizaf Rafaeli. "Studying Gamification: The Effect of Rewards and Incentives on Motivation." *Gamification in Education and Business*, edited by Torsten Reiners and Lincoln C. Woods. Springer, 2015, pp. 21–46.

Rizzolatti, Giacomo. "The Mirror Neuron System and Its Function in Humans." *Anatomy and Embryology*, vol. 210, no. 5, 2005, pp. 419–421. https://pubmed.ncbi.nlm.nih.gov/16222545/.

Robson, Jon, and Aaron Meskin. "Video Games as Self-Involving Interactive Fictions." *Journal of Aesthetics and Art Criticism*, vol. 74, 2016, pp. 165–177.

Rose, Jacqueline. *States of Fantasy*. Clarendon Press, 1996.

Rotundo, E. Anthony. *American Manhood: Transformations in Masculinity from the Revolution to the Modern Era*. Basic Books, 1994.

Rozario, Kevin. *Culture of Calamity: Disaster and the Making of Modern America*. University of Chicago Press, 2007.

Ruberg, Bonnie. *Video Games Have Always Been Queer*. New York University Press, 2019.

Ruberg, Bonnie, and Adrienne Shaw, eds. *Queer Game Studies*. University of Minnesota Press, 2017.

Rugnetta, Mike. "Can Bullet Hell Games Be Meditative?" *Idea Channel*, December 18, 2013. https://www.youtube.com/watch?v=DY-45DjRk_E.

Ryan, Marie-Laure. *Narrative across Media: The Languages of Storytelling*. University of Nebraska Press, 2004.

Rybczynski, Witold. *Home: A Short History of an Idea*. Penguin Books, 1986.

Sandler, Joseph, and Anne-Marie Sandler. "Phantasy and Its Transformations: A Contemporary Freudian View." *Unconscious Phantasy*, edited by Riccardo Steiner. Karnac Books, 2003, pp. 77–88.

———. "The 'Second Censorship,' the 'Three Box Model' and Some Technical Implications." *Psychoanalytic Inquiry*, vol. 4, 1983, pp. 413–425.

Scheler, Max. *The Nature of Sympathy*. Translated by Stephen Heath. Archon Books, 1922 [1970].

Scholz, Trebor, ed. *Digital Labor: The Internet as Playground and Factory*. Routledge, 2013.

Schroeder, Audra. "The Only Review of '*Grand Theft Auto V*' That Matters Is Set to Smooth Jazz." *Daily Dot*, September 9, 2013. https://www.dailydot.com/parsec/grand-theft-auto-leigh-alexander-review/.

Shafton, Anthony. *Dream Reader: Contemporary Approaches to the Understanding of Dreams*. State University of New York Press, 1995.

Shanton, Karen, and Alvin Goldman. "Simulation Theory." *Wiley Interdisciplinary Reviews: Cognitive Science*, vol. 1, no. 4, 2010, pp. 527–538.

Shaviro, Steven. "Post-cinematic Affect: On Grace Jones, *Boarding Gate* and *Southland Tales*." *Film-Philosophy*, vol. 14, no. 1, 2010, pp. 1–102.

Shaw, Adrienne. *Gaming at the Edge: Sexuality and Gender at the Margins of Gamer Culture*. University of Minnesota Press, 2015.

Shilling, Chris. *The Body and Social Theory*. Sage, 1993.

"Shooter Game." Wikipedia. Accessed May 3, 2016. https://en.wikipedia.org/wiki/Shooter_game.

Shusterman, Richard. *Thinking through the Body: Essays in Somaesthetics*. Cambridge University Press, 2012.

Siang, Ang Chee, and Radha Krishna Rao. "Theories of Learning: A Computer Game Perspective." *Proceedings of the IEEE Fifth International Symposium on Multimedia Software Engineering*. ACM, 2003, pp. 239–245.

Silverman, Kaja. *Male Subjectivity at the Margins*. Routledge, 1992.

———. *The Subject of Semiotics*. Oxford University Press, 1983.

Singer, Ben. *Melodrama and Modernity*. Columbia University Press, 2001.

Singer, Jerome. "Affect and Imagination in Play and Fantasy." *Emotions in Personality and Psychopathology*, edited by C. E. Izard. Plenum Press, 1979, pp. 11–34.

Smith, Kathy. "Reframing Fantasy: September 11 and the Global Audience." *The Spectacle of the Real: From Hollywood to "Reality" TV and Beyond*, edited by Geoff King. Intellect Books, 2005, pp. 59–70.

Sobchack, Vivian. *Carnal Thoughts: Embodiment and Moving Image Culture*. University of California Press, 2004.

Solomon, Robert, and Kathleen Higgins. *What Nietzsche Really Said*. Schocken Books, 2000.

Spigel, Lynn. *Make Room for TV: Television and the Family Ideal in Postwar America*. University of Chicago Press, 1992.

Springer, Claudia. "The Pleasure of the Interface." *Screen*, vol. 32, no. 3, 1991, pp. 303–323.

Spufford, Francis. *I May Be Some Time: Ice and the English Imagination*. Picador, 1997.

Squire, Kurt. *Video Games and Learning*. Teachers College Press, 2011.

Stallabrass, Julian. *Gargantua: Manufactured Mass Culture*. Verso, 1996.

Stewart, Sam. "The Origins of the 'Ken Combo.'" ESPN, February 24, 2017. www.espn
.com/esports/story/_/id/18760579/the-origins-ken-combo.

Stewart, Susan. *On Longing: Narratives of the Miniature, the Gigantic, the Souvenir, the
Collection*. Duke University Press, 1993.

Stickgold, Robert, April Malia, Denise Maguire, David Roddenberry, and Margaret
O'Connor. "Replaying the Game: Hypnagogic Images in Normals and Amnesics."
Science, vol. 290, 2000, pp. 350–353.

Stillar, Glenn. "Loops as Genre Resources." *Folia Linguistica*, vol. 39, nos. 1–2, 2005,
pp. 197–212.

Stockton, Kathryn Bond. *The Queer Child; or, Growing Sideways in the Twentieth
Century*. Duke University Press, 2009.

Suits, Bernard. *The Grasshopper: Games, Life, and Utopia*. University of Toronto Press,
1978.

Sutton-Smith, Brian. *The Ambiguity of Play*. Harvard University Press, 1997.

Swink, Steve. *Game Feel: A Game Designer's Guide to Virtual Sensation*. Morgan
Kaufmann, 2009.

Tannahill, Nick, Patrick Tissington, and Carl Senior. "Video Games and Higher
Education: What Can 'Call of Duty' Teach Our Students?" *Frontiers in Psychology*,
vol. 3, no. 210, 2012, pp. 1–3.

Tarlow, Sarah. "The Aesthetic Corpse in Nineteenth-Century Britain." *Thinking
through the Body: Archaeologies of Corporeality*, edited by Yannis Hamilakis, Mark
Pluciennik, and Sarah Tarlow. Kluwer, 2002, pp. 85–97.

Theweleit, Klaus. *Male Fantasies*, vol. 2. *Male Bodies: Psychoanalyzing the White Terror*.
Translated by Erica Carter and Chris Turner in collaboration with Stephen Conway.
University of Minnesota Press, 1989.

Treat, Shaun. "How America Learned to Stop Worrying and Cynically ENJOY! The
Post-9/11 Superhero Zeitgeist." *Communication and Critical/Cultural Studies*, vol. 6,
no. 1, 2009, pp. 103–109.

Trumpp, Laura. "Sol Duc Cabin: A Private Steelhead Fly Fishing Cabin." The Wading
List. Accessed October 10, 2020. https://www.thewadinglist.com/sol-duc-cabin/.

Turkle, Sherry. *Alone Together: Why We Expect More from Technology and Less from
Each Other*. Basic Books, 2011.

———. *The Second Self: Computers and the Human Spirit*. Simon & Schuster, 1984.

Turner, Jenny. "Reasons for Liking Tolkien." *London Review of Books*, vol. 23, no. 22,
2001. https://www.lrb.co.uk/the-paper/v23/n22/jenny-turner/reasons-for-liking
-tolkien.

"Turn Your Home into a Fortress." *ABC News Go*, January 6, 2006. https://abcnews.go
.com/Primetime/story?id=1231700&page=1.

Walkerdine, Valerie. "Video Replay: Families, Films and Fantasy." *Formations of
Fantasy*, edited by Victor Burgin, James Donald, and Cora Kaplan. Methuen, 1986,
pp. 167–199.

Wang, Chia-Chih, and Brent Mallinckrodt. "Differences between Taiwanese and U.S.
Cultural Beliefs about Ideal Adult Attachment." *Journal of Counseling Psychology*,
vol. 53, no. 2, 2006, pp. 192–204.

Ward, Paul. "Videogames as Remediated Animation." *ScreenPlay: Cinema / Videogames / Interfaces*, edited by Geoff King and Tanya Krzywinska. Wallflower Press,
2002, pp. 122–135.

Wardrip-Fruin, Noah. *Expressive Processing: Digital Fictions, Computer Games, and Software Studies*. MIT Press, 2009.

Ware, James. "The Norwegian Philosophy of Thriving in Winter: A Strategy for Getting through the Dark Days Ahead." *Forge*, October 20, 2020. https://forge.medium.com /the-norwegian-philosophy-of-thriving-in-winter-3a9a3a2582b9.

Warren, Tom. "Minecraft Still Incredibly Popular as Sales Top 200 Million and 126 Million Play Monthly." *The Verge*, May 18, 2020. https://www.theverge.com/2020/5 /18/21262045/minecraft-sales-monthly-players-statistics-youtube.

Whissel, Kristen. "The Digital Multitude." *Cinema Journal*, vol. 49, no. 4, 2010, pp. 90–110.

———. *Spectacular Digital Effects: CGI and Contemporary Cinema*. Duke University Press, 2014.

Williams, Linda. "Film Bodies: Gender, Genre, and Excess." *Film Quarterly*, vol. 44, no. 4, 1991, pp. 2–13.

———. *Hard Core: Power, Pleasure, and the "Frenzy of the Visible."* University of California Press, 1989.

———. "Mega-Melodrama! Vertical and Horizontal Suspensions of the 'Classical.'" *Modern Drama*, vol. 55, no. 4, 2012, pp. 523–543.

———. *Playing the Race Card: Melodramas of Black and White from Uncle Tom to O.J. Simpson*. Princeton University Press, 2001.

———. "'Tales of Sound and Fury . . .' or, The Elephant of Melodrama." *Melodrama Unbound: Across History, Media, and National Cultures*, edited by Christine Gledhill and Linda Williams. Columbia University Press, 2018, pp. 205–217.

———. "World and Time: Serial Television Melodrama in America." *Melodrama Unbound: Across History, Media, and National Cultures*, edited by Christine Gledhill and Linda Williams. Columbia University Press, 2018, pp. 169–183.

Wolff, Janet. "The Invisible Flâneuse." *Theory, Culture and Society*, vol. 2, no. 3, 1985, pp. 37–40.

Yates, Candida. "'Video Replay: Families, Films and Fantasy' as a Transformational Text: Commentary on Valerie Walkerdine's 'Video Replay.'" *Psychoanalysis, Culture & Society*, vol. 15, no. 4, 2010, pp. 404–411.

Yee, Nick. "The Labor of Fun: How Video Games Blur the Boundaries of Work and Play." *Games and Culture*, vol. 1, no. 1, 2006, pp. 68–71.

———. "Motivation for Play in Online Games." *CyberPsychology & Behavior*, vol. 9, no. 6, 2006, pp. 772–775.

Young, Damon R. "The Living End, or Love without a Future." *Queer Love in Film and Television: Critical Essays*, edited by Pamela Demory and Christopher Pullen. Palgrave Macmillan, 2013, pp. 13–22.

———. *Making Sex Public and Other Cinematic Fantasies*. Duke University Press, 2018.

Young, Iris Marion. *On Female Body Experience: "Throwing Like a Girl" and Other Essays*. Oxford University Press, 2005.

Žižek, Slavoj. "Cogito and the Sexual Difference." *Tarrying with the Negative*. Duke University Press, 1993, pp. 45–80.

———. *Looking Awry: An Introduction to Jacques Lacan through Popular Culture*. MIT Press, 1991.

———. *The Plague of Fantasies*. Verso, 1997 [2008].

Index

Note: Page numbers in *italics* indicate figures.

About the Author

CHRISTOPHER GOETZ completed his PhD in film and media at the University of California, Berkeley. He is currently an assistant professor in the Department of Cinematic Arts at the University of Iowa. His research focuses on fantasy and nostalgia in games, cinema, and other media. He is one of the founding organizers of the annual Queerness and Games Conference.

Printed and bound by CPI Group (UK) Ltd, Croydon, CR0 4YY

09/06/2025

14685742-0002